NSW Targeting Maths

Year 1

Katy Pike

PASCAL
PRESS

Contents

Term 1

Term 2

Term 3

Term 4

New Edition

Targeting Maths Australia's Favourite Maths Program

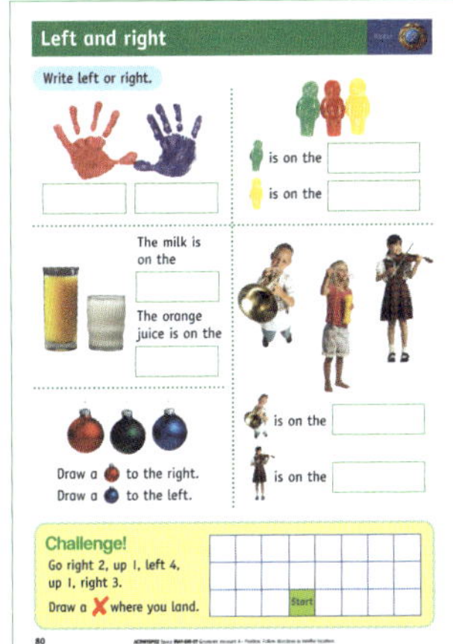

Australian Curriculum/NSW Alignment

This NEW Edition fully aligns each student page with both the new NSW Syllabus (2022) and the Australian Curriculum. The new NSW Syllabus outcome codes and content groups appear alongside the Australian Curriculum code and content descriptions on each student page.

iPad Apps

With an app for each year, from Kindergarten to Year 6, the Targeting Maths Apps include all the essential maths content that children need to know in an amazing app that makes learning maths fun, motivating and full of rewards. Look for it in Apple's App Store today! Made especially for the iPad and aligned to each student page in this book.

Integrated Problem-solving Program

Includes an integrated problem-solving program that actively builds students' problem solving capabilities.

In-stage Topic Alignment for Composite Classes

Great for composite classes too, the contents of each book in one stage, eg Year 1 and Year 2, match topic by topic.

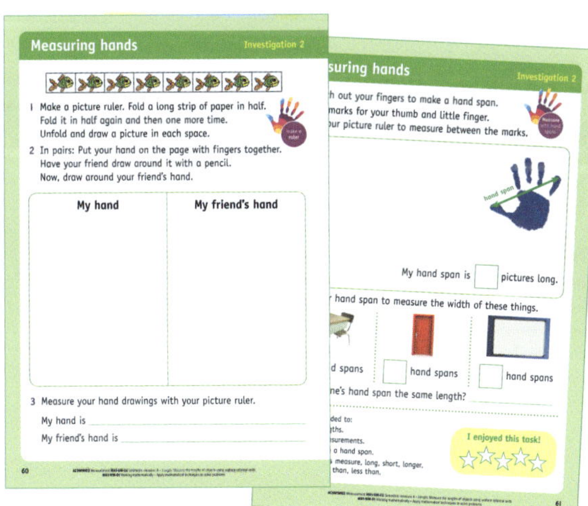

Term Investigations

Each term includes an investigation that will get students planning and working through an extended problem.

Regular Revision

Revision pages appear both at mid term and at the end of each term to revise key concepts.

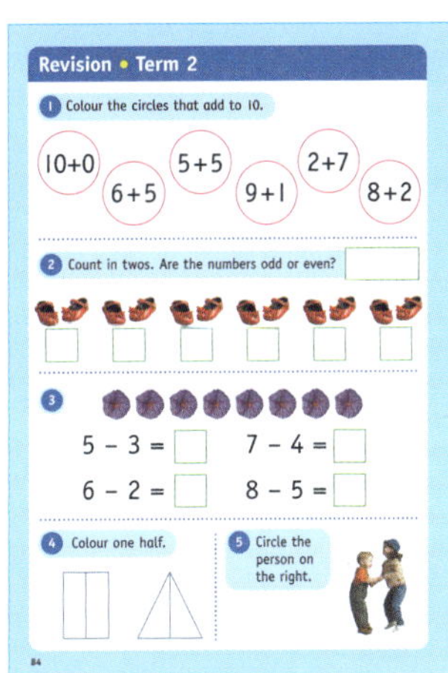

Hands-on Activities

Various hands-on activities are included in each term, asking students to measure and make, count and compare, using objects from around the classroom or home.

Year 1 Outcomes

Strand	NSW Syllabus Outcomes	Student pages
Working Mathematically	**MA1-WM-01** develops understanding and fluency in mathematics through exploring and connecting mathematical concepts	pages 2 to 168
	MA1-WM-01 develops understanding and fluency in mathematics through choosing and applying mathematical techniques to solve problems	8, 13, 19, 20, 21, 34, 52, 59, 60, 61, 67, 75, 83, 91, 96, 104, 105, 113, 123, 125, 135, 142, 148, 149, 156, 159, 164
	MA1-WM-01 develops understanding and fluency in mathematics through communicating their thinking and reasoning coherently and clearly	21, 34, 67, 83, 113, 123, 156, 164
Number and Algebra	**Representing whole numbers**	
	MA1-RWN-01 applies an understanding of place value and the role of zero to read, write and order two- and three-digit numbers	2, 3, 5, 6, 68, 69, 70, 71, 72, 73, 74, 86, 87, 88, 89, 90, 91, 128, 129, 130, 131
	MA1-RWN-02 reads numerals and represents whole numbers to at least 20	4, 5, 6, 7, 8, 20, 21, 86, 88, 89, 90, 91, 128, 129, 130, 131
	Combining and separating quantities	
	MA1-CSQ-01 uses number bonds and the relationship between addition and subtraction to solve problems involving partitioning	14, 15, 16, 17, 18, 19, 28, 29, 30, 31, 32, 33, 34, 44, 45, 46, 47, 48, 49, 50, 51, 52, 56, 57, 58, 59, 108, 109, 110, 111, 112, 113, 136, 137, 138, 139, 140, 141, 142
	Forming groups	
	MA1-FG-01 uses the structure of equal groups to solve multiplication problems, and shares or groups to solve division problems	70, 71, 72, 73, 74, 75, 100, 101, 102, 103, 104, 105, 123, 152, 153, 154, 155, 156
Measurement and Space	**Geometric measure**	
	MA1-GM-01 represents and describes the positions of objects in familiar locations	80, 81, 82, 83
	MA1-GM-02 measures, records, compares and estimates lengths and distances using uniform informal units, as well as metres and centimetres	53, 54, 55, 94, 95, 104, 105
	MA1-GM-03 creates and recognises halves, quarters and eighths as part measures of a whole length	38, 39, 118, 119, 120, 121, 122
	Two-dimensional spatial structure	
	MA1-2DS-01 recognises, describes and represents shapes including quadrilaterals and other common polygons	9, 10, 11, 12, 13, 97, 98, 99
	MA1-2DS-02 measures and compares areas using uniform informal units in rows and columns	92, 93, 96
	Three-dimensional spatial structure	
	MA1-3DS-01 recognises, describes and represents familiar three-dimensional objects	64, 65, 66, 67, 160, 161, 162, 163, 164
	MA1-3DS-02 measures, records, compares and estimates internal volumes (capacities) and volumes using uniform informal units	40, 41, 143, 144, 145, 146, 147, 148, 149
	Non-spatial measure	
	MA1-NSM-01 measures, records, compares and estimates the masses of objects using uniform informal units	35, 36, 37, 157, 158, 159
	MA1-NSM-02 describes, compares and orders durations of events, and reads half- and quarter-hour time	24, 25, 26, 27, 114, 115, 116, 117, 132, 133, 134, 135
Statistics & Probability	**Data**	
	MA1-DATA-01 gathers and organises data, displays data in lists, tables and picture graphs	76, 77, 124, 125, 165
	MA1-DATA-02 reasons about representations of data to describe and interpret the results	76, 77, 165
	MA1-CHAN-01 recognises and describes the element of chance in everyday events	78, 79, 166

Strand	Australian Curriculum Content Descriptions *Students learn to:*	Student pages
Number	**AC9M1N01** recognise, represent and order numbers to at least 120 using physical and virtual materials, numerals, number lines and charts	2, 3, 4, 5, 6, 20, 21, 86, 87, 90, 91, 131
	AC9M1N02 partition one- and two-digit numbers in different ways using physical and virtual materials, including partitioning two-digit numbers into tens and ones	5, 91, 128, 129
	AC9M1N03 quantify sets of objects, to at least 120, by partitioning collections into equal groups using number knowledge and skip counting	6, 7, 88, 89
	AC9M1N04 add and subtract numbers within 20, using physical and virtual materials, part-part-whole knowledge to 10 and a variety of calculation strategies	14, 15, 16, 17, 18, 30, 31, 32, 33, 44, 45, 46, 47, 48, 49, 56, 57, 108, 109, 110, 136, 137, 139, 140, 141
	AC9M1N05 use mathematical modelling to solve practical problems involving additive situations, including simple money transactions; represent the situations with diagrams, physical and virtual materials, and use calculation strategies to solve the problem	8, 19, 28, 29, 34, 50, 51, 52, 58, 59, 111, 112, 113, 138, 142
	AC9M1N06 use mathematical modelling to solve practical problems involving equal sharing and grouping; represent the situations with diagrams, physical and virtual materials, and use calculation strategies to solve the problem	75, 100, 101, 102, 103, 123, 152, 153, 154, 155, 156
Algebra	**AC9M1A01** recognise, continue and create pattern sequences, with numbers, symbols, shapes and objects, formed by skip counting, initially by twos, fives and tens	68, 69, 70, 71, 72, 73, 74, 86, 105, 130, 131
	AC9M1A02 recognise, continue and create repeating patterns with numbers, symbols, shapes and objects, identifying the repeating unit	10
Measurement	**AC9M1M01** compare directly and indirectly and order objects and events using attributes of length, mass, capacity and duration, communicating reasoning	35, 36, 37, 40, 41, 144, 145, 146, 147, 157, 158, 159
	AC9M1M02 measure the length of shapes and objects using informal units, recognising that units need to be uniform and used end-to-end	53, 54, 55, 54, 55, 94, 95, 104
	AC9M1M03 describe the duration and sequence of events using years, months, weeks, days and hours	24, 25, 26, 27, 132, 133, 134, 135
Space	**AC9M1SP01** make, compare and classify familiar shapes; recognise familiar shapes and objects in the environment, identifying the similarities and differences between them	9, 11, 12, 13, 64, 65, 66, 67, 92, 97, 98, 99, 160, 161, 162, 163, 164
	AC9M1SP02 give and follow directions to move people and objects to different locations within a space	80, 81, 82, 83
Statistics	**AC9M1ST01** acquire and record data for categorical variables in various ways including using digital tools, objects, images, drawings, lists, tally marks and symbols	124, 125
	AC9M1ST02 represent collected data for a categorical variable using one-to-one displays and digital tools where appropriate; compare the data using frequencies and discuss the findings	76, 77, 125, 165

How to Solve a Problem

Read • Plan • Work • Check

Read the problem carefully. Underline the question. Circle the facts.

Plan what you will do: +, –, × (multiply) or ÷ (share).

Work Write or draw a picture to work it out. Write the answer.

Check your answer! Did you answer the question?

Draw a diagram

Draw a simple picture.

Here are some pictures and what they mean:

take away	8 – 3 =	
add	6 + 7 =	
equal groups	4 × 4 =	
share	share 6 between 3	

Looking for patterns

If you can see a pattern, use it to help find the answer.

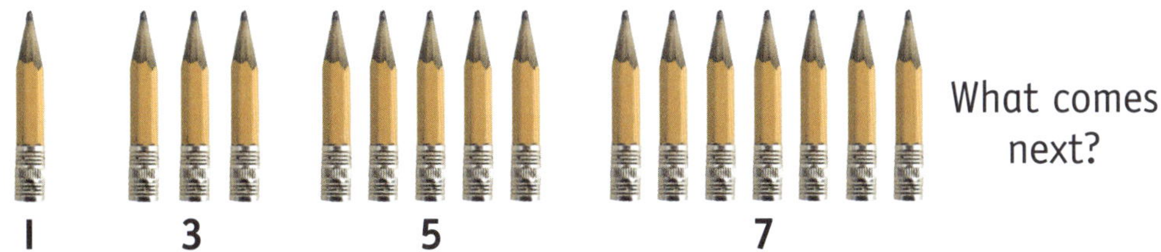

What comes next?

Act it out

Do something. You can use objects, or cut-outs, or move things around.

Trial and error

Make a good guess and write it down. Check if it is right. If it's wrong, try again. Should it be higher or lower?

Dictionary

addition (+)

Six balls and two balls makes eight balls.

$6 + 2 = 8$

area

The amount of space something covers.

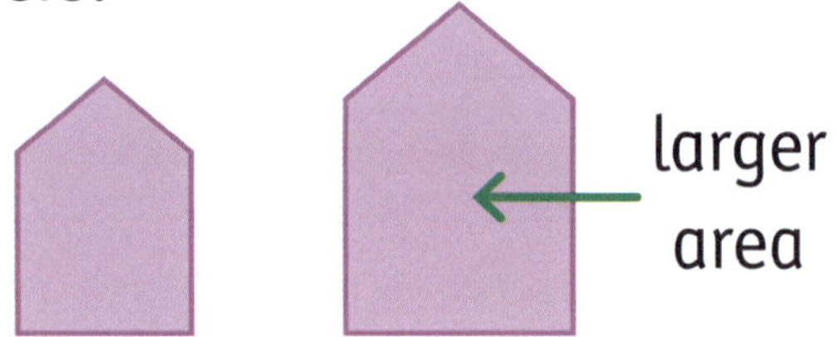

capacity

The amount it can hold.

The jug holds more.

clocks

half-past ten

digital

analog

corner

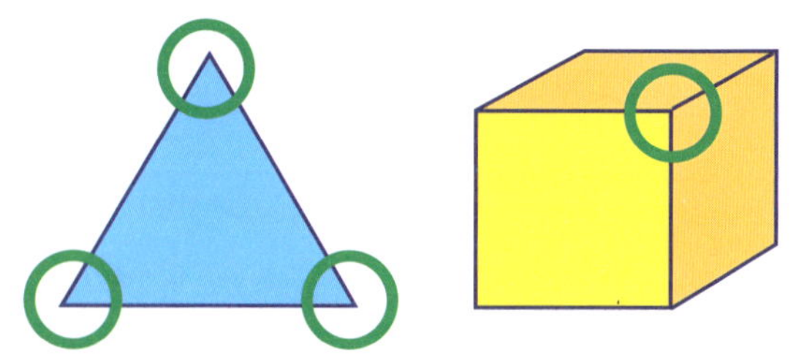

days

Sunday
Monday
Tuesday
Wednesday
Thursday
Friday
Saturday

face

The flat surface of a solid object.

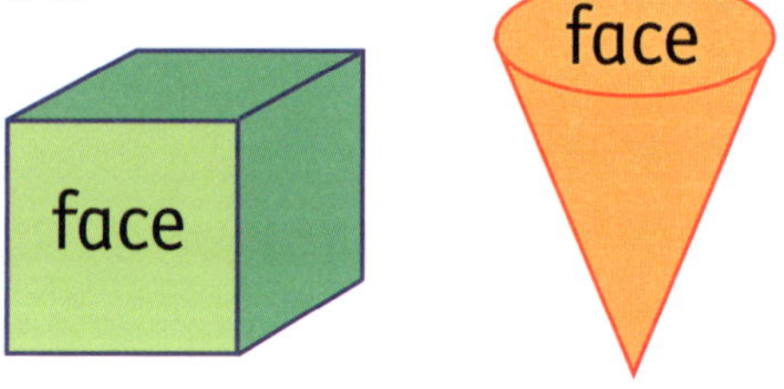

fractions

halves = two equal parts

half a length

Dictionary

fractions

quarters = four equal parts.

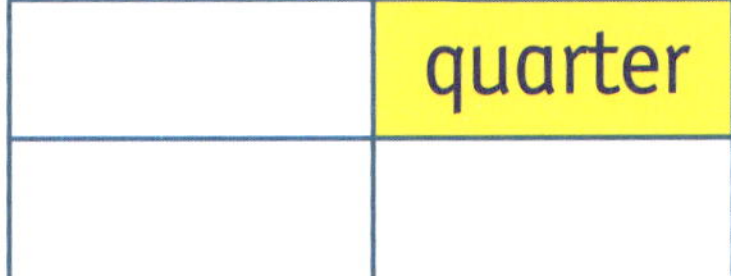

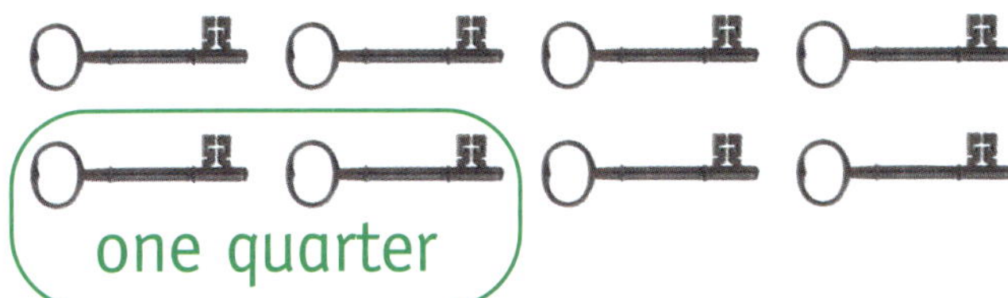

one quarter

quarter lengths

groups

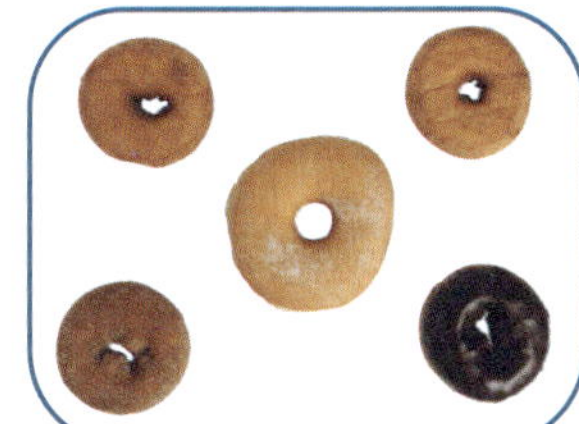

I group of 5

3 groups of 7

length

mass

money

coins

notes

Dictionary

months

January
February
March
April
May
June
July
August
September
October
November
December

Seasons

Summer
December
January
February

Autumn
March
April
May

Winter
June
July
August

Spring
September
October
November

numbers

Even numbers can be grouped in pairs evenly.

Odd numbers grouped into pairs have an odd one left.

Ordinal numbers tell position.

1st 2nd 3rd 4th 5th 6th

position

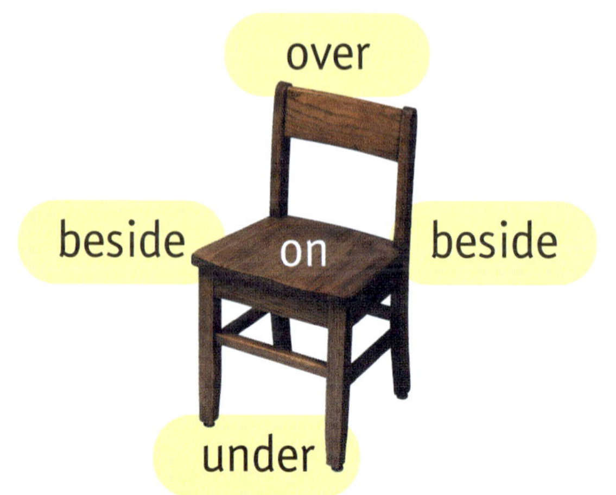

Dictionary

subtraction (–)

Nine rabbits take away three rabbits leaves six rabbits.

9 – 3 = 6

two-dimensional (2D) shapes

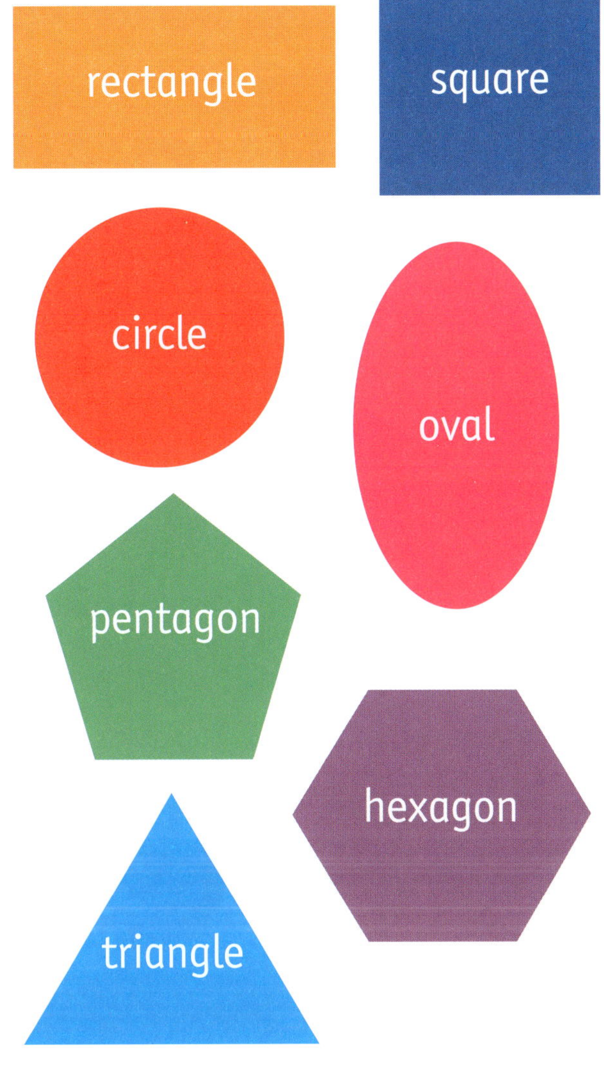

three-dimensional (3D) objects

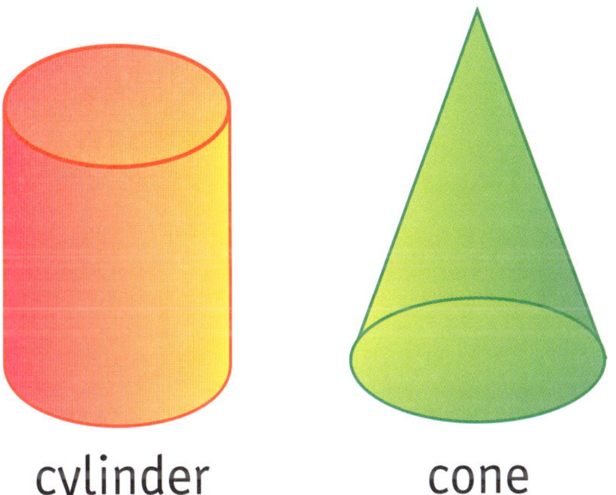

cylinder

cone

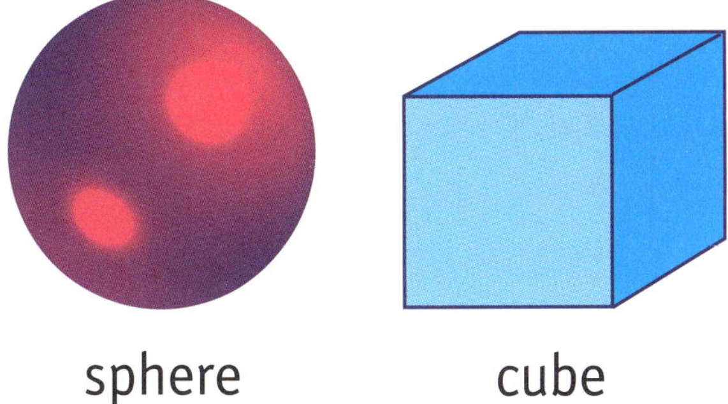

sphere

cube

volume

The space it takes up.

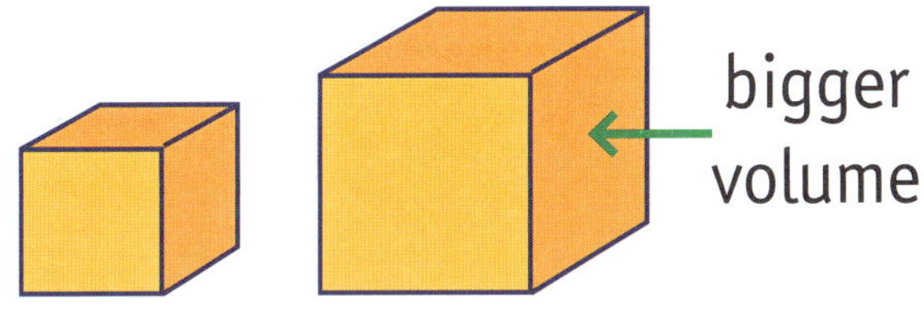

Numbers to twenty

Write the missing numbers.

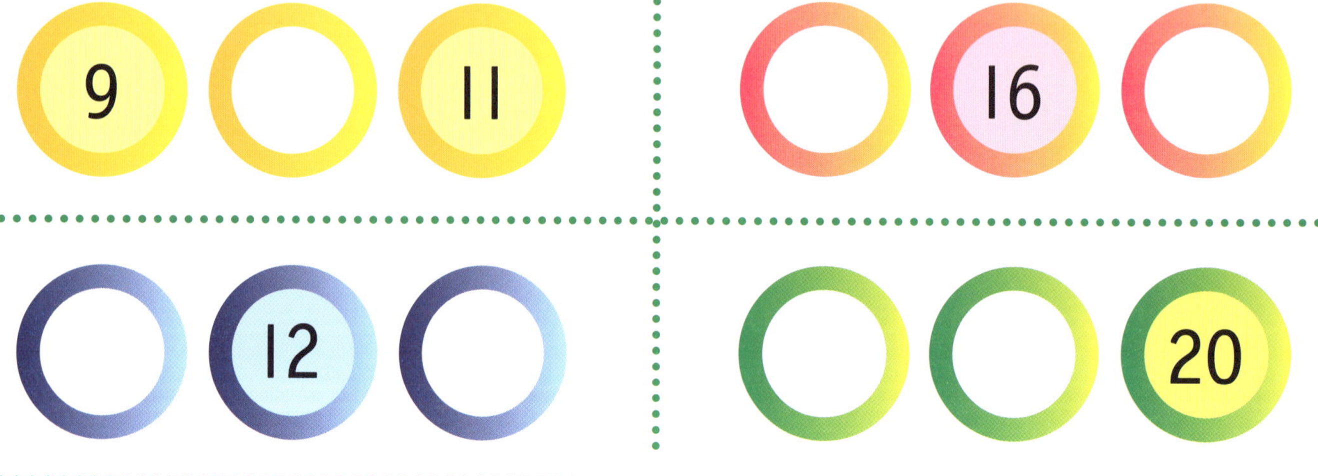

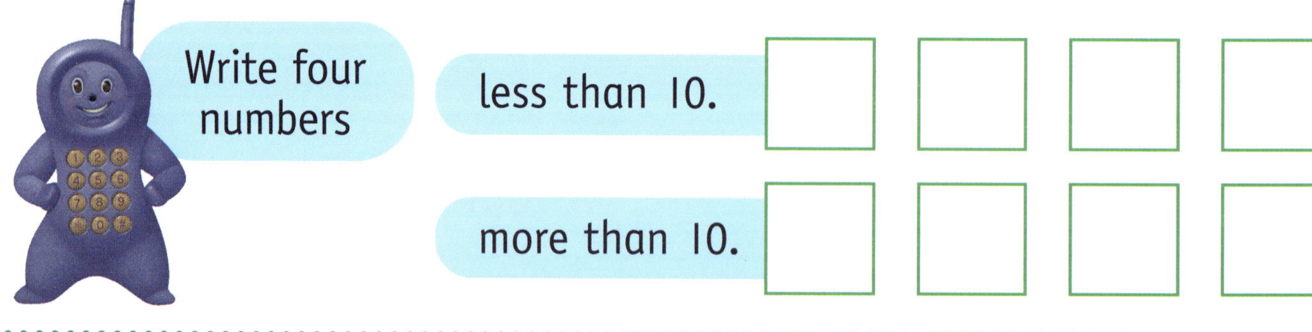

Write four numbers

less than 10.

more than 10.

Challenge! Write your own numbers in order.

More than and less than

Make each price $1 **more.**

 $8 

 $5 

 $9 

 $10  $15 

 $11 

One **more** than 12  16  19

Two **more** than 9  15  20

Make each price $1 **less.**

 $6 

 $8 

 $10 

 $13 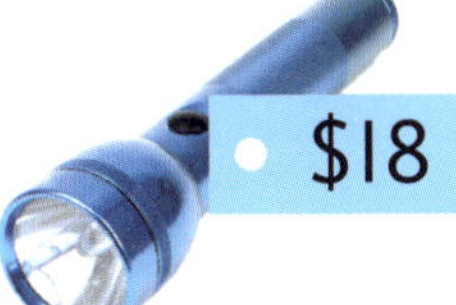 $18 

 $20 

One **less** than 9  14  17 

Two **less** than 7  12  15 

Counting to thirty

How many?

red		
green		
long		
big, round		
small, round		
long, green		
round, red		
bugs altogether		

AC9M1N01 Number **MAE-RWN-02** Representing whole numbers A • Use counting sequences of ones with two-digit numbers and beyond

Numbers to 30

Write these numerals.

Match to a number.

eleven

fifteen

sixteen

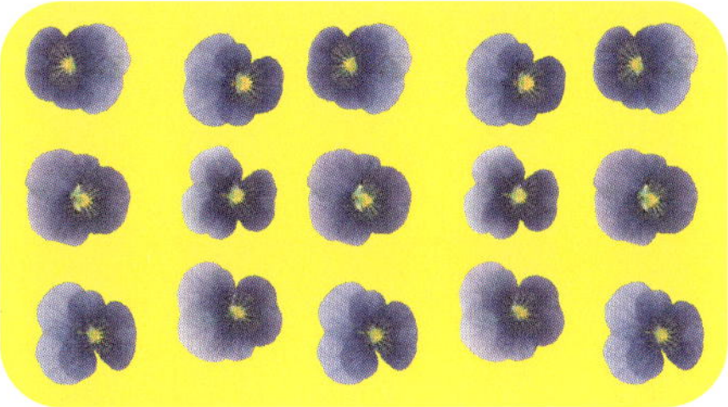

fourteen

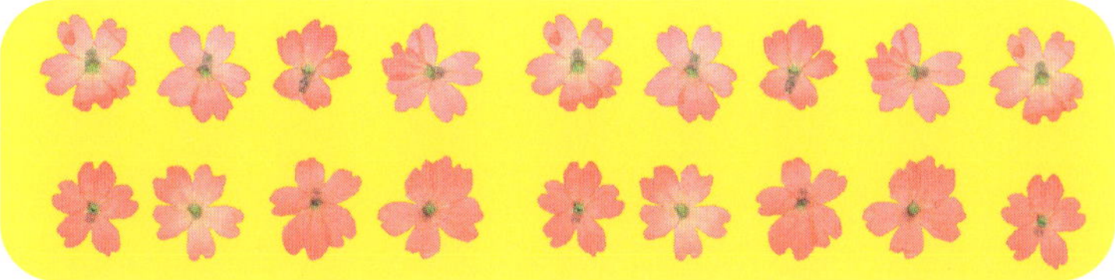

twelve

nineteen

thirteen

eighteen

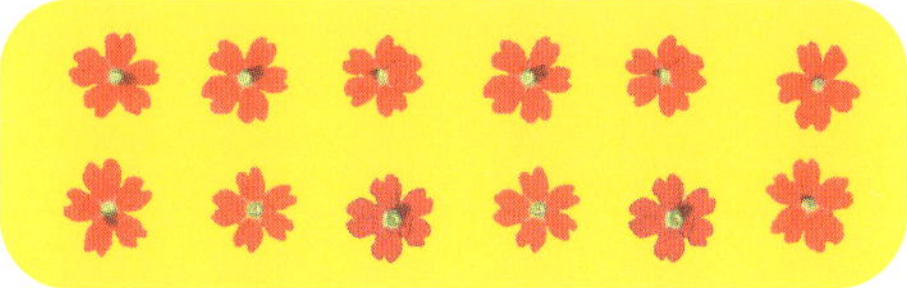

seventeen

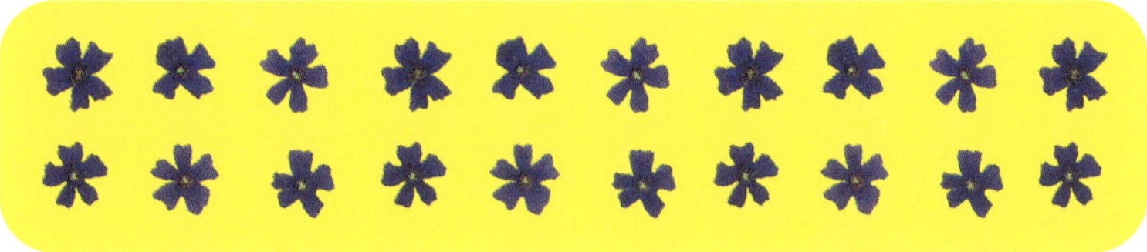

twenty

How many?

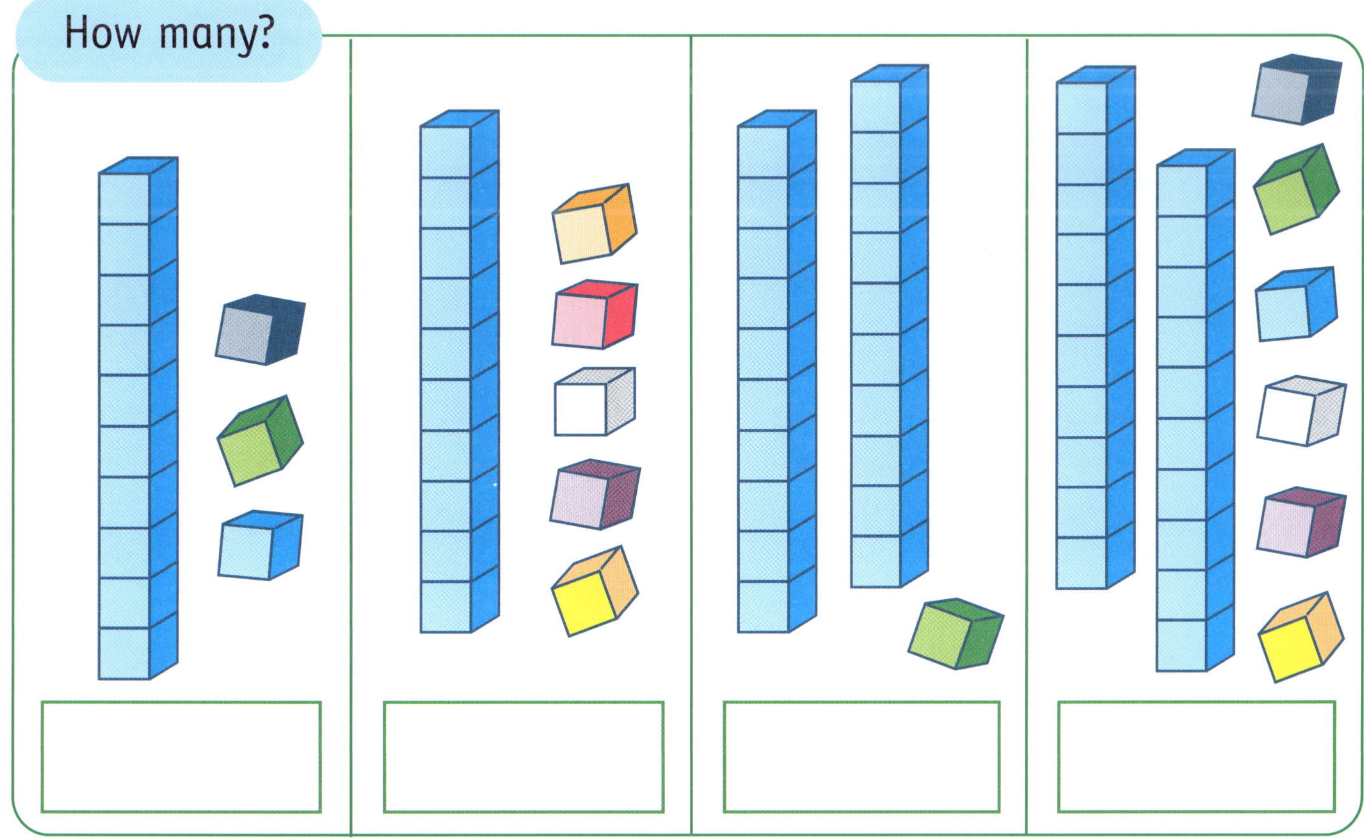

Numbers to fifty

Complete.

1	2	3				7	8		10
11	12	13			16				20
21			24	25		27			30
31	32		34		36		38		40
	42	43		45		47		49	

How many bugs altogether? ☐ Count in tens.

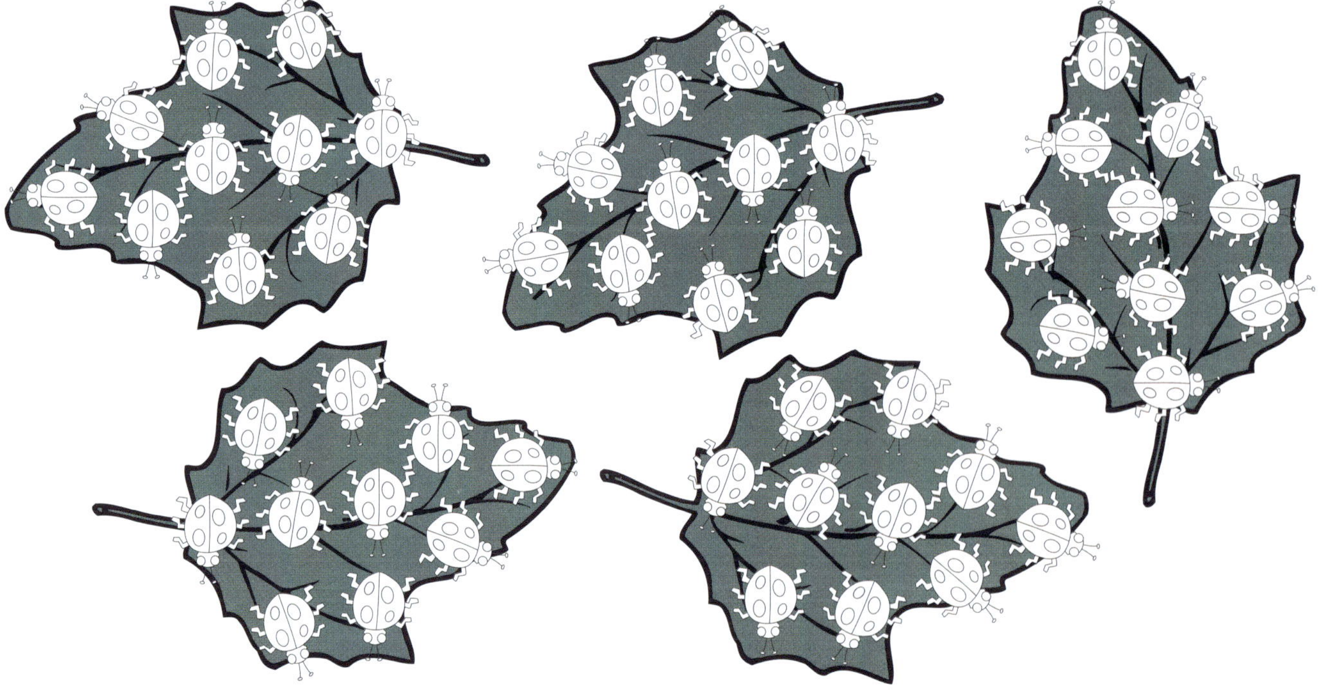

Colour. 24 bugs **red** 12 bugs **green** 14 bugs **blue**

Estimation

Here are 20 balloons.

Zac sells balloons.

How many balloons did Zac sell on:

1 Monday?

guess

check

2 Tuesday?

guess

check

3 Wednesday?

guess

check

4 Thursday?

guess

check

5 Friday?

guess

check

Mastery Checklist

I can:

- ☐ identify the number before and after a number.
- ☐ count by ones to 50.
- ☐ use 10 to make numbers from 11 to 20.
- ☐ count large sets of objects by grouping in tens.
- ☐ estimate the number of objects in a collection.

Problem solving

Lily has some pets.
Altogether the pets have 20 legs.
What pets could she have?
Draw the pets.

Write your answer.

I can solve a problem by:

☐ counting to 20. ☐ drawing a picture.

AC9M1N05 Number **MAE-RWN-02** Representing whole numbers A • Represent the structure of groups of ten in whole numbers
MA1-WM-01 Working mathematically • Apply mathematical techniques to solve problems

2D shapes

Horizontal lines go side-to-side across the page. Vertical lines go up and down.

	Colour vertical lines green. Colour horizontal lines red.	Draw the shape
square		
circle		
triangle		
rectangle		
hexagon		

Shape patterns

Colour squares (■) **red**, triangles (▲) **green** and circles (●) **blue**.

Draw the missing shapes. Colour.

Draw your own patterns.

Sides and corners

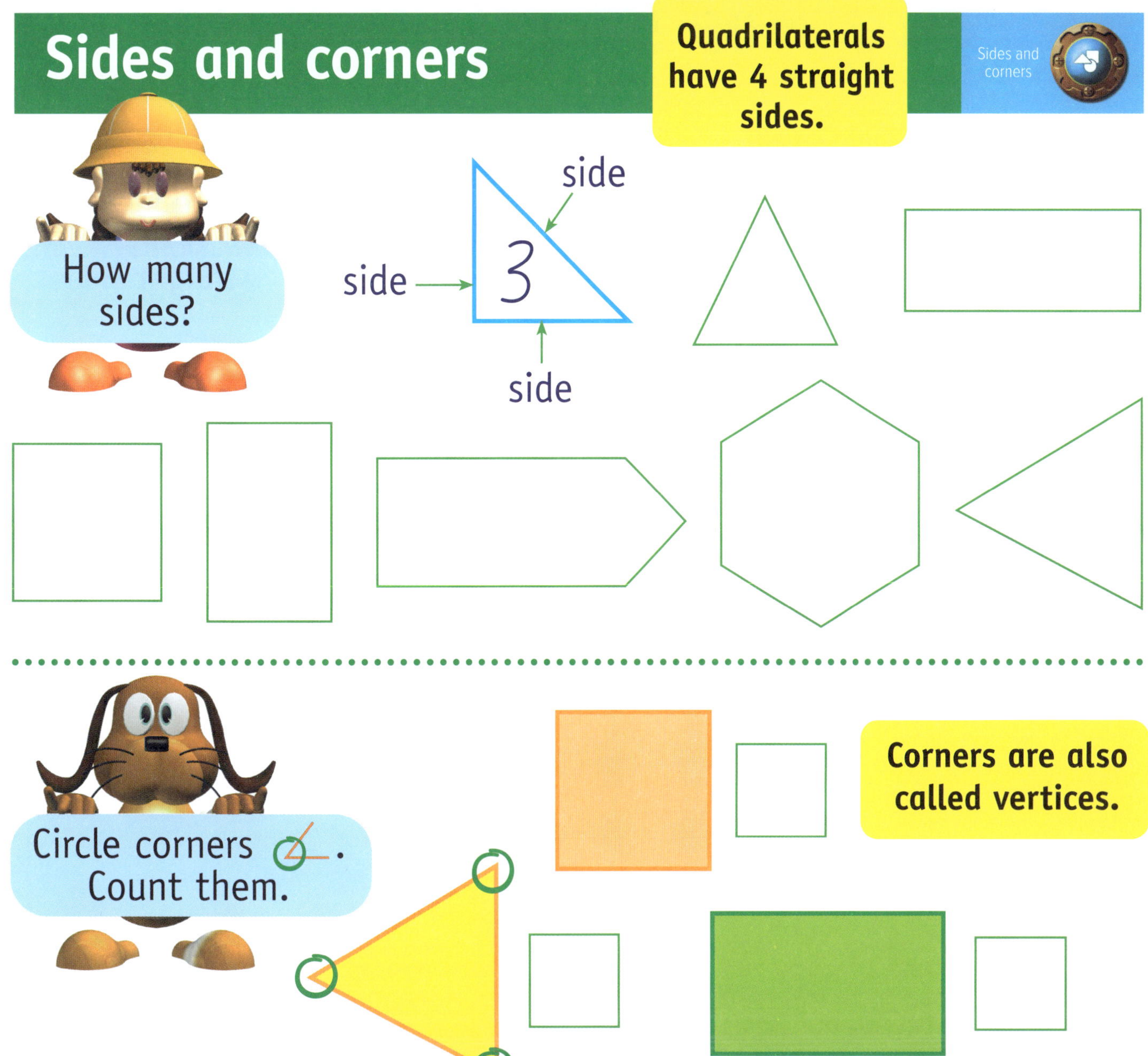

	Sides	Vertices	Quadrilateral?(yes or no)
triangle			
square			
rectangle			

Polygons

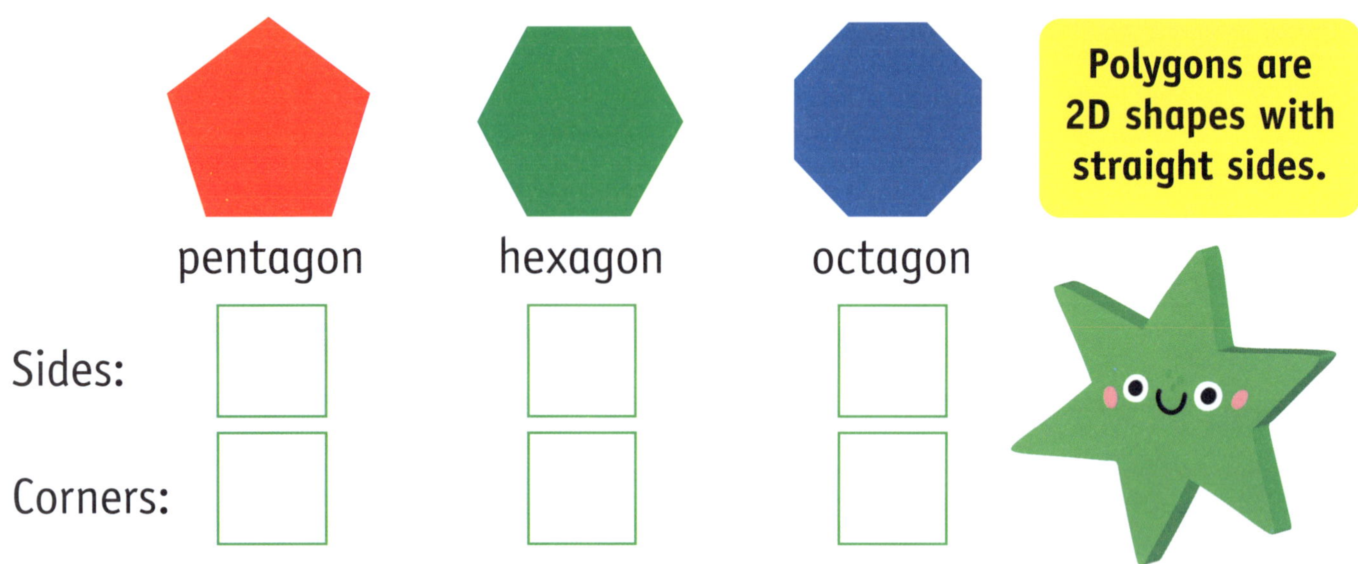

Polygons are 2D shapes with straight sides.

Colour pentagons **red**, hexagons **green**, octagons **blue**.

Challenge!

How many different triangles can you draw?

Mastery Checklist

I can:

- [ ] identify features of 2D shapes.
- [ ] create repeating patterns with shapes.
- [ ] classify polygons by the number of sides or corners.
- [ ] identify polygons with different side lengths.

Problem solving

2D shapes

Draw and name each shape.

3 corners

6 sides

4 sides the same length

5 sides of different lengths

2 short vertical sides, 2 long horizontal sides

I can solve a problem by:

☐ naming a shape from its features. ☐ drawing a picture.

Addition

and, plus, + all mean add

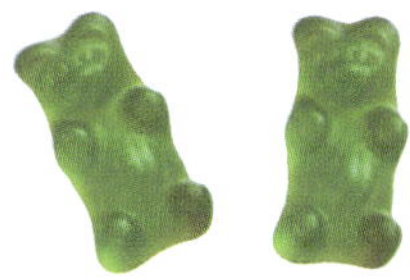  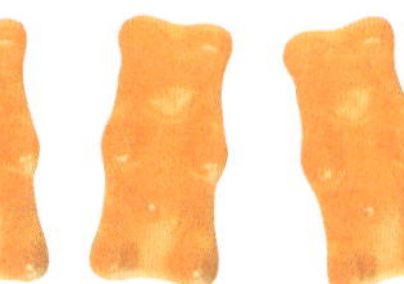  

☐ and ☐ makes ☐

☐ and ☐ makes ☐

 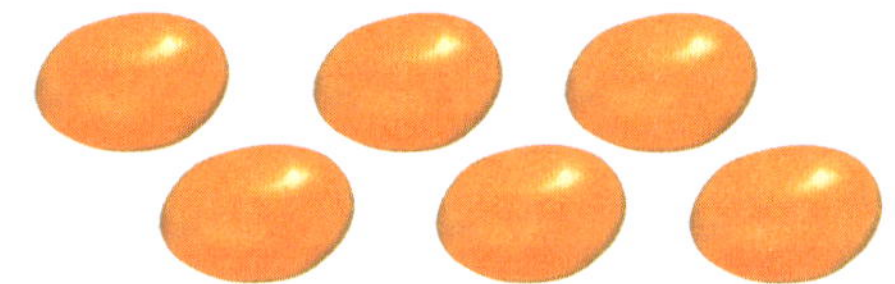  

☐ and ☐ makes ☐

☐ and ☐ makes ☐

 plus  equals  

☐ + ☐ = ☐

 plus  equals 

☐ + ☐ = ☐

 plus  equals 

☐ + ☐ = ☐

Addition

**This is the plus sign.
It means add.**

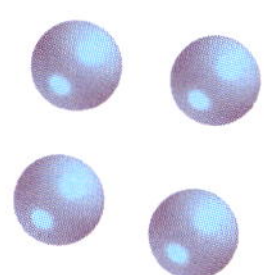  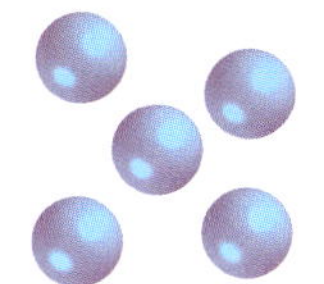

4 + 1 = ☐

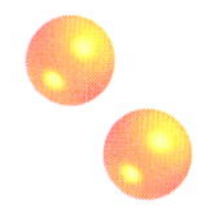

☐ + ☐ = ☐

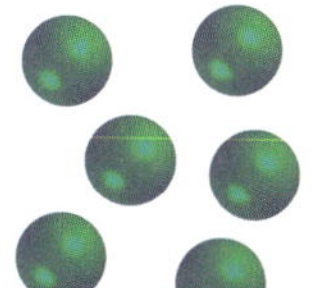 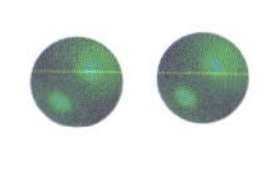

☐ + ☐ = ☐

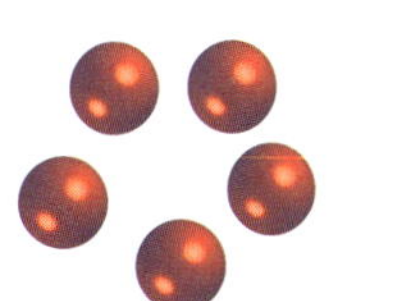

☐ + ☐ = ☐

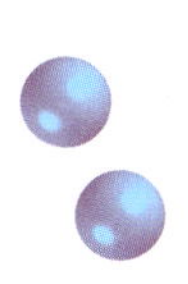 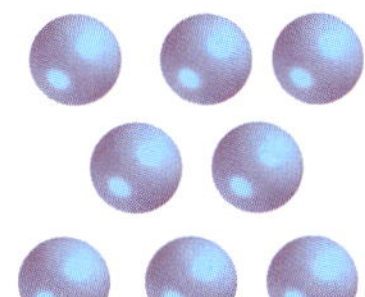

☐ + ☐ = ☐

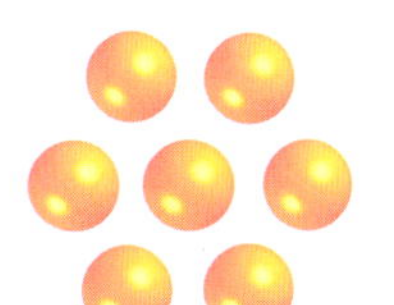

☐ + ☐ = ☐

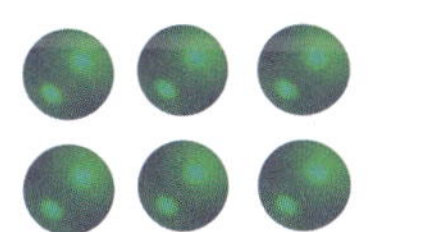 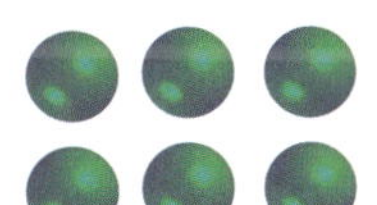

☐ + ☐ = ☐

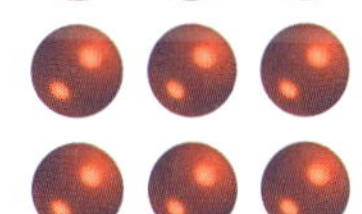

☐ + ☐ = ☐

Challenge!

6 black dogs 3 white dogs 2 puppies

How many dogs altogether? 

Addition on a number line

Jump along the number line to add.

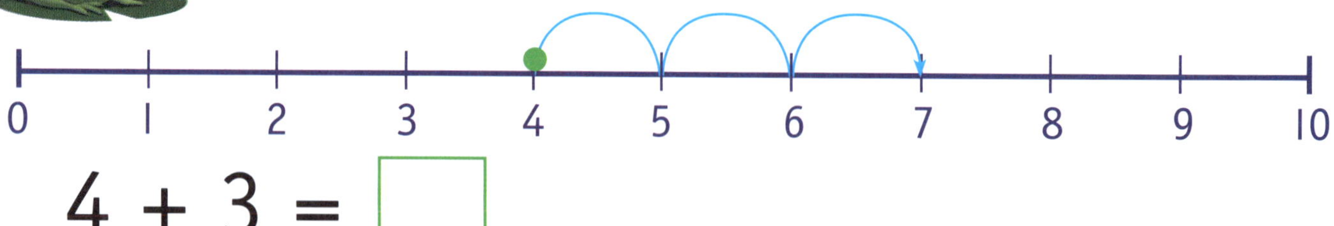

4 + 3 = ☐

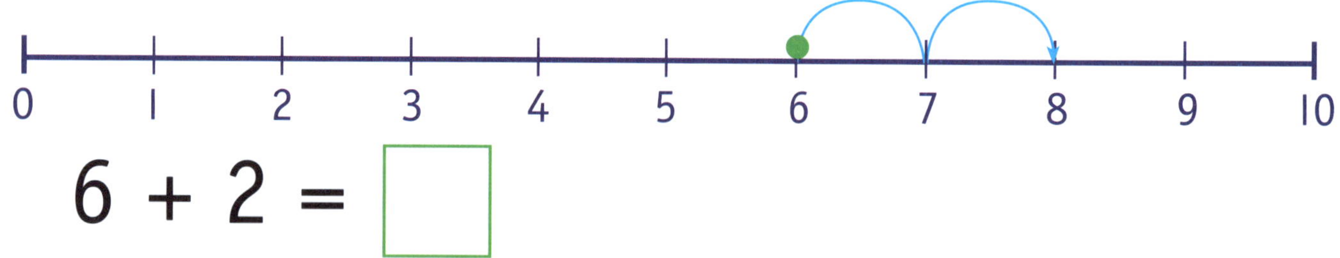

6 + 2 = ☐

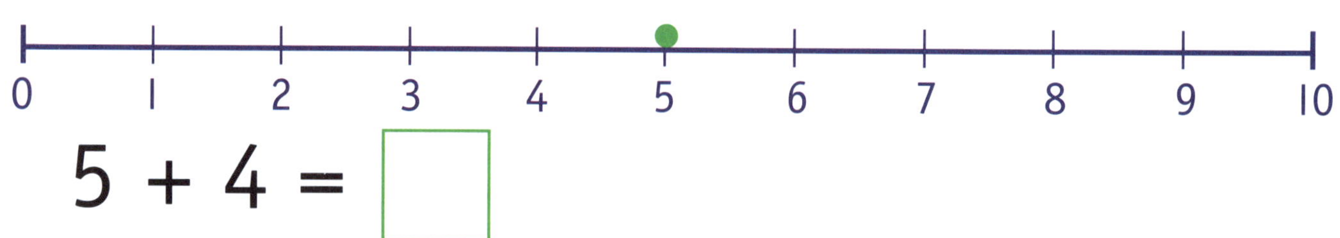

5 + 4 = ☐

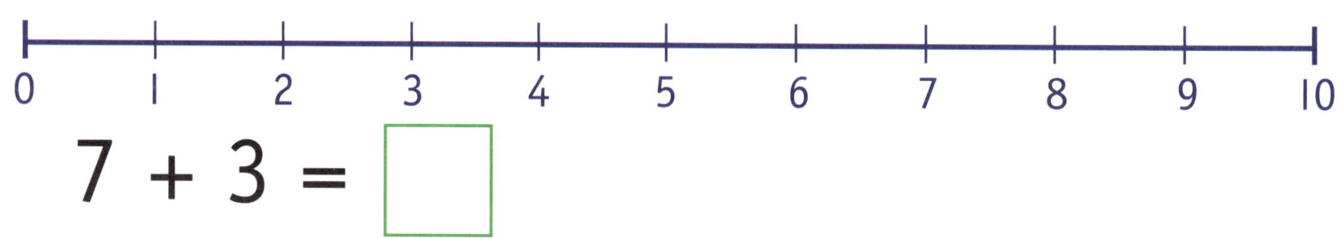

7 + 3 = ☐

Choose your own numbers.

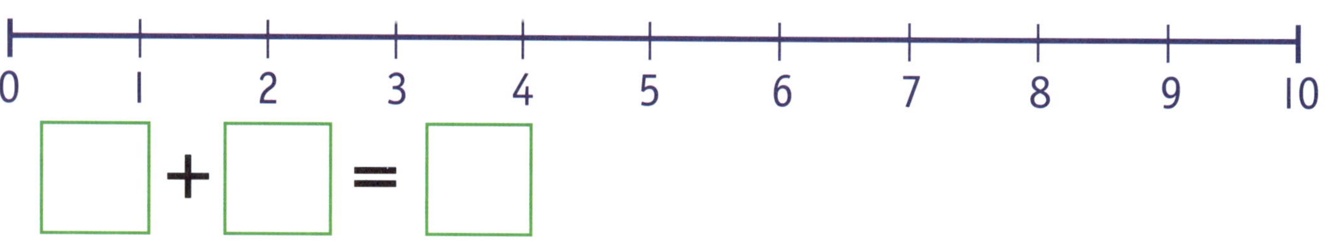

☐ + ☐ = ☐

AC9M1N04 Number **MA1-CSQ-01** Combining and separating quantities A • Use advanced count-by-one strategies to solve addition problems

Making ten

How many more to make 10?

3 + ☐ = 10

6 + ☐ = 10

2 + ☐ = 10

☐ + ☐ = 10

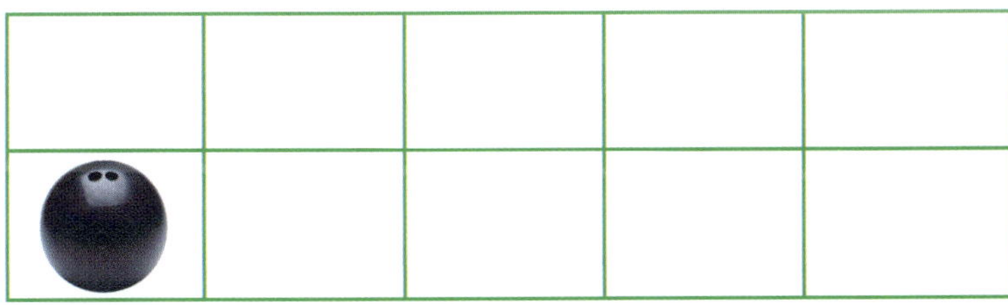

☐ + ☐ = 10

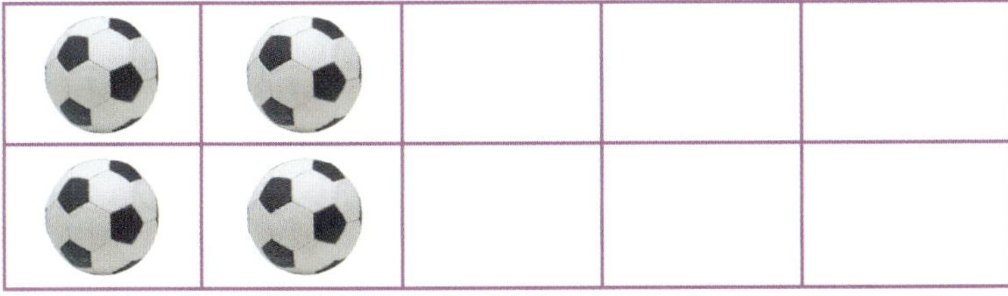

☐ + ☐ = 10

☐ + ☐ = 10

Doubles

Draw the same number of dots.

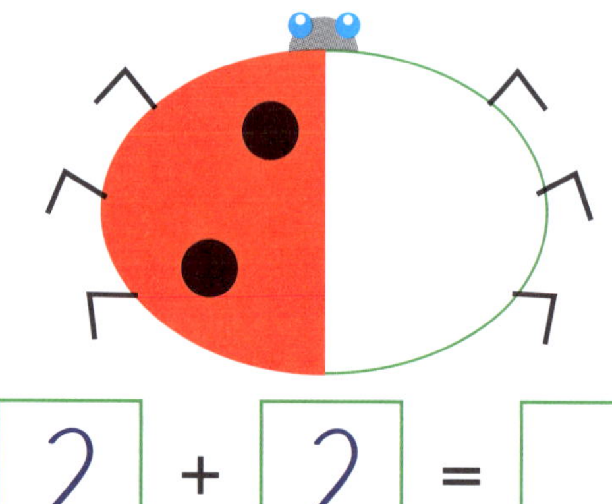

2 + 2 = ☐

Double 2 = ☐

☐ + ☐ = ☐

Double 3 = ☐

☐ + ☐ = ☐

Double 4 = ☐

☐ + ☐ = ☐

Double 5 = ☐

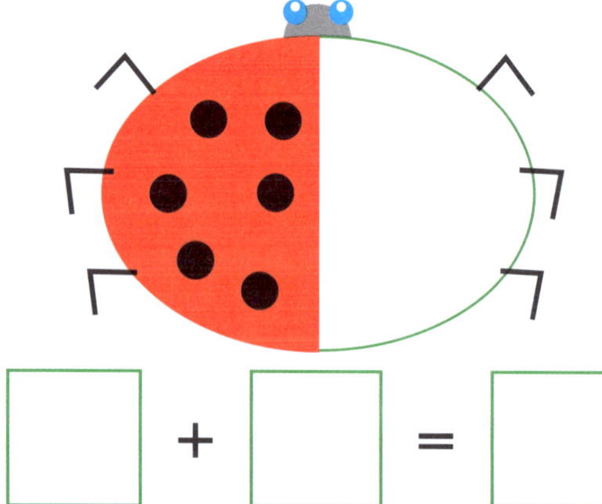

☐ + ☐ = ☐

Double 6 = ☐

Mastery Checklist

I can:

- ☐ use the symbols for plus (+) and equals (=).
- ☐ use count-by-one strategies to add.
- ☐ record pairs of numbers that add up to 10.
- ☐ describe adding two of the same number as 'doubles'.

Problem solving

Little Red Riding Hood

Little Red is going to Grandma's house. She packs a basket.
She puts in 5 apples, then doubles the number.
She puts in 3 cakes, then doubles the number.
She puts in 4 pies, and doubles that number too.
What did she take? Draw the items in the basket.
List each item and how many.

____

____

____

I can solve a problem by:

☐ doubling numbers to 5. ☐ drawing a picture and writing a list.

How many can you see?

Investigation 1

1 Count each group. Match to a box. Write the number of items in the box.

gems

fruit

blocks

less than 20

19 gems

butterflies

more than 20

animals

books

leaves

AC9M1N01 Number **MAE-RWN-02** Representing whole numbers A • Represent the structure of groups of ten in whole numbers
MA1-WM-01 Working mathematically • Apply mathematical techniques to solve problems • Communicate their thinking and reasoning coherently and clearly

How many can you see?

Investigation 1

2 How many windows in your classroom?

Circle your estimate:

- less than 10
- more than 10

Count them. ______

Draw them.

3 How many pencils on your table?

Circle your estimate:

- less than 20
- more than 20

Count them. ______

Draw them.

4 How many children in your class today?

Circle your estimate:

- less than 20
- more than 20

Count them. ______

Draw them.

5 Count one group in a different way. How did you do it?

____

____

To do this, I needed to:

- ☐ count to thirty or more.
- ☐ estimate numbers to 20.
- ☐ understand the terms 'more' and 'less'.
- ☐ use strategies that help me count.

I enjoyed this task! ☆☆☆☆☆

Revision

1 How many?

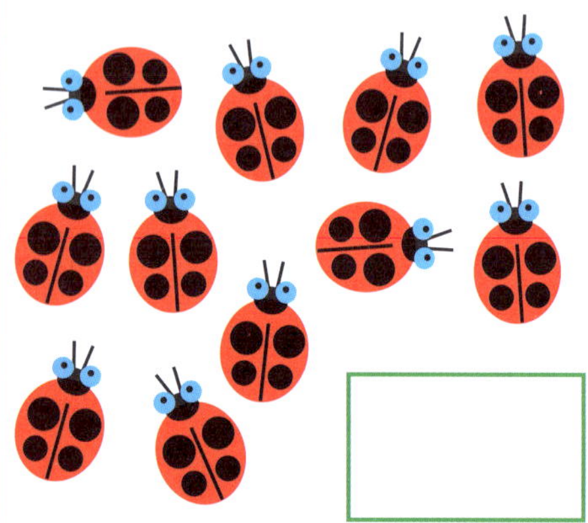

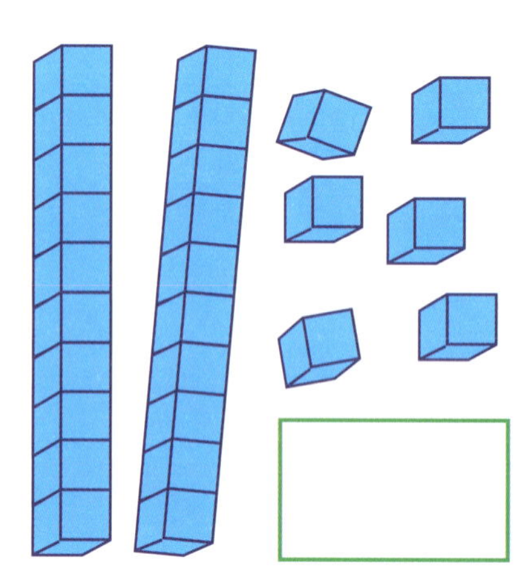

2 Write the numerals.

twelve

eighteen

twenty

fifteen

3 Match. Then circle the largest shape.

triangle

rectangle

square

circle

4 Add.

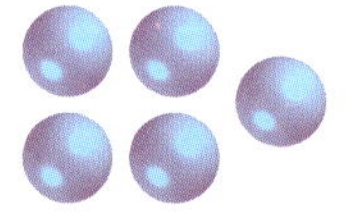

3 + 5 =

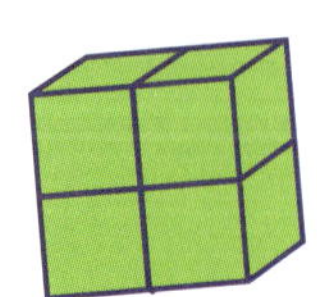

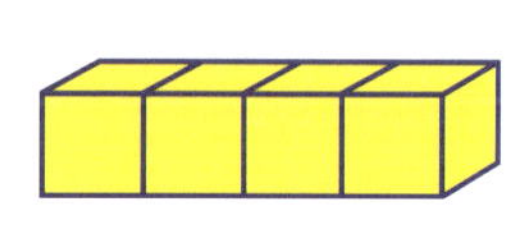

+ =

Revision

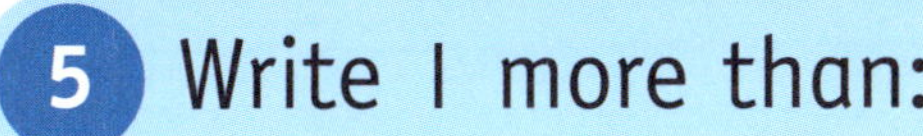

7 ☐ 14 ☐ 11 ☐ 19 ☐

6 Match.

quadrilateral | pentagon | hexagon | octagon

7 Make 10:

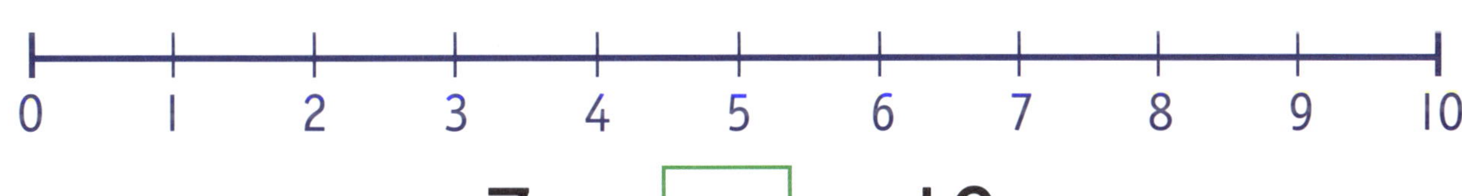

7 + ☐ = 10

8 Draw and write.

Double 4 = ☐

Double 3 = ☐

Double 5 = ☐

The days of the week

Write and draw something you do on each day.

		Draw
Sunday		
Monday		
Tuesday		
Wednesday		
Thursday		
Friday		
Saturday		

Which day comes after:

Sunday? ____________________ Thursday? ____________________

Which day comes before:

Wednesday? ____________________ Sunday? ____________________

Revise: **AC9M1M03** Measurement **MA1-NSM-02** Non-spatial measure A • Time: Name and order the cycle of months

O'clock

What time is it?

☐ o'clock

☐ o'clock

☐ o'clock

☐ o'clock

☐ o'clock

☐ o'clock

☐ o'clock

☐ o'clock

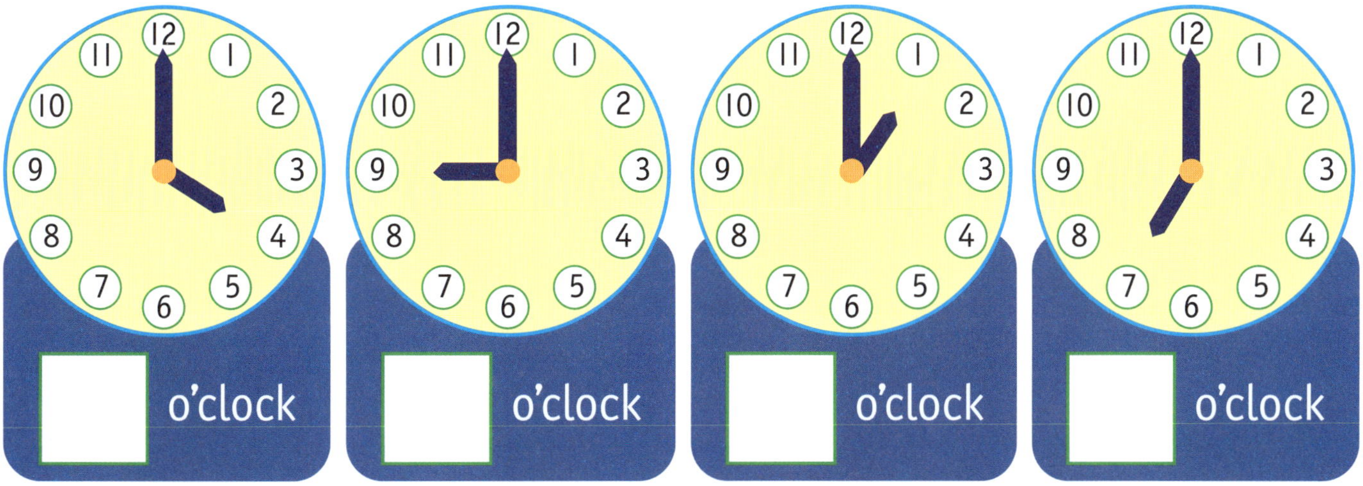

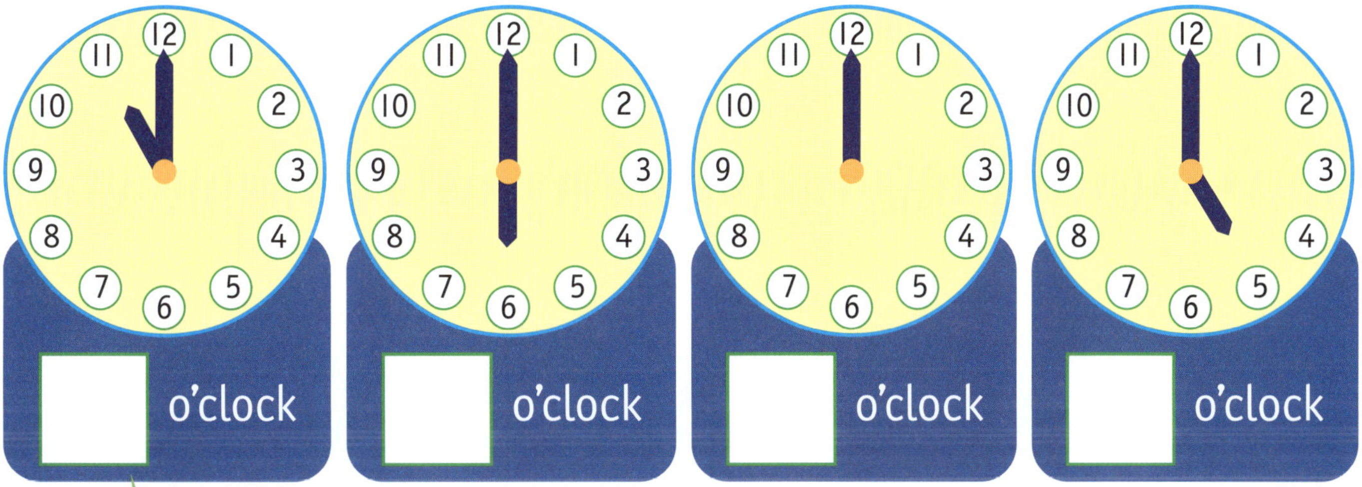

Draw hands.

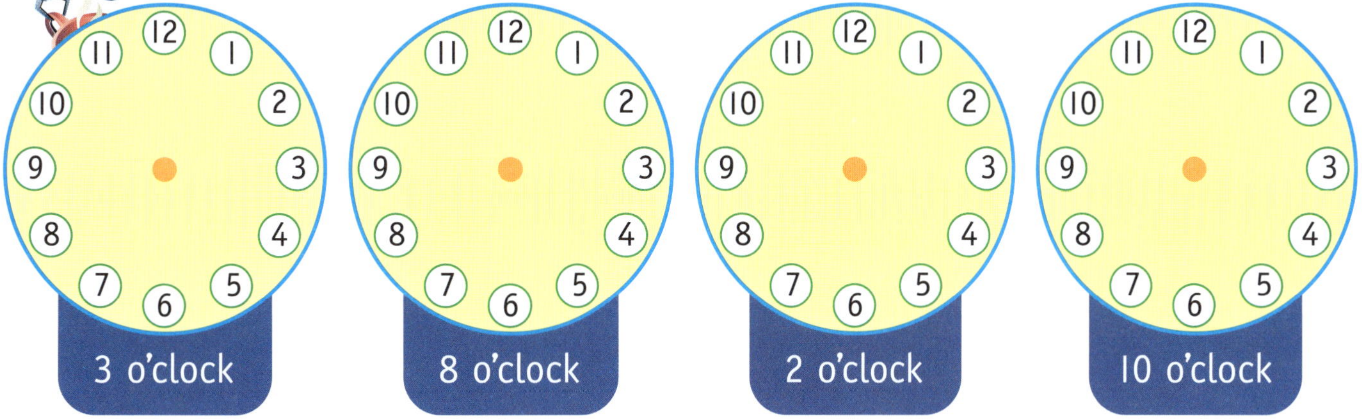

3 o'clock

8 o'clock

2 o'clock

10 o'clock

Months of the year

Match. Write the missing months.

May

February

July

October

August

January	Summer
March	Autumn
April	
June	Winter
September	Spring
November	
December	Summer

Which month is:

1st? ____________ 4th? ____________

When is your birthday? ____________

Reading digital clocks

What time is it?

3:00	7:00	8:00	10:00
3 o'clock	o'clock	o'clock	o'clock
5:00	1:00	11:00	12:00
o'clock	o'clock	o'clock	o'clock

Colour to match.

2:00

6 o'clock

2 o'clock

6:00

Challenge!

What time is it 1 hour after?

4:00 o'clock

o'clock

Mastery Checklist

I can:
- ☐ name the days of the week.
- ☐ read analog and digital clocks to the hour.
- ☐ write time on the hour using the word 'o'clock'.
- ☐ name and order the months of the year.

Take away

Word problems

Cross out to take away.

1

☐ take away 2 = ☐

2

☐ take away 2 = ☐

Draw pictures.

3 7 cats, 3 run away.

How many left?

☐

4 6 fish, 4 swim away.

How many left?

☐

5 9 children, 4 go home.

How many left?

6 Write your own story.

____

____

Subtraction stories

Tell a story about the picture to a friend.

☐ children. ☐ boys.

How many girls?

☐ – ☐ = ☐

☐ children. ☐ girls.

How many boys?

☐ – ☐ = ☐

Write your own subtraction story.

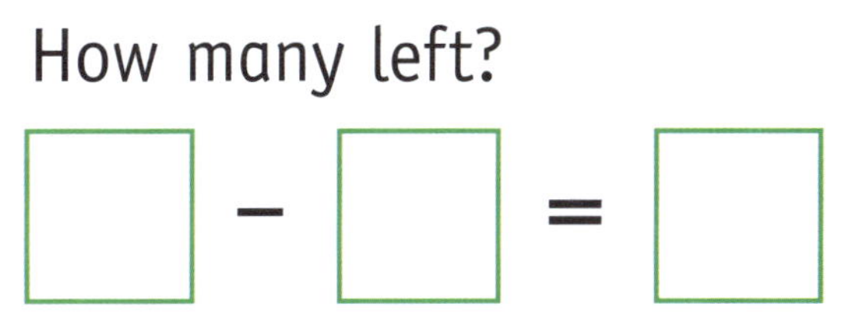

☐ apples. ☐ eaten.

How many left?

☐ – ☐ = ☐

Subtraction

This sign means take away.

8 – 3 = ☐

5 – 2 = ☐

7 – 5 = ☐

6 – 3 = ☐

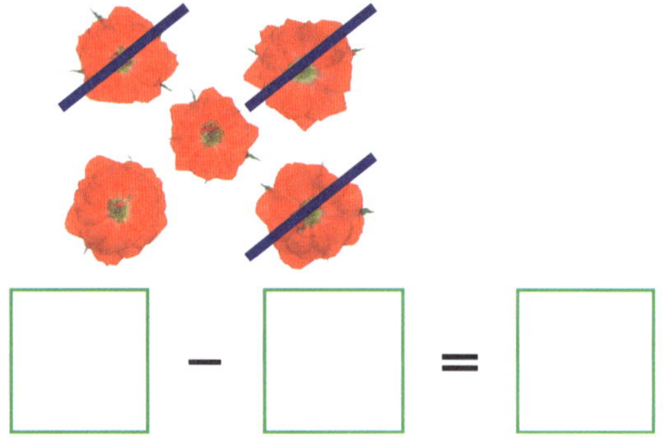

☐ – ☐ = ☐

☐ – ☐ = ☐

☐ – ☐ = ☐

☐ – ☐ = ☐

Challenge!

10 cakes.
Kate eats 2.
Jim eats 5.

How many left? ☐

Counting back

− means take away.

Count back 2.

$6 - 2 = \square$

1 2 3 4 5 6 7 8 9 10

$3 - 2 = \square$

1 2 3 4 5 6 7 8 9 10

$9 - 2 = \square$

1 2 3 4 5 6 7 8 9 10

$7 - 2 = \square$

Count back 3.

$8 - 3 = \square$

$5 - 3 = \square$

1 2 3 4 5 6 7 8 9 10

$10 - 3 = \square$

1 2 3 4 5 6 7 8 9 10

$9 - 3 = \square$

Take away

1 2 3 4 5 6 7 8 9 10

Count back.

6 − [3] = ☐

10 − [2] = ☐

8 − [5] = ☐

7 − [6] = ☐

Throw a [die]. Draw the dots.

9 − ☐ = ☐

6 − ☐ = ☐

7 − ☐ = ☐

10 − ☐ = ☐

6 − ☐ = ☐

8 − ☐ = ☐

8 − ☐ = ☐

9 − ☐ = ☐

AC9M1N04 Number **MA1-CSQ-01** Combining and separating quantities A • Use advanced count-by-one strategies to solve subtraction problems

Subtraction on a number line

Jump back to take away.

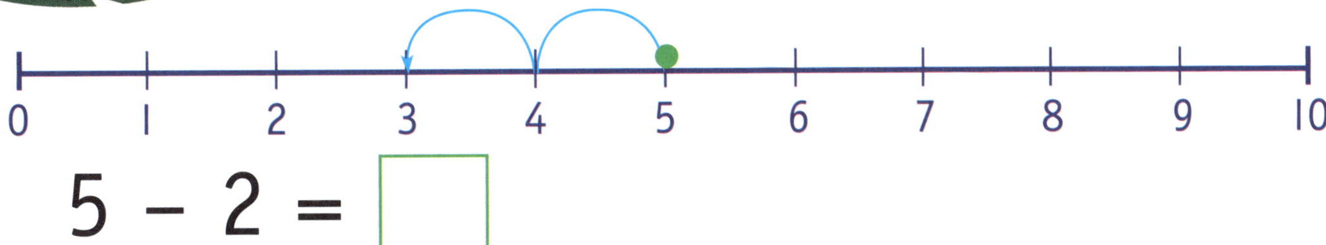

5 – 2 = ☐

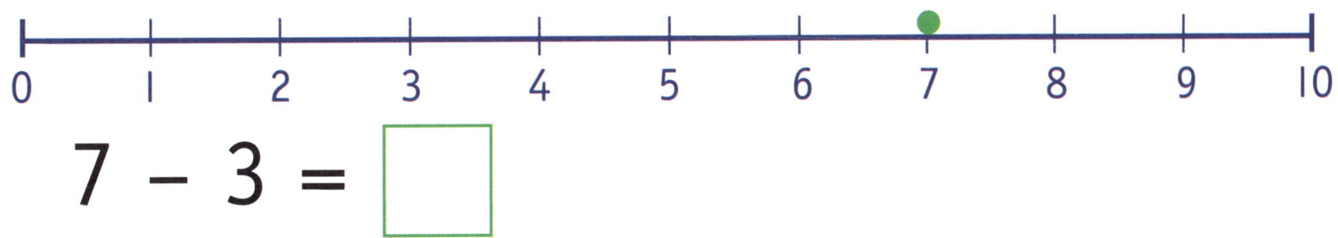

7 – 3 = ☐

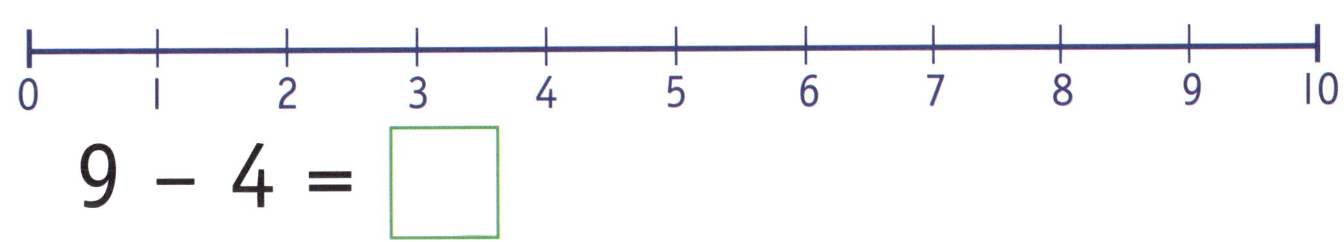

9 – 4 = ☐

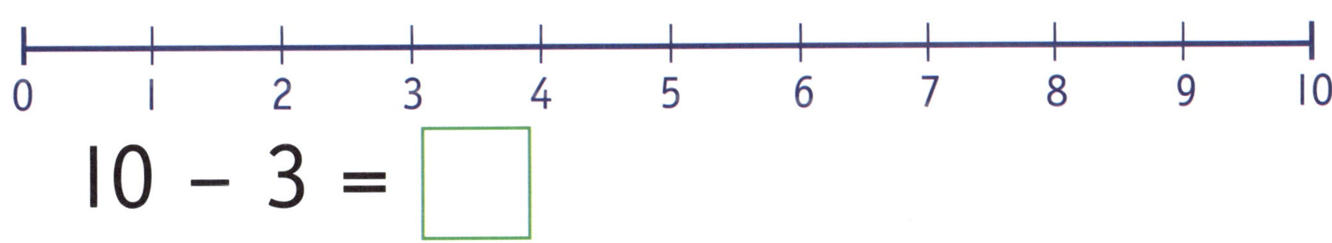

10 – 3 = ☐

Challenge!

Choose your own numbers. Draw a number line to take away.

Mastery Checklist

I can:

- ☐ use the symbols for minus (–) and equals (=).
- ☐ record number sentences.
- ☐ use count-by-one strategies to subtract.
- ☐ count back to solve subtraction problems.

Problem solving

Lisa cooked 2 trays of muffins.

Freya ate 1. The twins ate 1 each. Katy ate 2. Ned ate 3.

4 friends are coming to visit.

Will they get one each?

Will Lisa have any left?

Draw your answer.

Write about how you got your answers.

I can solve a problem by:

☐ counting back to take away.

☐ drawing a picture.

AC9M1N05 Number **MA1-CSQ-01** Combining and separating quantities A • Use advanced count-by-one strategies to solve addition and subtraction problems
MA1-WM-01 Working mathematically • Apply mathematical techniques to solve problems • Communicate their thinking and reasoning coherently and clearly

Comparing mass

Circle ◯ the heavier one. Draw a ✗ on the lighter one.

Draw something heavier.

Draw something lighter.

Draw two different things that weigh the same.

Compare and measure mass

Match.

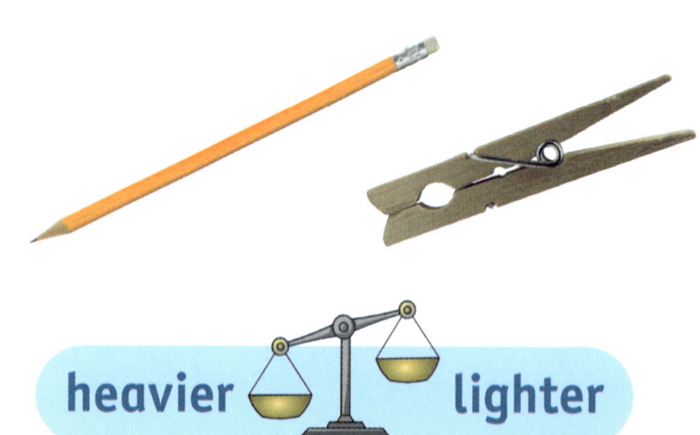

Weigh items against 20 blocks.

Draw an item that matches each word:

Measure **mass** on a scale

 heavier	 lighter	 about the same

__________ is heavier than 20 blocks.

__________ is lighter than 20 blocks.

__________ weighs about the same as 20 blocks.

Compare and measure mass

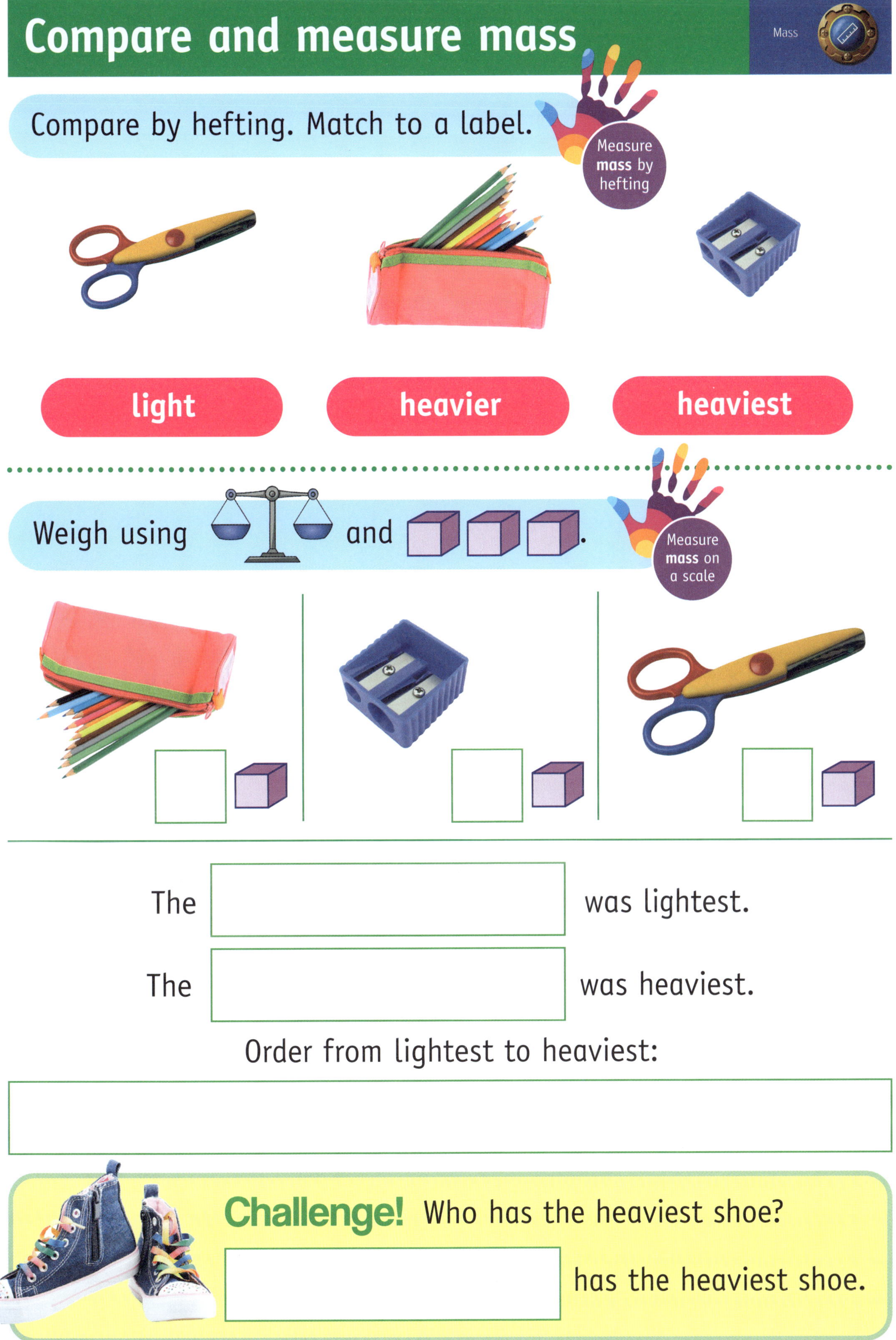

Compare by hefting. Match to a label.

light

heavier

heaviest

Weigh using [balance] and [cubes].

The [ ] was lightest.

The [ ] was heaviest.

Order from lightest to heaviest:

Challenge! Who has the heaviest shoe?

[ ] has the heaviest shoe.

Half

Colour half.

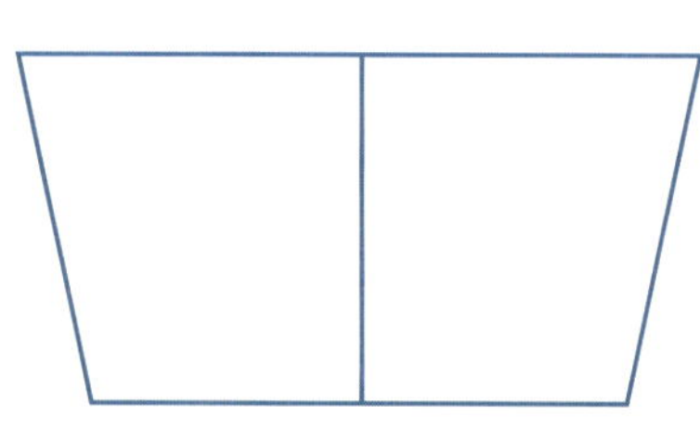

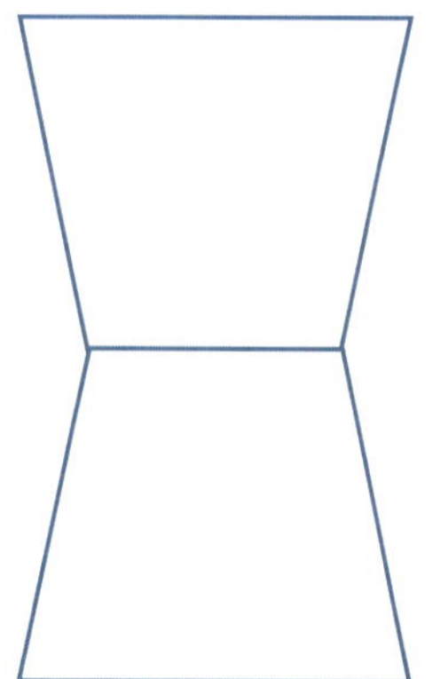

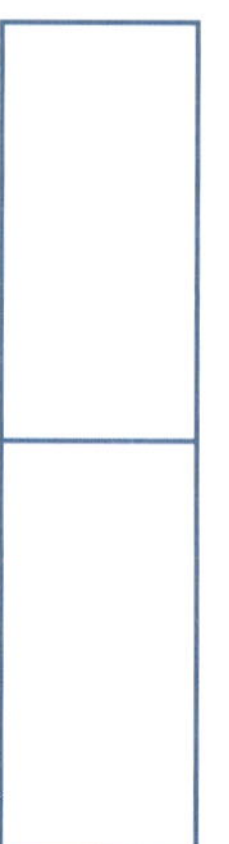

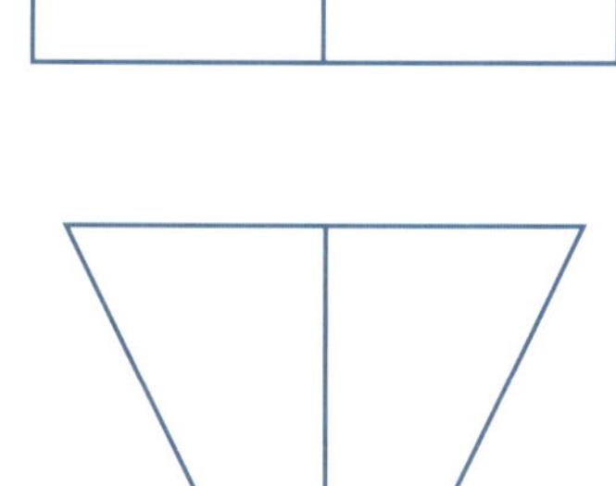

Share between two. Draw a line to cut each into halves.

AC9M1SP01 Space **MA1-GM-03** Geometric measure • Length: Subdivide lengths to find halves and quarters

Halves

Tick the lines cut in half.

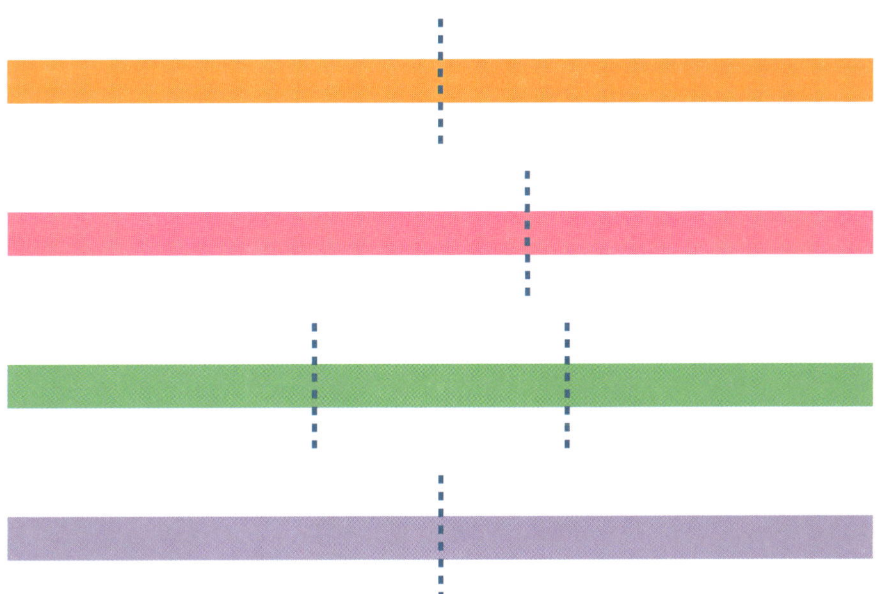

Colour $\frac{1}{2}$ of each shape.

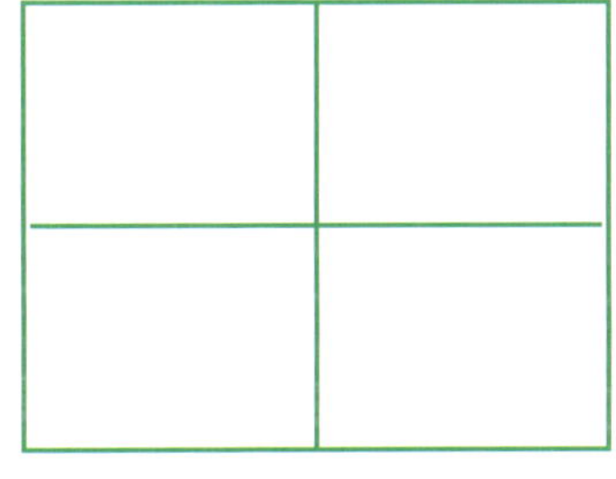

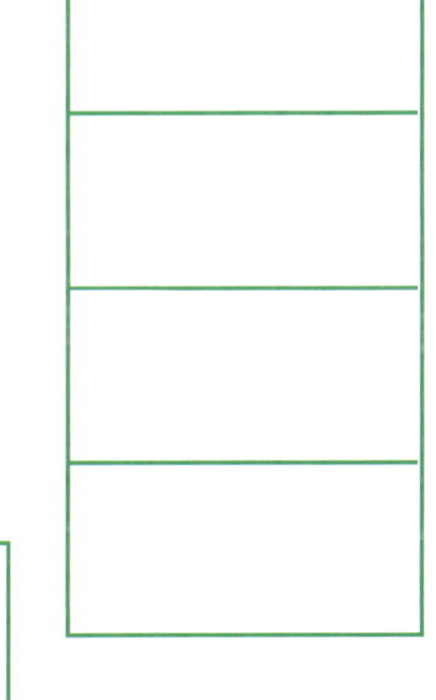

Challenge! Colour one half. Make each one different.

$\frac{1}{2}$

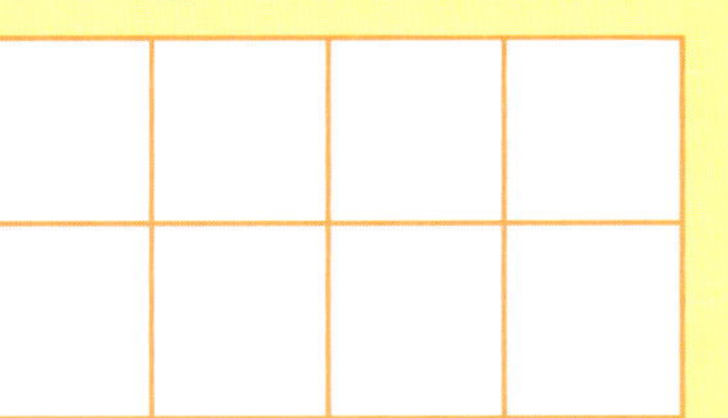

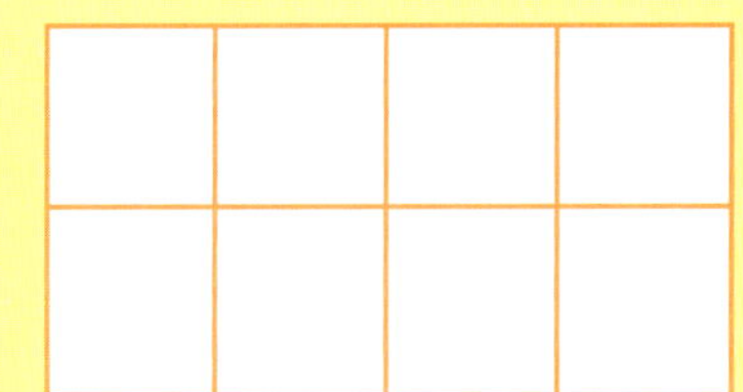

AC9M1SP01 Space **MA1-GM-03** Geometric measure • Length: Subdivide lengths to find halves and quarters

Comparing capacity

Circle the one that holds more.

How many  ?

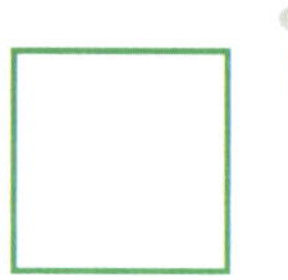

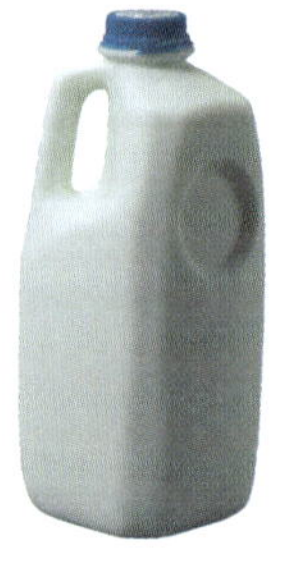

 holds most  holds least

Challenge! Compare lunchboxes. Order four lunchboxes from holds least to holds most.

AC9M1M01 Measurement **MA1-3DS-02** Three-dimensional spatial structure A • Volume: Measure and compare the internal volumes (capacities) of containers by filling

Measuring capacity

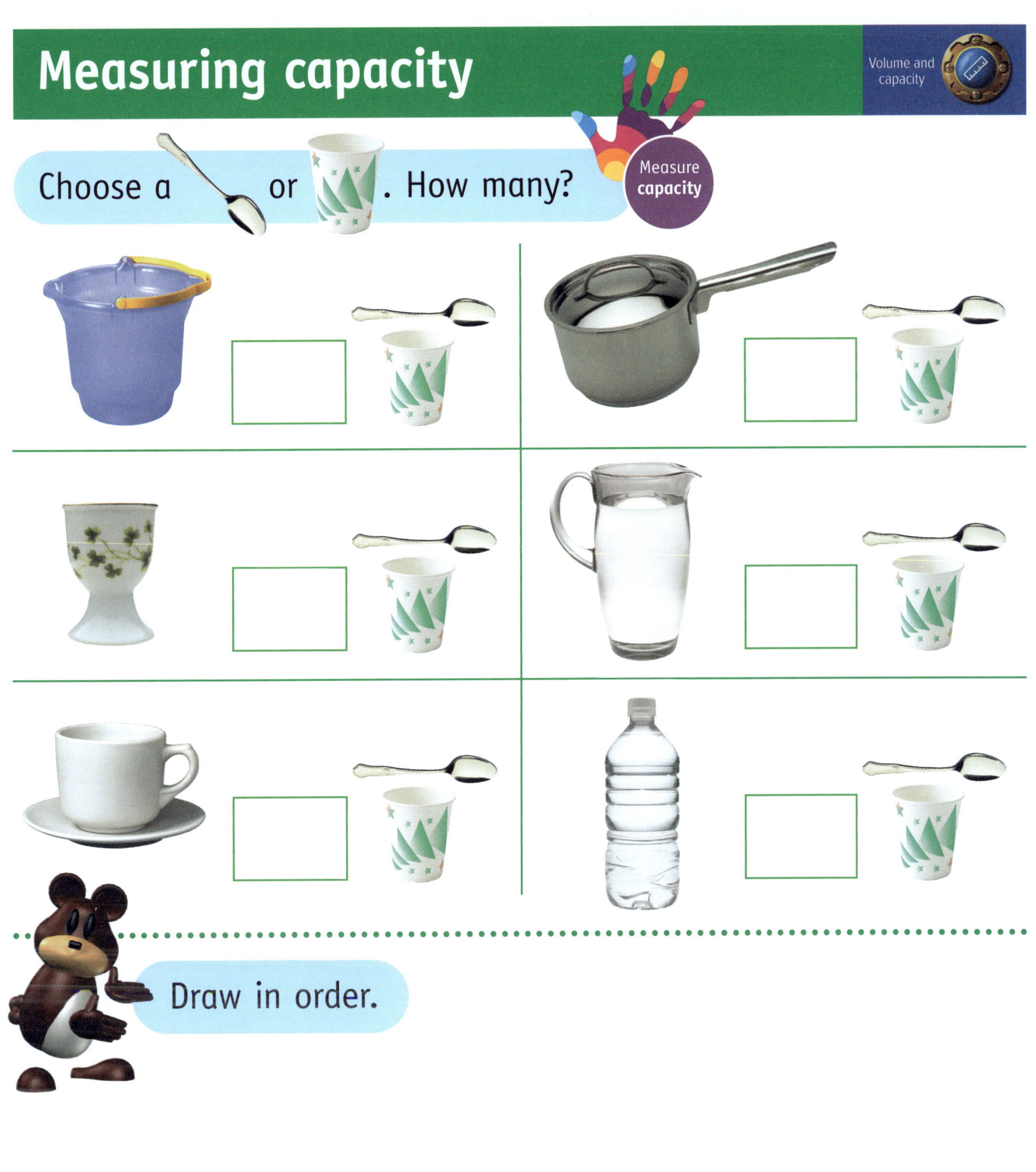

Draw in order.

holds least

holds most

Mastery Checklist

I can:
- [ ] compare the masses of objects by hefting, and check using an equal-arm balance.
- [ ] identify items cut into halves.
- [ ] choose units to measure the capacities of containers.
- [ ] compare the capacities of two or more containers.

Revision • Term 1

1 Write the missing numbers.

2 What time is it?

3 Circle each shape that is a:

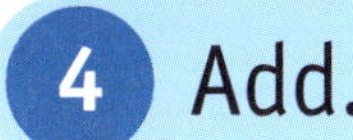

4 Add.

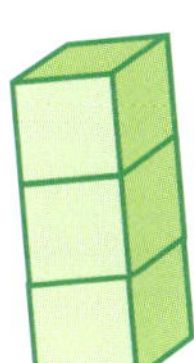

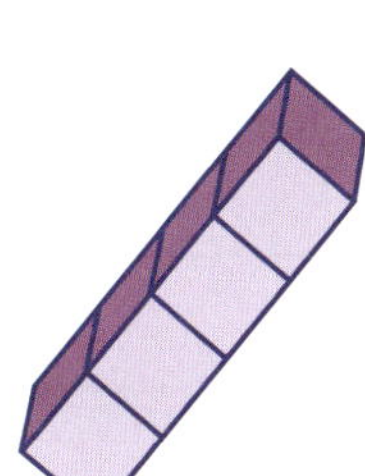

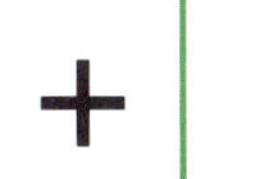

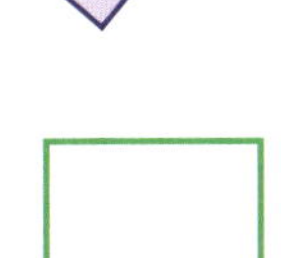
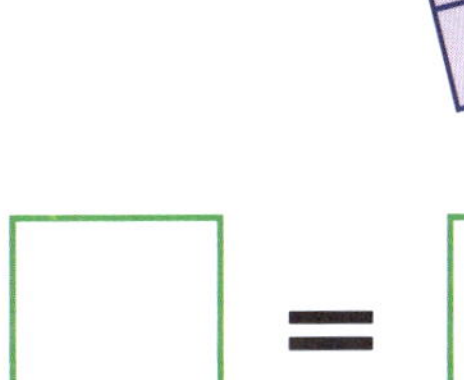

5 Colour half of each shape.

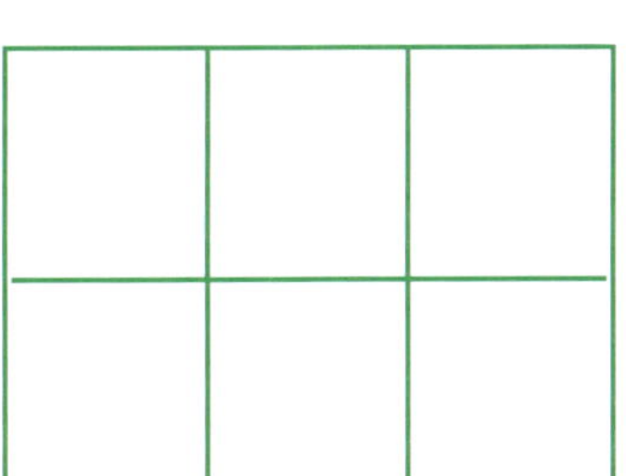
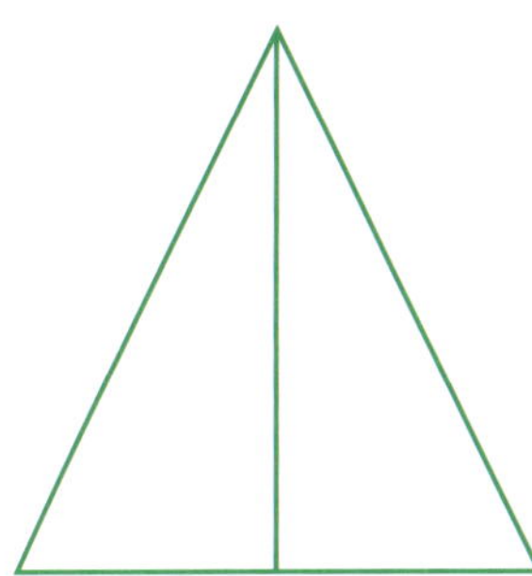

6

5 jelly beans. 3 eaten.

How many left? ☐

7 What day is it today?

☐

Doubles

Draw the same number of dots. Write the double.

 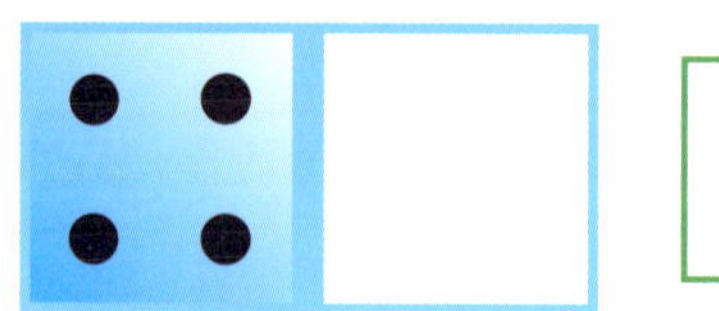

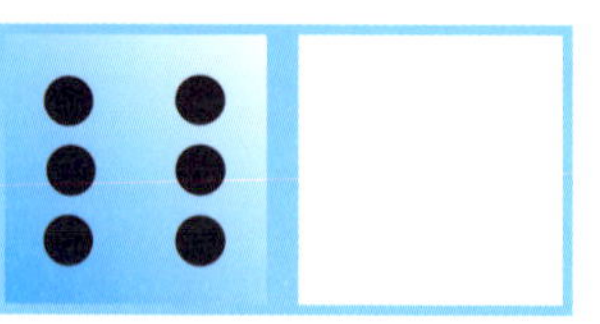 

Write the double.

Double 4 is

2 groups of 4 =

Double 3 is

2 groups of 3 =

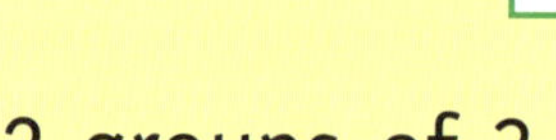

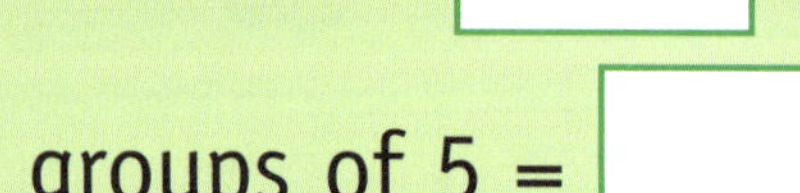

Double 5 is

2 groups of 5 =

Double 7 is

2 groups of 7 =

Challenge!

The price doubles as animals get bigger. How much is the chicken?

Near doubles

Double plus 1.

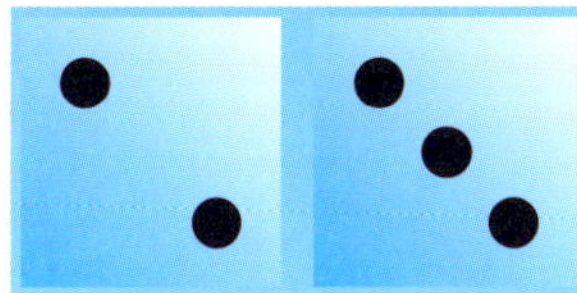

2 + 3 = double 2 plus 1

2 + 2 + 1 = ☐

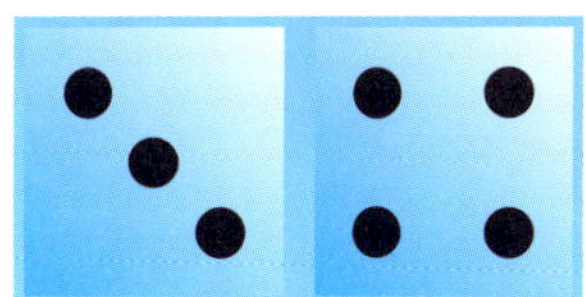

3 + 4 = double ☐ plus 1

☐ + ☐ + 1 = ☐

Write the near doubles.

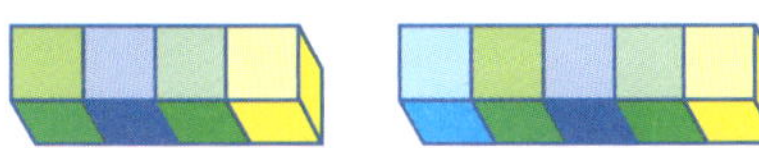

4 + 5 = ☐ + ☐ + 1 = ☐

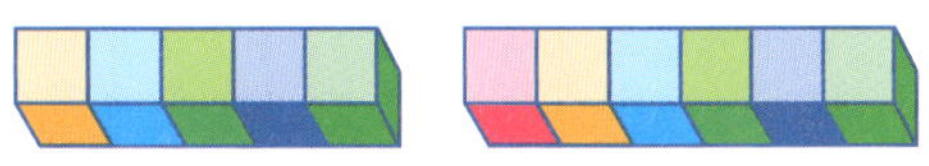

5 + 6 = ☐ + ☐ + 1 = ☐

Draw and write near doubles.

Min has 6 cats and 7 dogs.
How many pets?

☐ + ☐ = ☐

Kim has 7 birds and 8 fish.
How many pets?

☐ + ☐ = ☐

Number facts for 5, 7, 8

Draw dots to match.
Make each domino different.

5

4 + 1 = 5

☐ + ☐ = 5

☐ + ☐ = 5

7

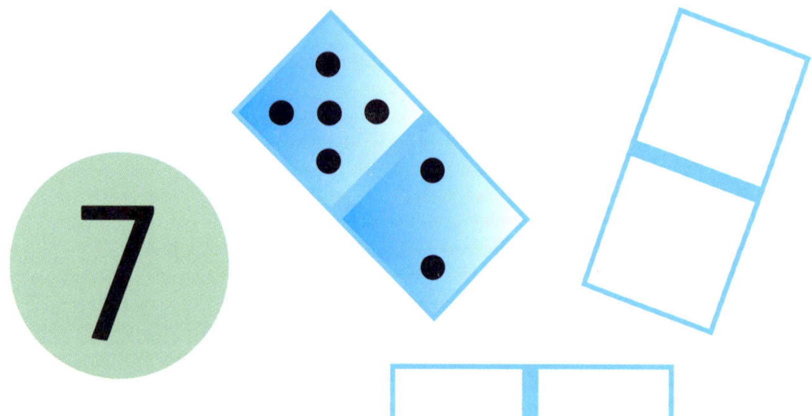

☐ + ☐ = 7

☐ + ☐ = 7

☐ + ☐ = 7

8

☐ + ☐ = 8

☐ + ☐ = 8

☐ + ☐ = 8

Addition patterns

1 Continue each pattern.

a 5

5 + 0 = 5
4 + ☐ = 5
3 + ☐ = 5
2 + ☐ = 5
1 + ☐ = 5
0 + ☐ = 5

b 6

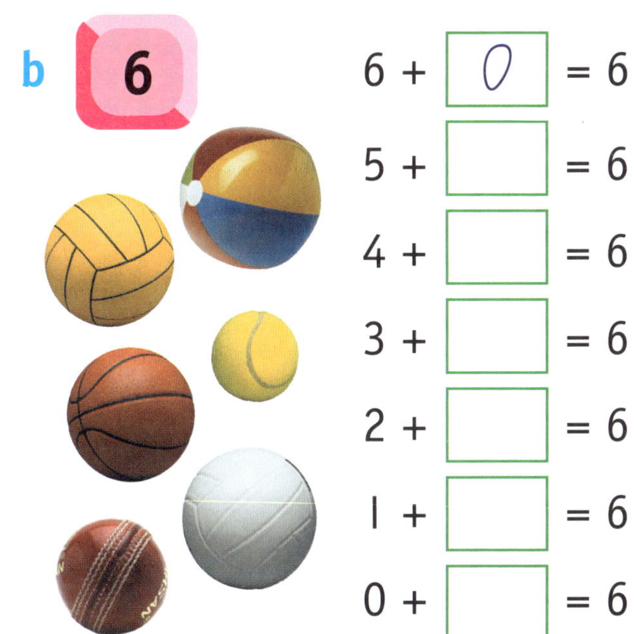

6 + 0 = 6
5 + ☐ = 6
4 + ☐ = 6
3 + ☐ = 6
2 + ☐ = 6
1 + ☐ = 6
0 + ☐ = 6

2 Write the addition pattern for:

a 7

7 + 0 = 7

b 9

9 + 0 = 9

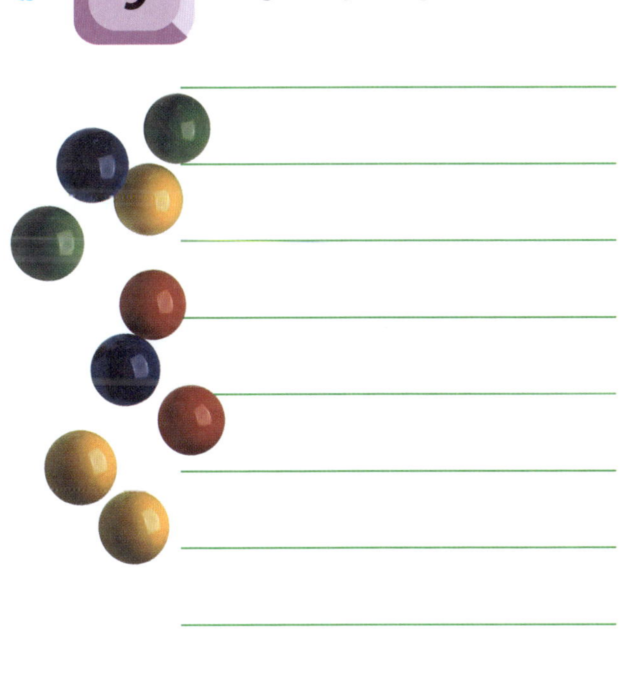

Looking for patterns

5 ☐ 6 ☐ 7 ☐ 9 ☐

How many additions for each number? What do you notice? Is it the same for all numbers?

Addition pairs for ten

Colour pairs that add to ten.

Make 10.

5 + ☐ = 10	4 + ☐ = 10
3 + ☐ = 10	2 + ☐ = 10
☐ + 9 = 10	☐ + 7 = 10
☐ + 8 = 10	☐ + 0 = 10

Make 10.

Addition to ten

1

3 + 6 = ☐

☐ + ☐ = ☐

☐ + ☐ = ☐

☐ + ☐ = ☐

☐ + ☐ = ☐

☐ + ☐ = ☐

2 Colour balls that match.

8 + 1 | 7 + 1 | 4 + 4 | 6 + 3 | 3 + 7

3 + 3 | 4 + 2 | 3 + 7 | 3 + 5 | 5 + 1

10 + 0 | 5 + 5 | 8 + 2 | 4 + 7 | 6 + 5

Challenge! Can you find 3 balls that add to 25?

Coins

Complete.

5c	c	c	c
five		twenty	fifty
	cents		

Make 20c.

Use 2 coins.

Use 3 coins.

Use 4 coins.

Challenge! How many ways can you make 50c?

Australian dollars

Write the missing numbers.

Australian dollars

$1 $2
$5 $10
$20 $50
$100

How many dollars?

$ ______

$ ______

$ ______

$ ______

$ ______

$ ______

Mastery Checklist

I can:

- ☐ add using doubles and near doubles.
- ☐ record all pairs of numbers adding to numbers up to 10.
- ☐ recognise coins and notes.
- ☐ select and apply strategies to solve addition problems.

Problem solving

Equal amounts

Here is Lin's shopping list.
Draw coins she can use to make each amount.

apple	15c	
water bottle	80c	
cheese stick	30c	
salad	65c	

If Lin has no 10c pieces, how can she make these amounts?

15c	
80c	
30c	
65c	

I can solve a problem by:

☐ making equal amounts. ☐ drawing a picture.

AC9M1N05 Number **MA1-CSQ-01** Combining and separating quantities A • Use flexible strategies to solve addition and subtraction problems • Represent equality
MA1-WM-01 Working mathematically • Apply mathematical techniques to solve problems

Measuring length

Make a picture ruler.

Measure things with your picture ruler.

Measure these with cubes and your picture ruler.

	Number of cubes	Picture ruler

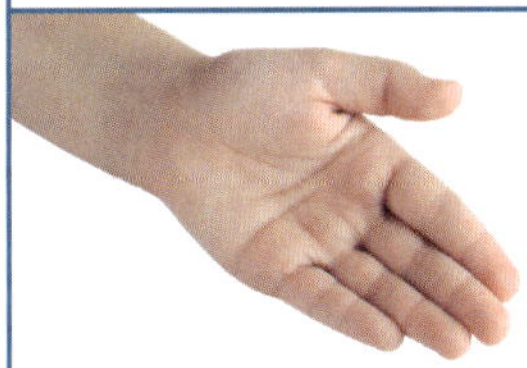		
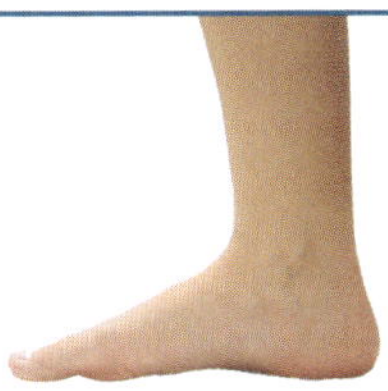		

Measure and compare length

Find something that fits in this box.

Draw it.

How many beads long is each thing?

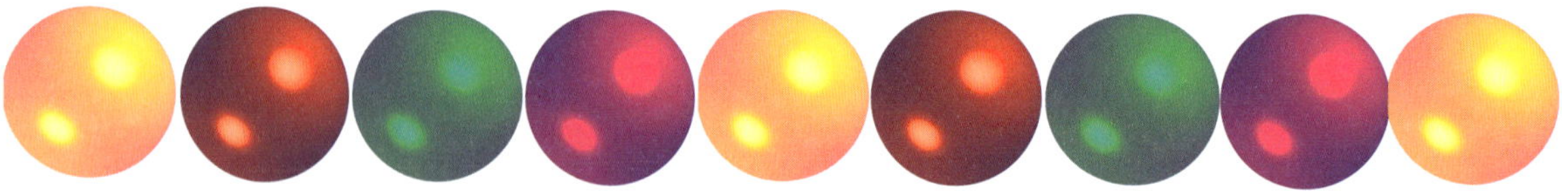

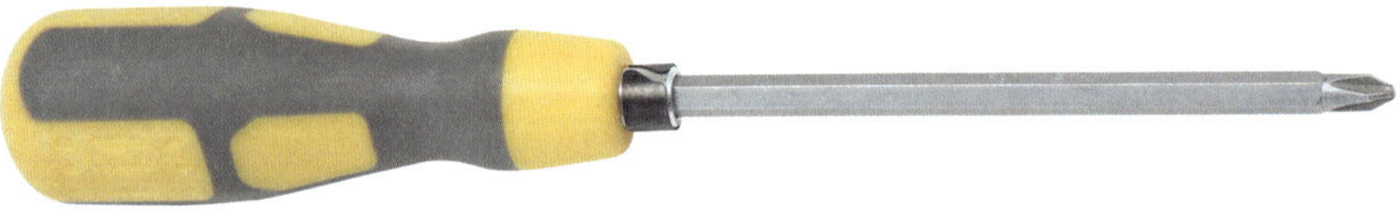

✗ longer than 5 beads

O shorter than 5 beads

Which is: longest?

shortest?

Lengths

Use string to measure each path.

Draw the length of each path.

frog	
rabbit	
bird	

Whose path is the shortest?	
Whose path is the longest?	

Measure each path using blocks.

frog ☐ blocks rabbit ☐ blocks bird ☐ blocks

Measure each string using blocks.

frog ☐ blocks rabbit ☐ blocks bird ☐ blocks

Did you get the same numbers? Why? ______________________________

____

____

Difference

How many?

The difference between 8 and 5 is ☐.

The difference between ☐ and ☐ is ☐.

The difference between ☐ and ☐ is ☐.

The difference between ☐ and ☐ is ☐.

Number line difference

What is the difference? Count the jumps.

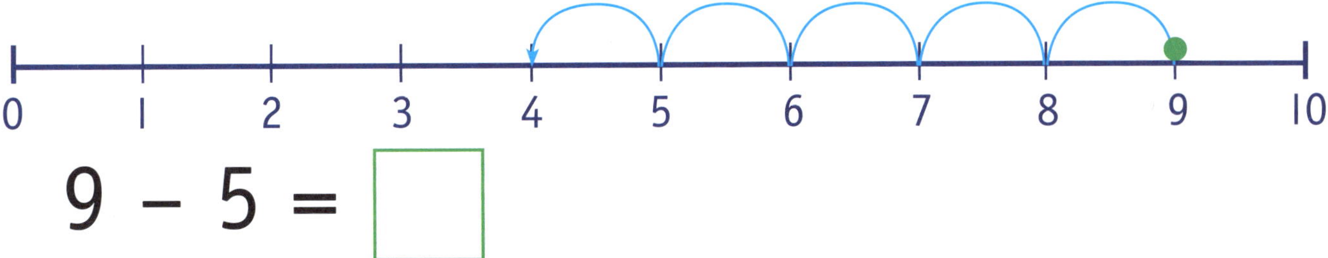

$9 - 5 = \square$

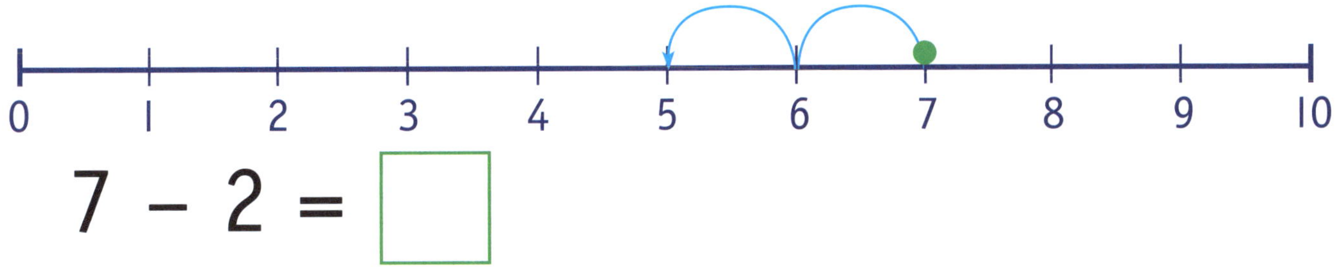

$7 - 2 = \square$

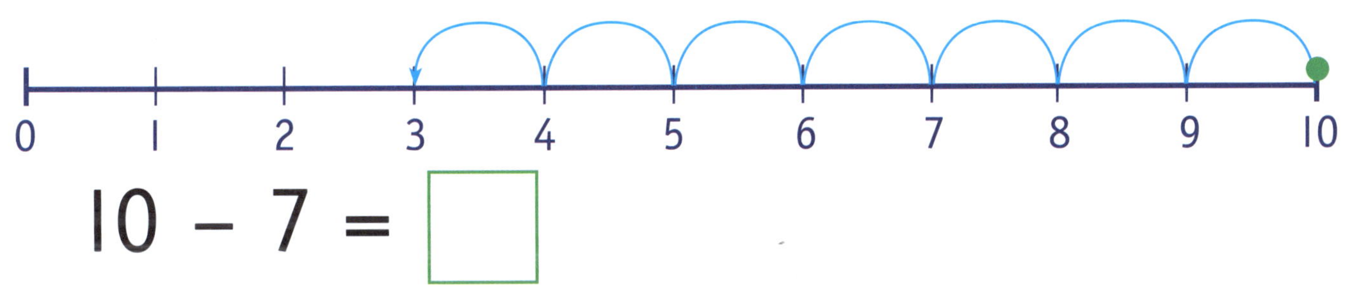

$10 - 7 = \square$

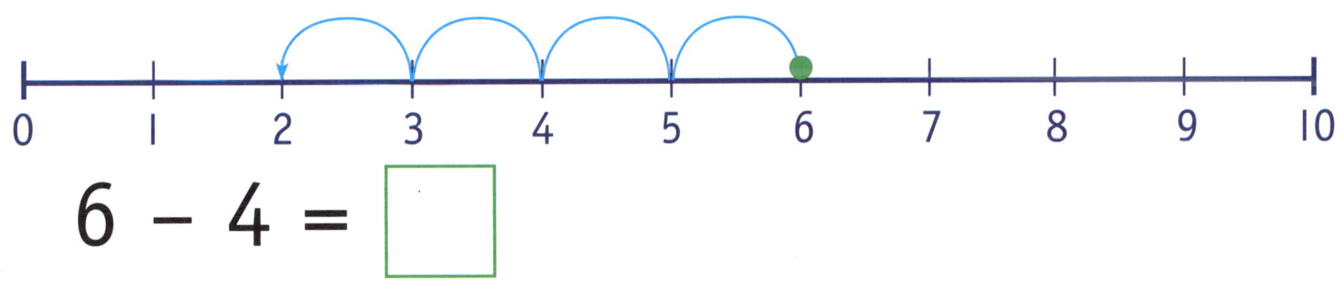

$6 - 4 = \square$

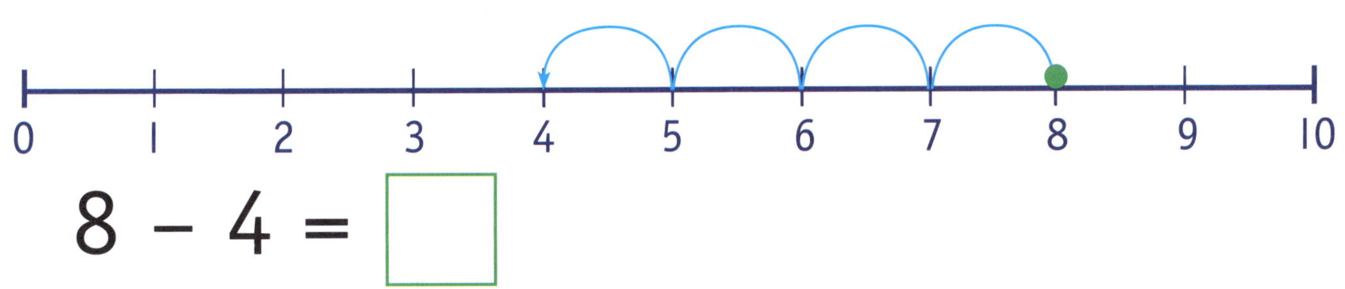

$8 - 4 = \square$

Change from $5 and $10

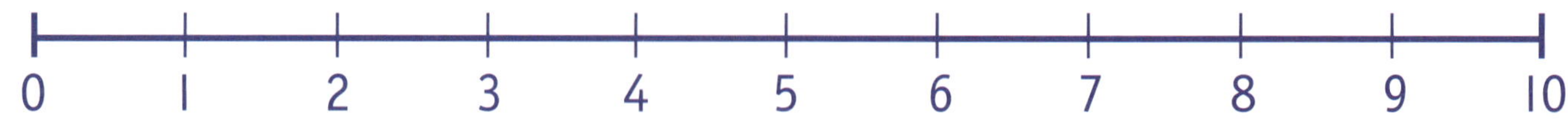

How much change?

change $

change $

change $

change $

change $

change $

change $

change $

Challenge!

change $

Mastery Checklist

I can:
- [ ] measure lengths by placing units end to end.
- [ ] compare the lengths of two or more objects using units.
- [ ] find the difference between two numbers.
- [ ] use a number line to subtract and find difference.

AC9M1N05 Number **MA1-CSQ-01** Combining and separating quantities A • Use advanced count-by-one strategies to solve addition and subtraction problems • Recognise and recall number bonds up to ten

Subtraction problems

Ben has 10 balls. Jen has 6 balls.
What is the difference?

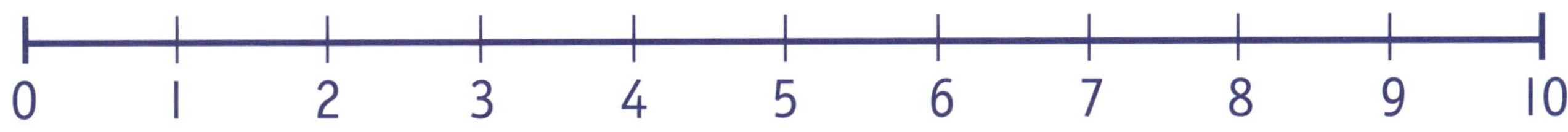

Luke makes 10 pies. The dog eats 5 of them.
How many pies are left?

Polly has 10 dolls. She gives 3 to Matt.
Then she gives 3 to Jane. How many left?

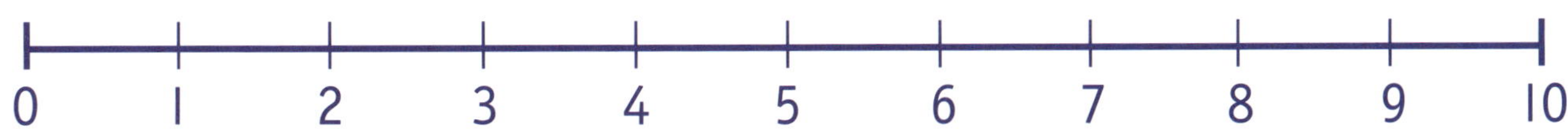

I can solve a problem by:

☐ counting back to subtract. ☐ using a number line.

Measuring hands

Investigation 2

1 Make a picture ruler. Fold a long strip of paper in half. Fold it in half again and then one more time. Unfold and draw a picture in each space.

make a **ruler**

2 In pairs: Put your hand on the page with fingers together. Have your friend draw around it with a pencil. Now, draw around your friend's hand.

My hand	**My friend's hand**

3 Measure your hand drawings with your picture ruler.

My hand is ____________________

My friend's hand is ____________________

AC9M1M02 Measurement **MA1-GM-02** Geometric measure A • Length: Measure the lengths of objects using uniform informal units
MA1-WM-01 Working mathematically • Apply mathematical techniques to solve problems

Measuring hands

Investigation 2

4 Stretch out your fingers to make a hand span.
Draw marks for your thumb and little finger.
Use your picture ruler to measure between the marks.

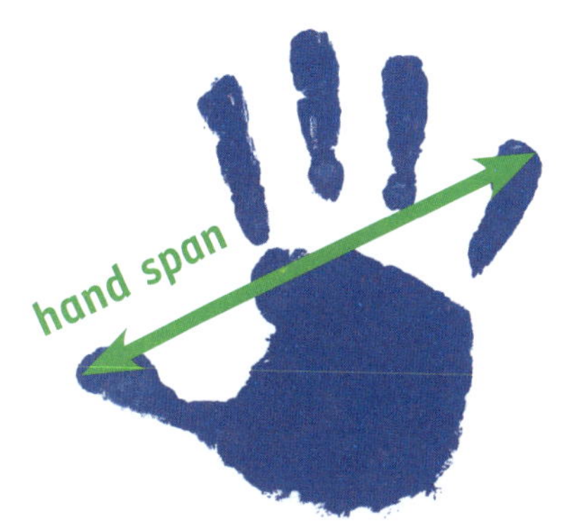

My hand span is ☐ pictures long.

5 Use your hand span to measure the width of these things.

☐ hand spans

☐ hand spans

☐ hand spans

6 Is everyone's hand span the same length? ____________

To do this, I needed to:

- ☐ measure lengths.
- ☐ compare measurements.
- ☐ measure with a hand span.
- ☐ use the words measure, long, short, longer, shorter, more than, less than.

I enjoyed this task!

Revision

1 Write the missing numbers.

31	32	33	34		36		38	39	40
41			44	45		47	48	49	

2 How many cubes long?

3 Make 10.

5 + ☐ = 10

8 + ☐ = 10

3 + 7 = ☐

0 + ☐ = 10

4 What time is it?

☐ o'clock

☐ o'clock

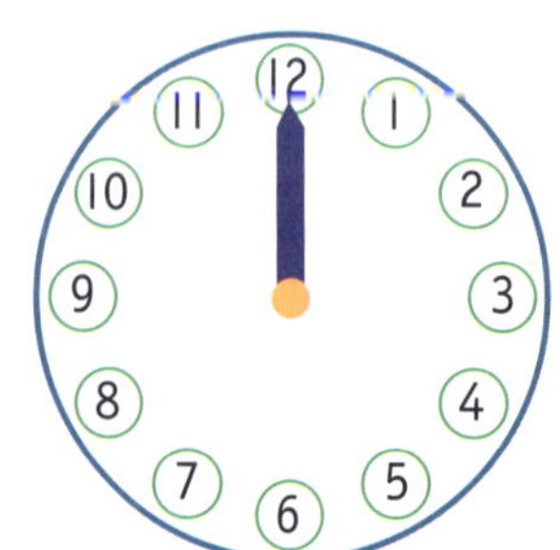

☐ o'clock

Revision

5 How much?

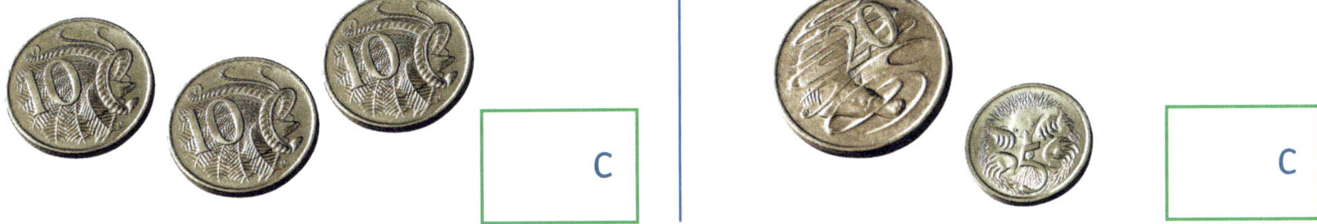

6 Count back on the number line.

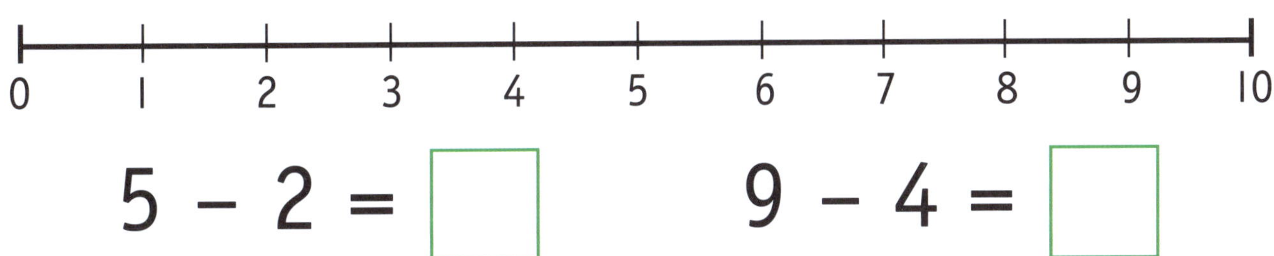

5 − 2 = ☐

9 − 4 = ☐

7 Use doubles to add.

5 + 5 = ☐

4 + 5 = ☐

8 Write an addition for each number.

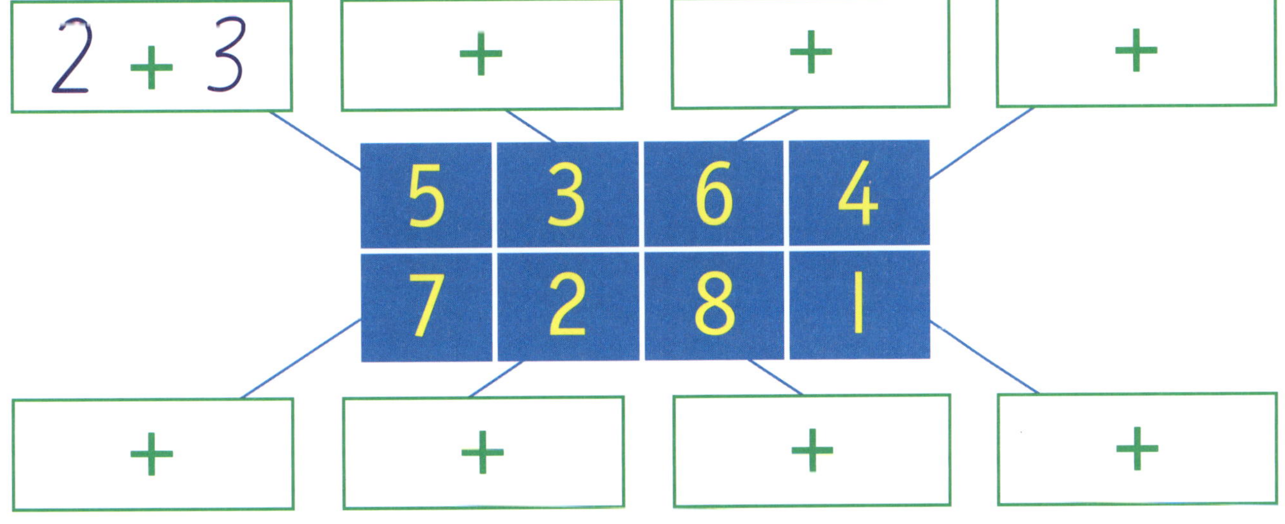

3D objects

3D objects are not flat.

Circle things that are shaped like each 3D object.

3D object	Things
 cone	   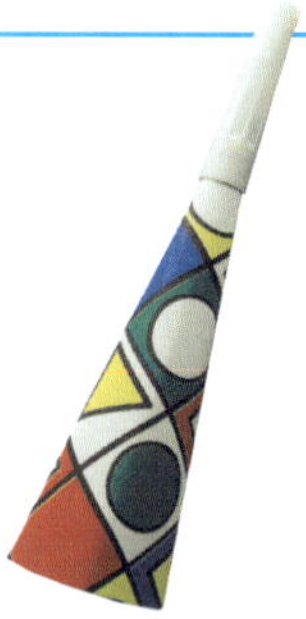
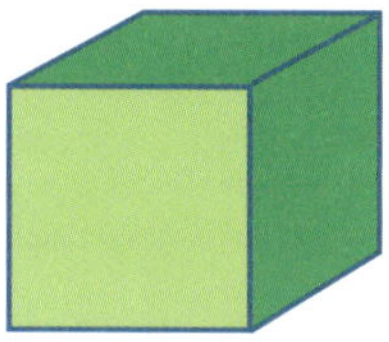 cube	   
 cylinder	   
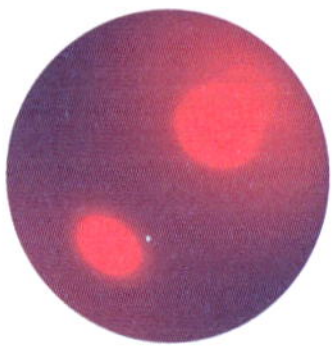 sphere	   

Challenge!

Name the 3D objects.

3D objects

Colour the drawings that match.

 cone	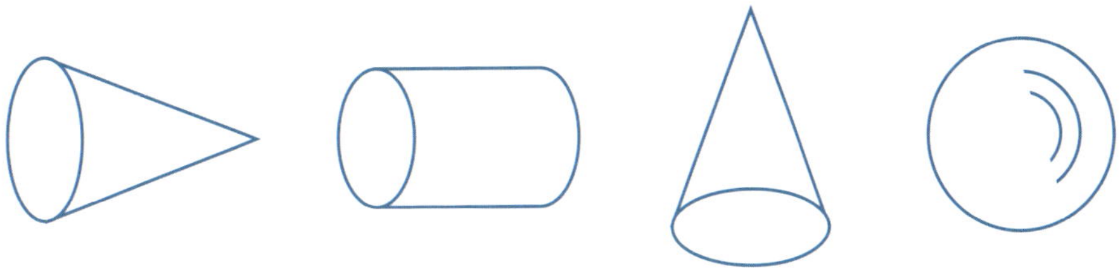
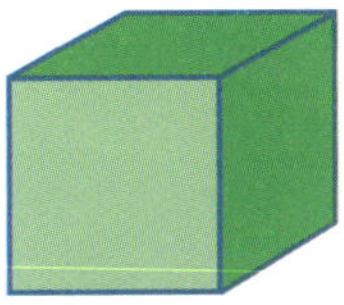 cube	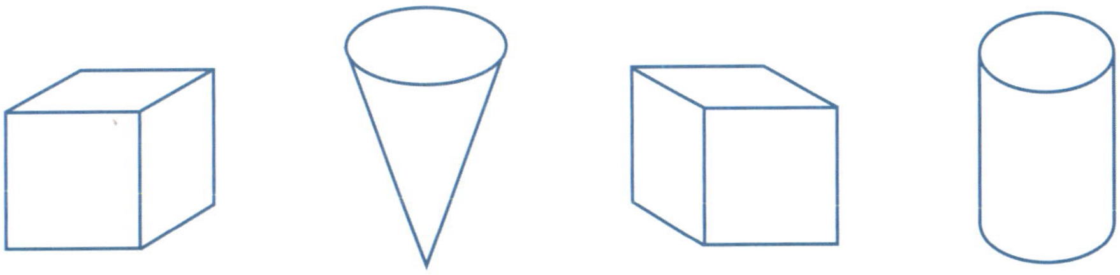
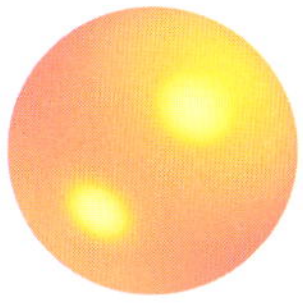 sphere	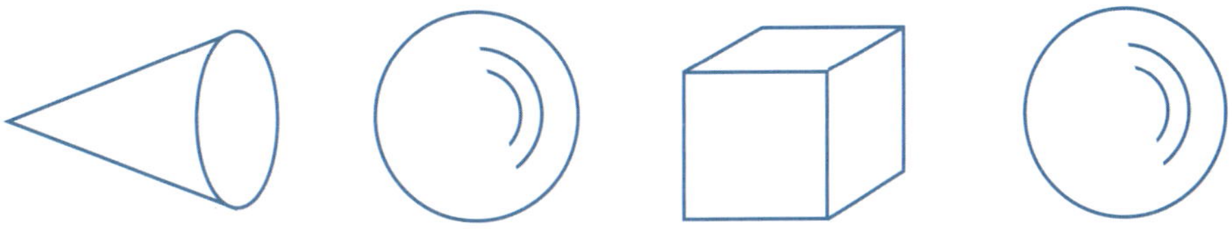
 cylinder	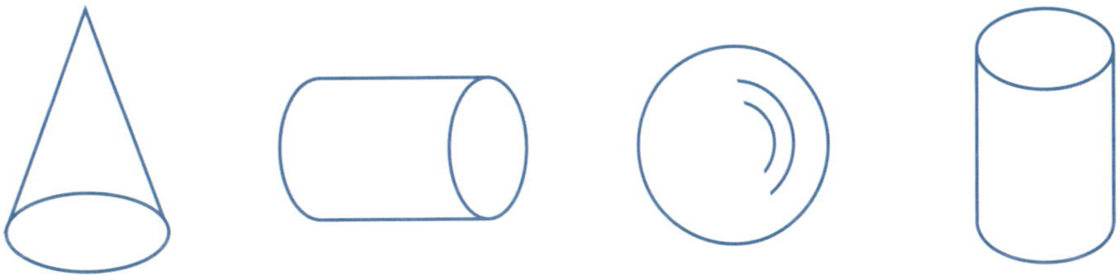
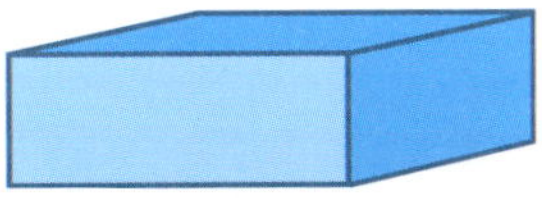 rectangular prism	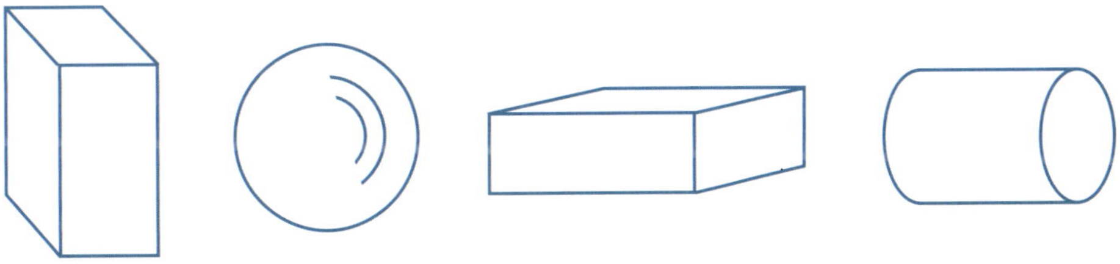

Challenge!

Draw these 3D objects. Name them.

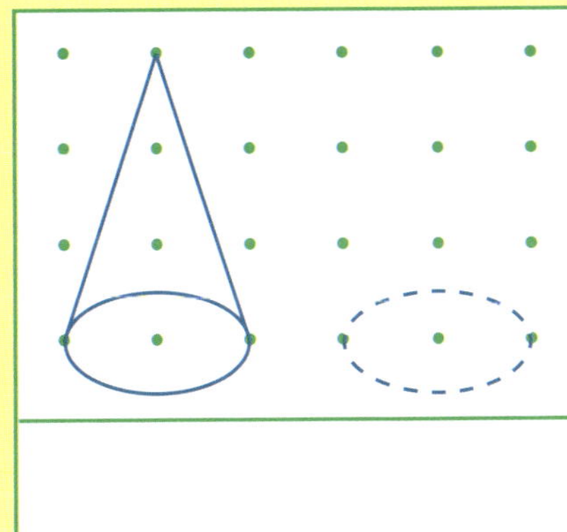

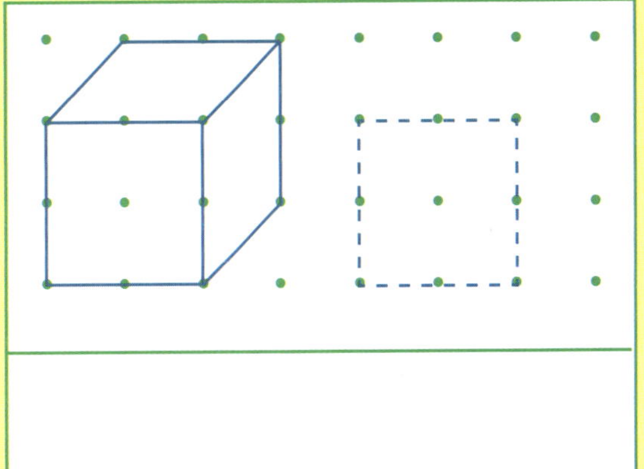

Sorting 3D objects

3D objects have flat faces and curved surfaces.

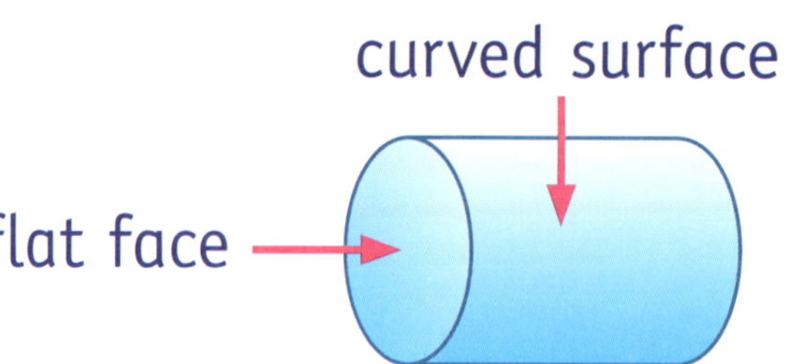

What is the arrow pointing to? Circle the correct answer.

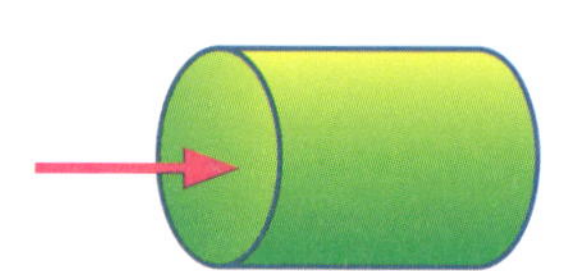 curved surface flat face	 curved surface flat face	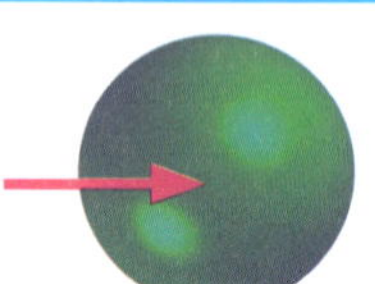 curved surface flat face

How many?

	curved surfaces	flat faces
 cone		
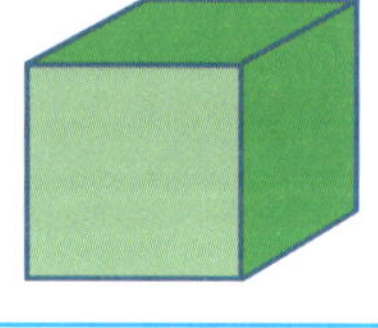 cube		
 sphere		
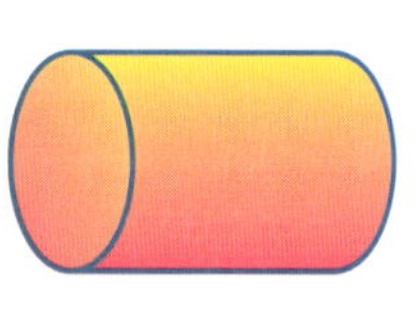 cylinder		

Mastery Checklist

I can:
- ☐ identify 3D objects.
- ☐ identify flat faces and curved surfaces on 3D objects.
- ☐ describe 3D objects.

Problem solving

3D Objects

Name each 3D object and describe it.

I can solve problems by:

☐ describing a 3D object. ☐ writing a description.

Odd and even

Even numbers can be put into pairs (groups of 2).

How many shoes?

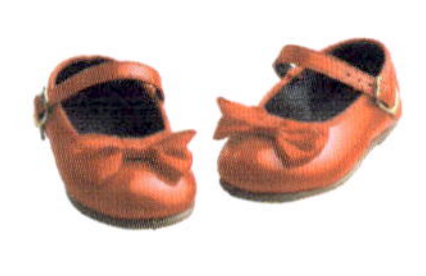

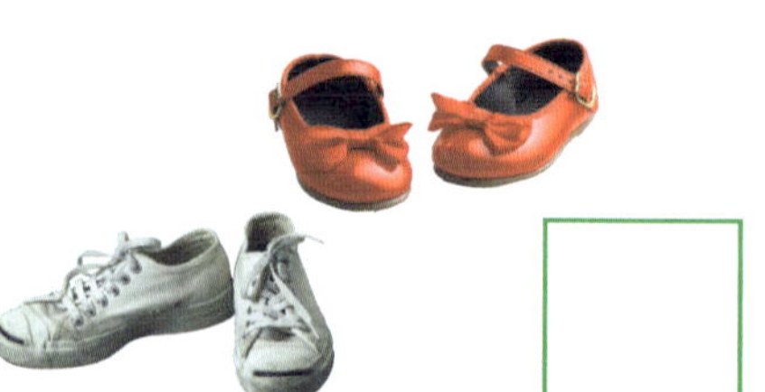

Write the even numbers in order.

2

How many socks?

Write the odd numbers in order.

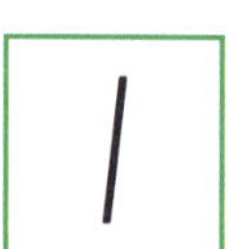

Odd and even

Odd numbers put into pairs have one left over.

How many triangles? Colour even **blue** and odd **red**.

6

Write in order.

Even numbers 2 4 6

Odd numbers

Counting in twos

Count by twos

1 Count in twos.

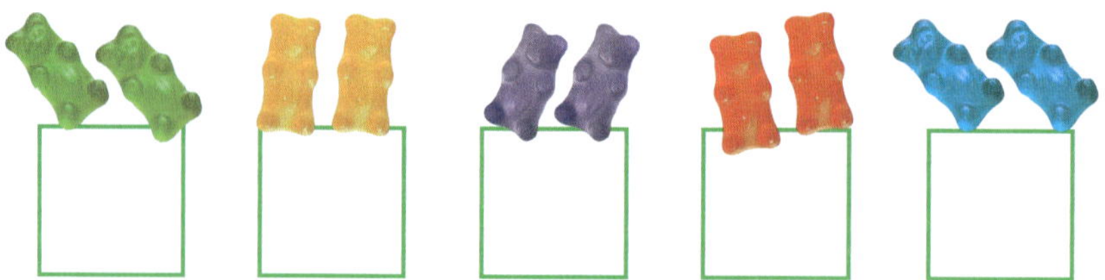

a

2 + 2 = ☐

2 groups of 2 = ☐

b

2 + 2 + 2 = ☐

3 groups of 2 = ☐

c

2 + 2 + 2 + 2 = ☐

4 groups of 2 = ☐

d

2+2+2+2+2= ☐

5 groups of 2 = ☐

2

6 groups of 2 = ☐

7 groups of 2 = ☐

3 Make jumps of 2. Write the numbers you land on.

0 5 10 15 20

2

AC9M1A01 Algebra MA1-RWN-01 Representing whole numbers A • Continue and create number patterns
MA1-FG-01 Forming groups A • Count in multiples using rhythmic and skip counting

Counting in fives

0	5	10	15	20	25	30	35	40	45	50

Count in 5s to find how many.

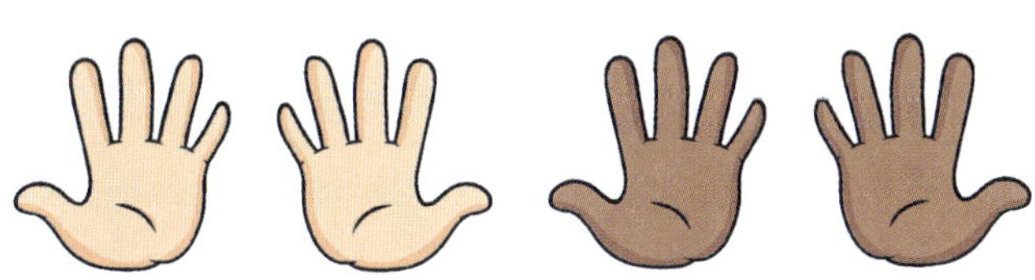

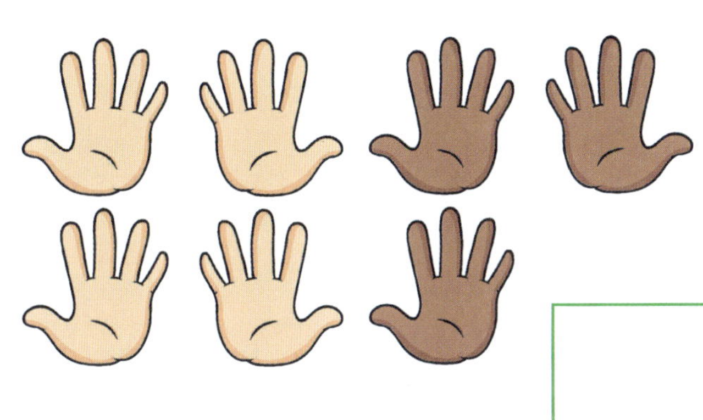

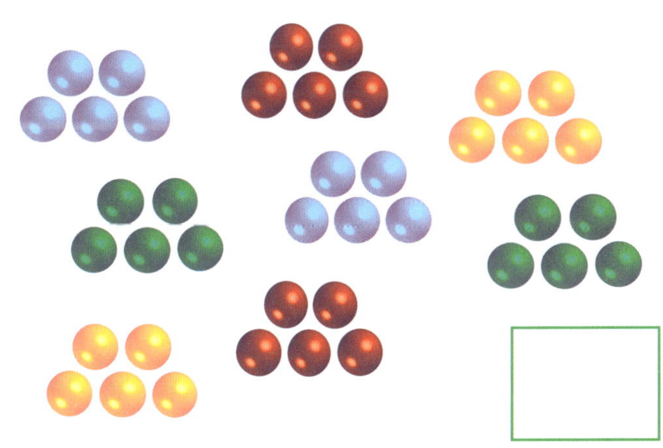

Challenge!

50 55 ☐ 65 ☐ ☐ 80 ☐ 90 ☐ 100

Number patterns

What numbers come next?

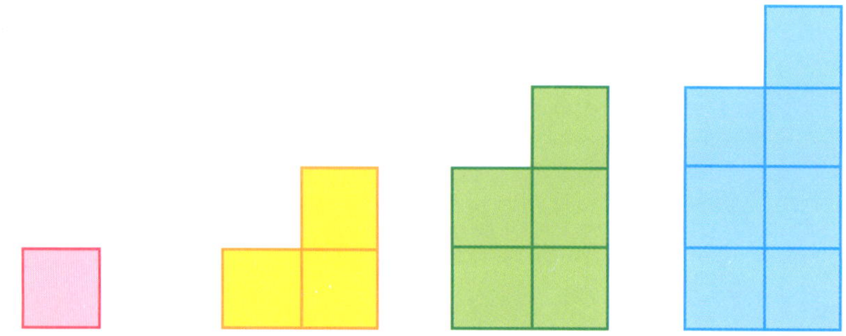

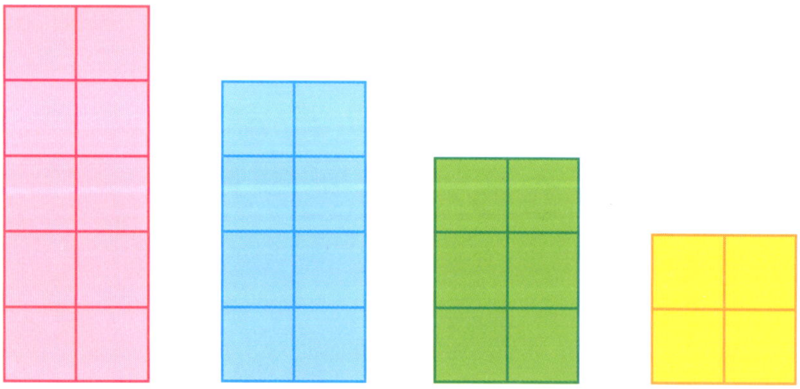

How do you know what comes next?

AC9M1A01 Algebra MA1-RWN-01 Representing whole numbers A • Continue and create number patterns
MA1-FG-01 Forming groups A • Count in multiples using rhythmic and skip counting

Calculator patterns

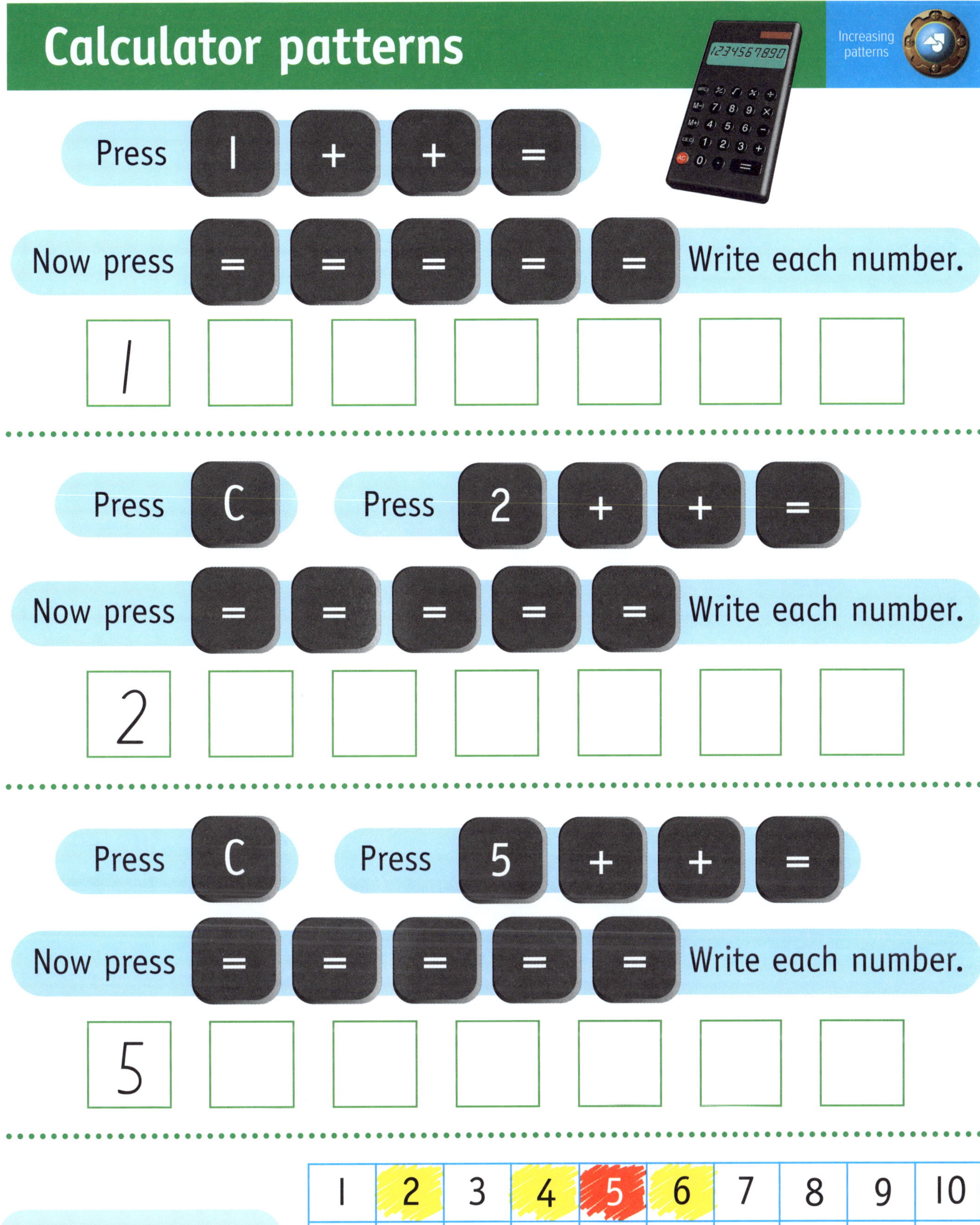

Colour the 2 pattern yellow and the 5 pattern red.

1	2	3	4	5	6	7	8	9	10
11	12	13	14	15	16	17	18	19	20
21	22	23	24	25	26	27	28	29	30
31	32	33	34	35	36	37	38	39	40
41	42	43	44	45	46	47	48	49	50

Skip counting

What is the pattern? Jump to the end of the line.

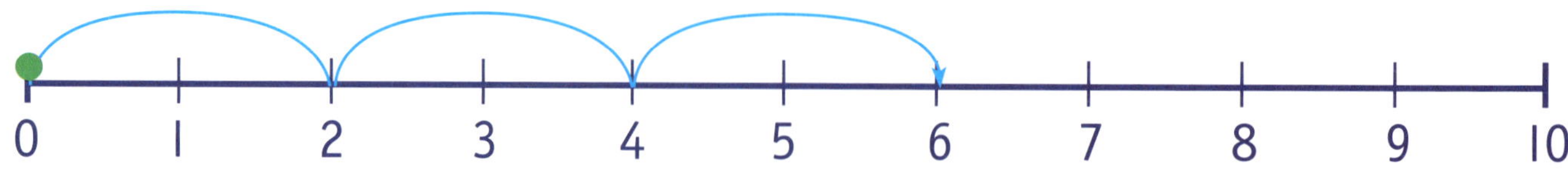

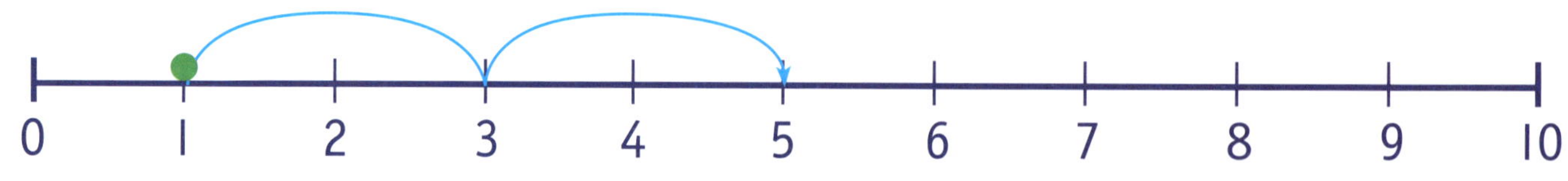

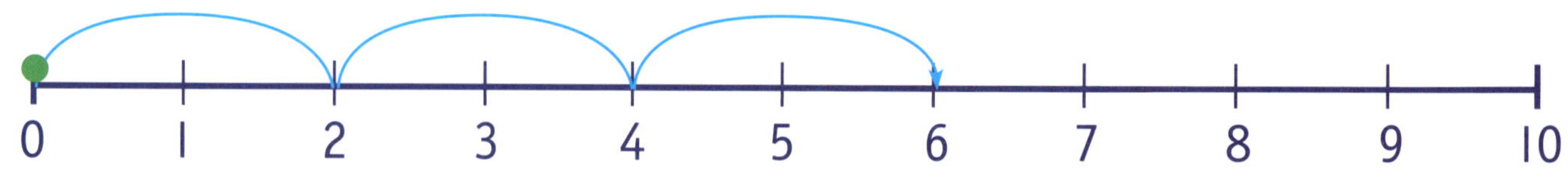

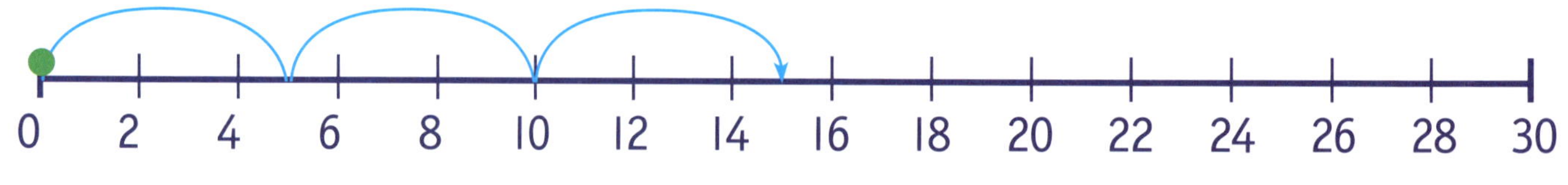

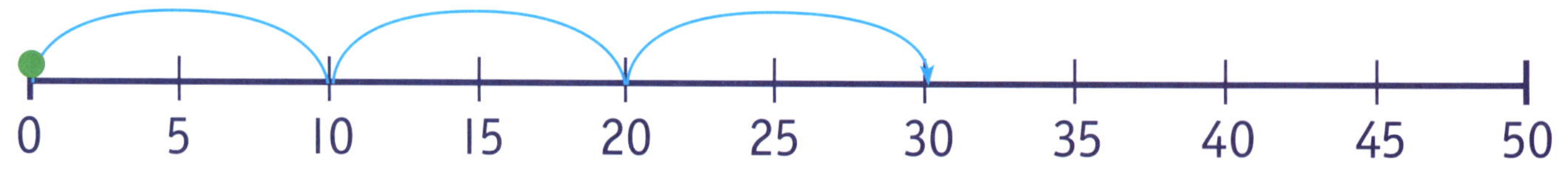

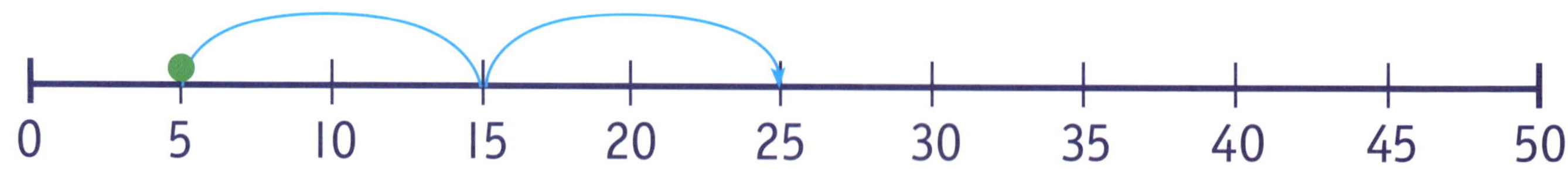

Mastery Checklist

I can:
- ☐ identify odd and even numbers.
- ☐ count by 2s and 5s.
- ☐ identify patterns skip counting by twos, fives and tens.
- ☐ add to patterns skip counting by twos, fives and tens.

AC9M1A01 Algebra **MA1-RWN-01** Representing whole numbers A • Continue and create number patterns
MA1-FG-01 Forming groups A • Count in multiples using rhythmic and skip counting • Use skip counting patterns

Problem solving

Zac's cookies

Zac made six cookies. How many Smarties could he put on each cookie if he had:

12 Smarties? Draw the cookies.

18 Smarties? Draw the cookies.

I can solve a problem by:

☐ sharing a set of items equally into groups. ☐ drawing a picture.

Graphs

Year One's Pets

How many?     

Complete the graph.

Pets of Year 1

How many more fish than cats?

Challenge! There are 2 fish in each fish tank.

How many fish tanks?

Graphing data

Colour

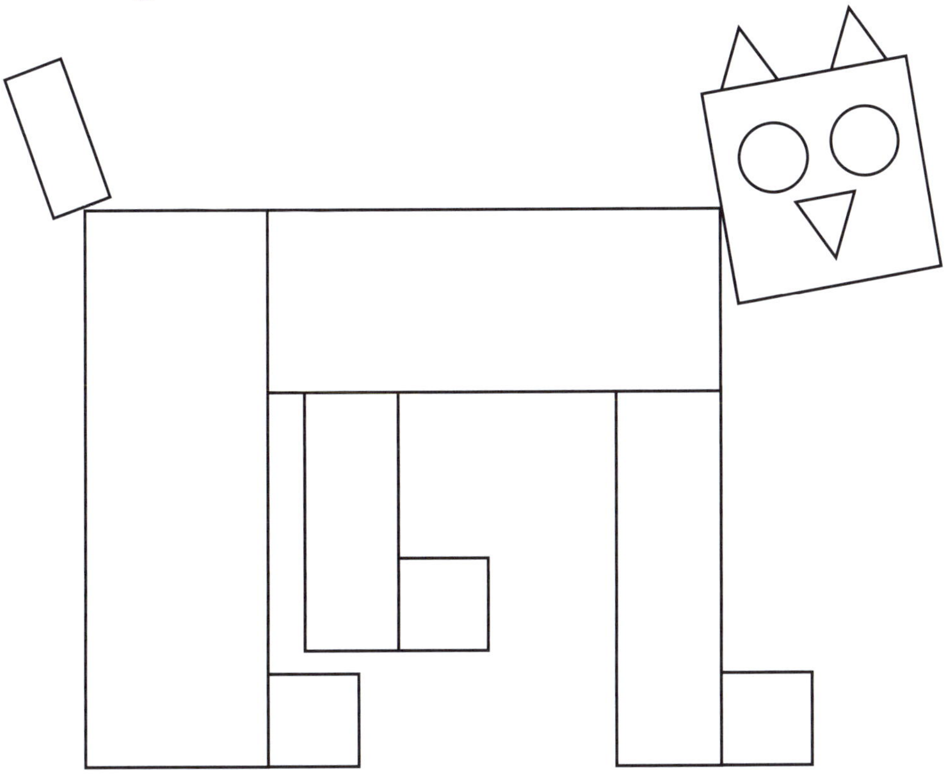

How many?

Draw.

Shapes in the Cat

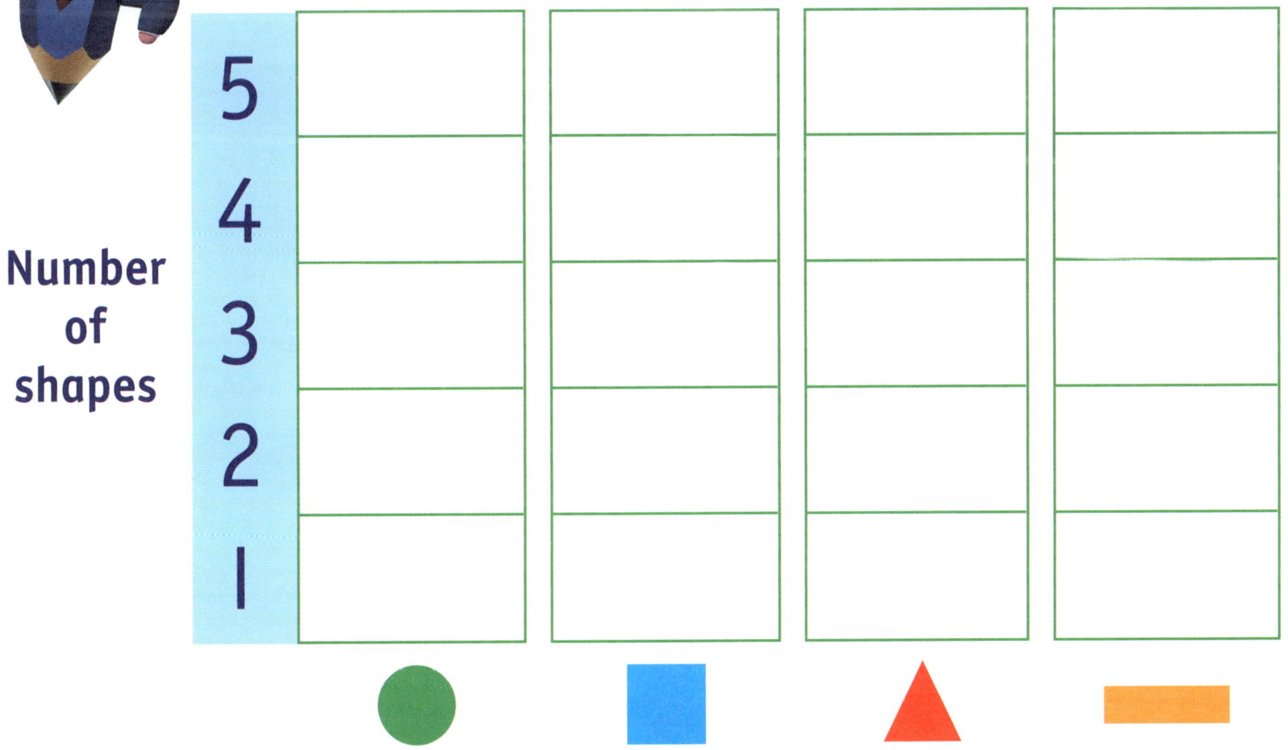

Number of shapes				
5				
4				
3				
2				
1				

Possible or impossible?

Use one of these words to describe each event. **possible** **impossible**

You write with a pencil.

You walk home from school.

You eat a house.

Bananas grow teeth.

You learn to fly tomorrow.

It rains this week.

You watch TV today.

Worms grow wings and wear hats.

More or less likely?

Chance

Compare the two events. Which is more likely to happen? Which is less likely?

1

more likely

2

3

4 Draw your own. Label.

Left and right

Write left or right.

is on the

is on the

The milk is on the

The orange juice is on the

Draw a to the right.

Draw a to the left.

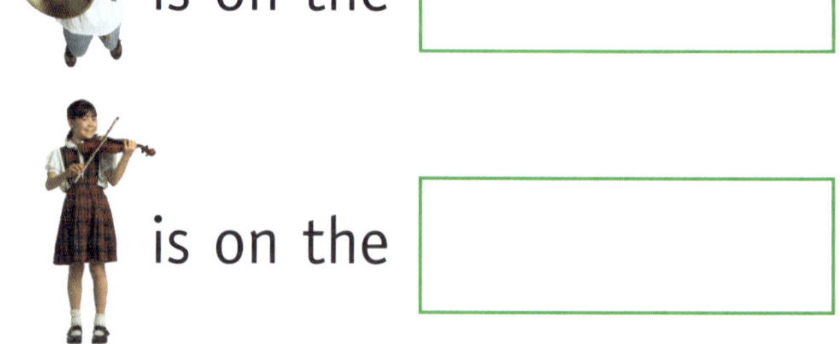

is on the

is on the

Challenge!

Go right 2, up 1, left 4, up 1, right 3.

Draw a X where you land.

Position words

Draw the shape that is

below [diamond] ☐

above [arrow] ☐

beside [question mark] ☐

above [heart] ☐

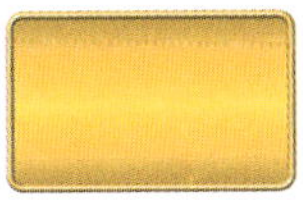

next to [rectangle] ☐

below [triangle] ☐

between [$] and [heart] ☐

between [star] and [oval] ☐

Challenge! Draw your own shape grid. Ask a partner position questions about your grid.

Following instructions

Draw a clock   **above** the bed.

Draw a football  **below** the desk.

Draw a lamp  **between** the bed and the desk.

Draw a picture frame  to the **left** of the bookshelves.

Draw a trophy  on the **right** side of the top shelf.

Challenge!

Write a description of this room. Ask a friend to draw the room using your description. How close did they get?

Mastery Checklist

I can:

- [ ] sort and count data to make a graph.
- [ ] describe the chance of an event happening.
- [ ] identify and describe position.
- [ ] follow directions and instructions.

Problem solving

Buried treasure

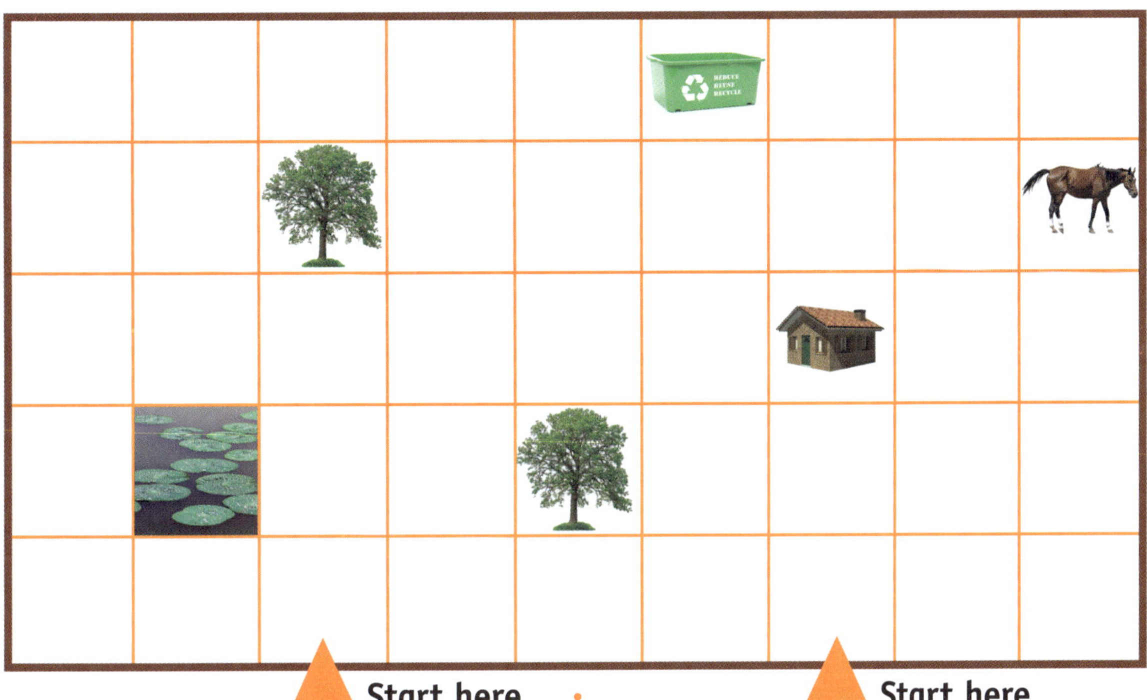

Start here to find treasure.

Up 3. Left 2. Up 2. Right 3.

Draw an ✕ in the square.

Draw an ✕ above the horse.

Write how to get there.

____

____

____

____

Draw one more item on the map. Write how to get there.

____

____

____

I can solve a problem by:

☐ giving and following directions. ☐ using a grid map.

Revision • Term 2

1 Colour the circles that add to 10.

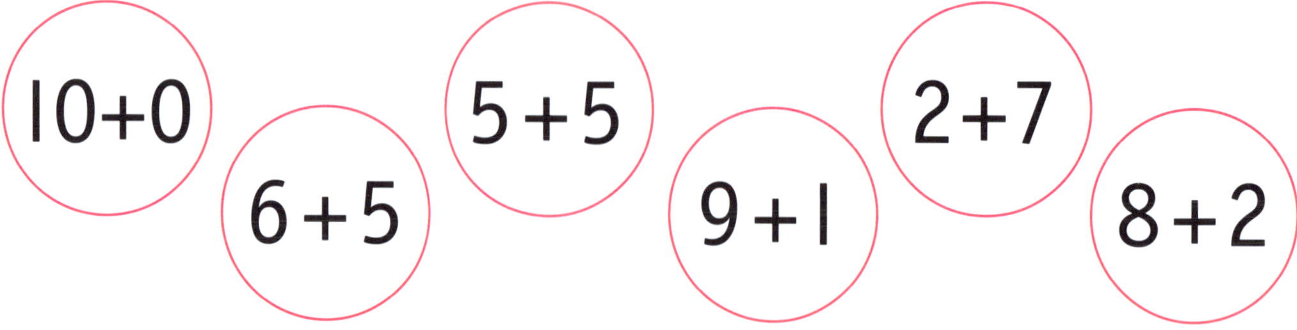

2 Count in twos. Are the numbers odd or even?

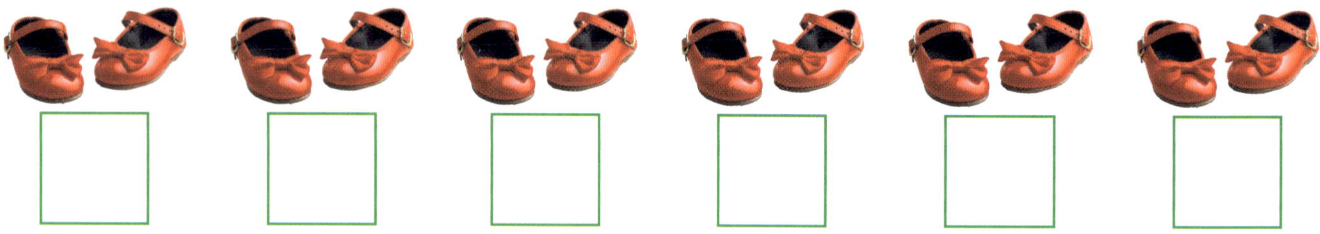

3

$5 - 3 = \square$ $7 - 4 = \square$

$6 - 2 = \square$ $8 - 5 = \square$

4 Colour one half.

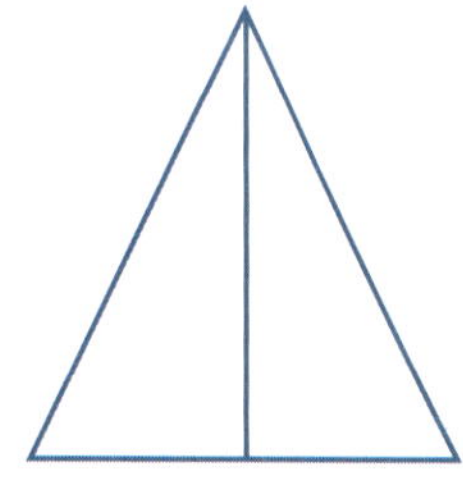

5 Circle the person on the right.

Revision • Term 2

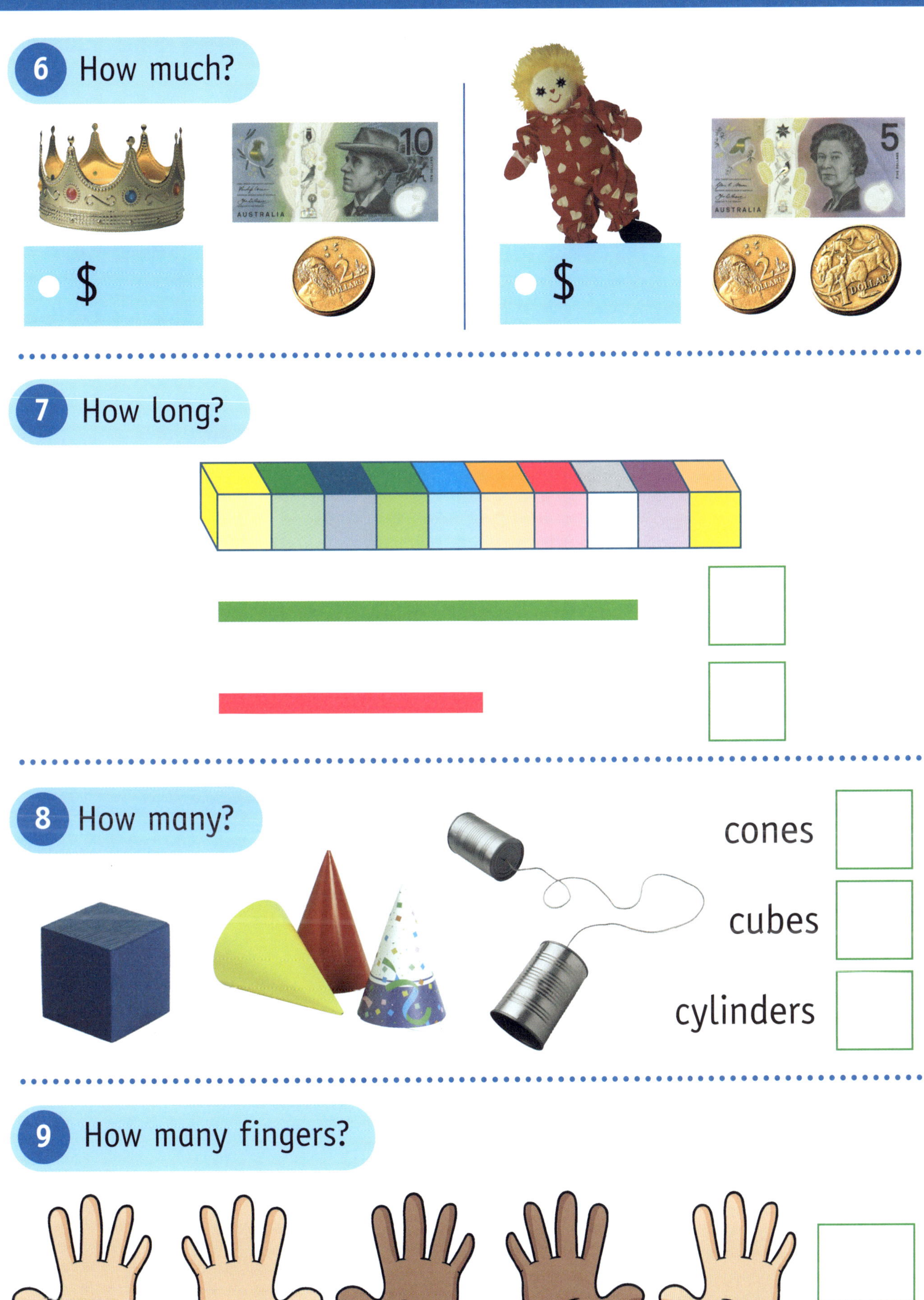

Numbers to one hundred

Write the missing numbers.

1	2	3	4	5		7	8	9	10
11	12	13	14	15	16	17	18		20
21	22	23		25	26	27	28	29	30
31	32	33	34	35	36	37		39	40
	42	43	44	45	46	47	48	49	50
51		53	54	55	56	57	58	59	60
61	62	63	64	65	66	67	68	69	
71	72	73	74		76	77	78	79	80
81		83	84	85	86	87	88	89	90
91	92	93	94	95	96		98	99	100

Count by 2s and colour them **yellow.**

Count by 5s and colour them **blue.**

Count by 10s and colour them **green.**

Number sense

What is the nearest ten?

17 → ☐   19 → ☐   12 → ☐

13 → ☐   15 → ☐   14 → ☐

What is the nearest ten? Use the number chart on page 86.

25 → ☐   36 → ☐   41 → ☐

58 → ☐   64 → ☐   73 → ☐

Which number is **after**?

5 ☐   37 ☐   81 ☐   96 ☐

Which number is **before**?

25 ☐   53 ☐   71 ☐   20 ☐

Which number is **between**?

40 ☐ 42   74 ☐ 76

Counting in tens

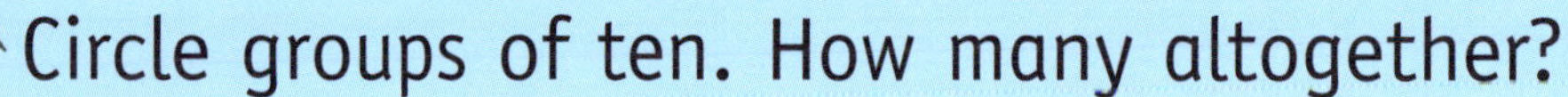

Circle groups of ten. How many altogether?

Make 43 ▲.

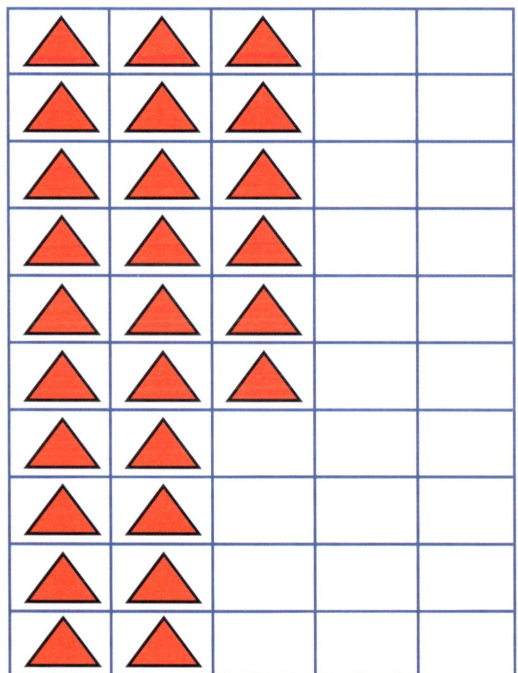

Make 54 ●.

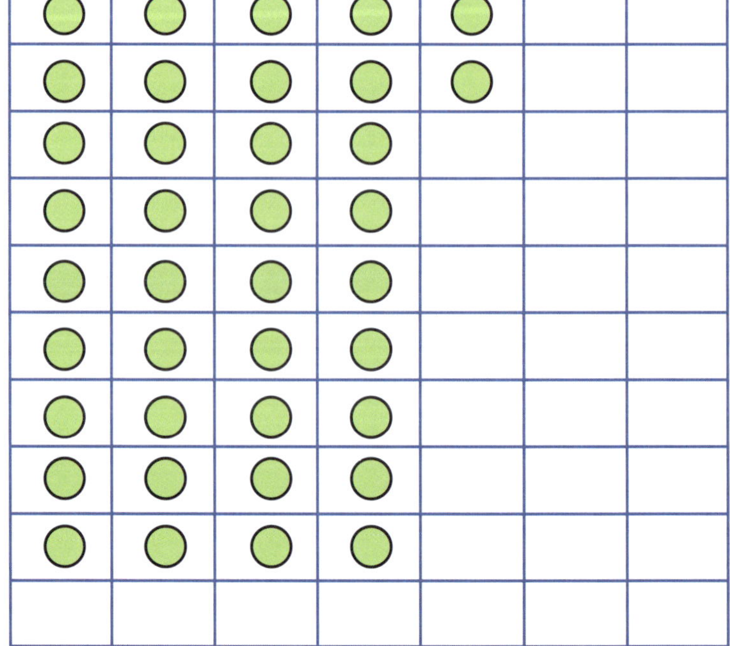

Counting in tens

How much money?

How many?

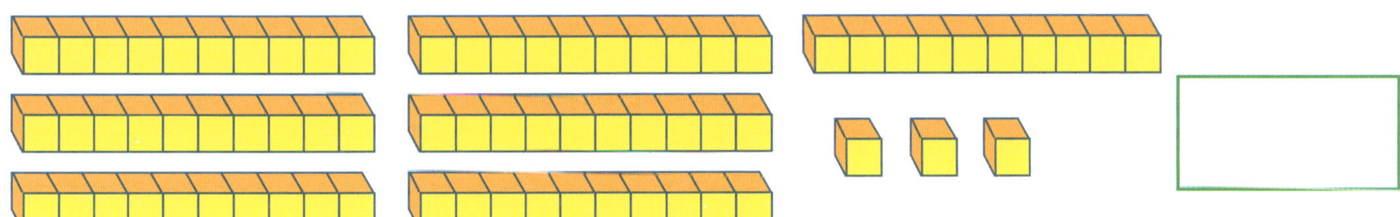

Challenge! Join the numbers that add to 100.

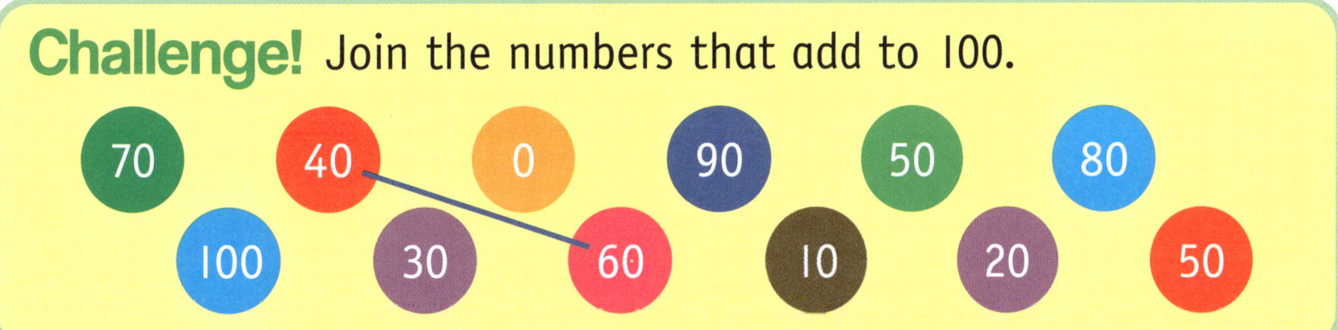

Ordering numbers to one hundred

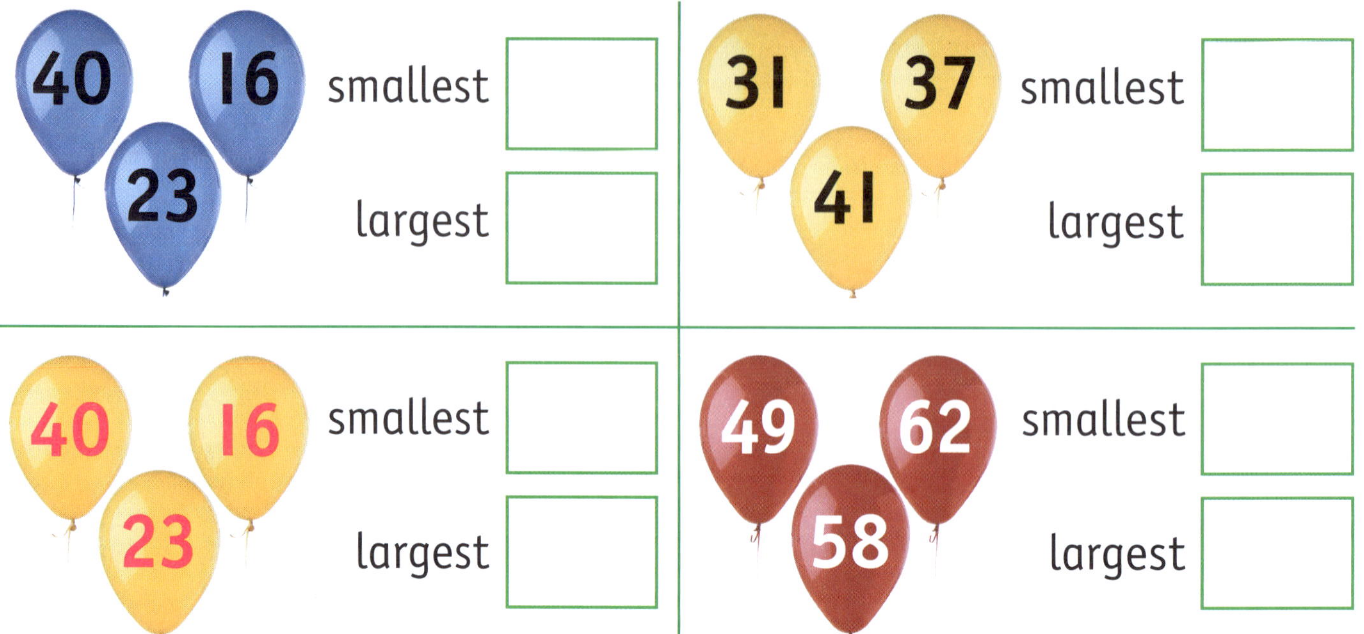

Order from smallest to largest.

Mastery Checklist

I can:

- [ ] find the nearest ten to a number.
- [ ] identify tens and ones in a two-digit number.
- [ ] count items using groups of ten.
- [ ] compare and order two-digit numbers.

Challenge!

Write all the numbers on this page in order from smallest to largest.

AC9M1N01 Number **MA1-RWN-01 • MAE-RWN-02** Representing whole numbers A • Use counting sequences of ones with two-digit numbers and beyond • Represent the structure of groups of ten in whole numbers

Problem solving

Representing two-digit numbers

Choose a two-digit number. Write it in the green boxes.

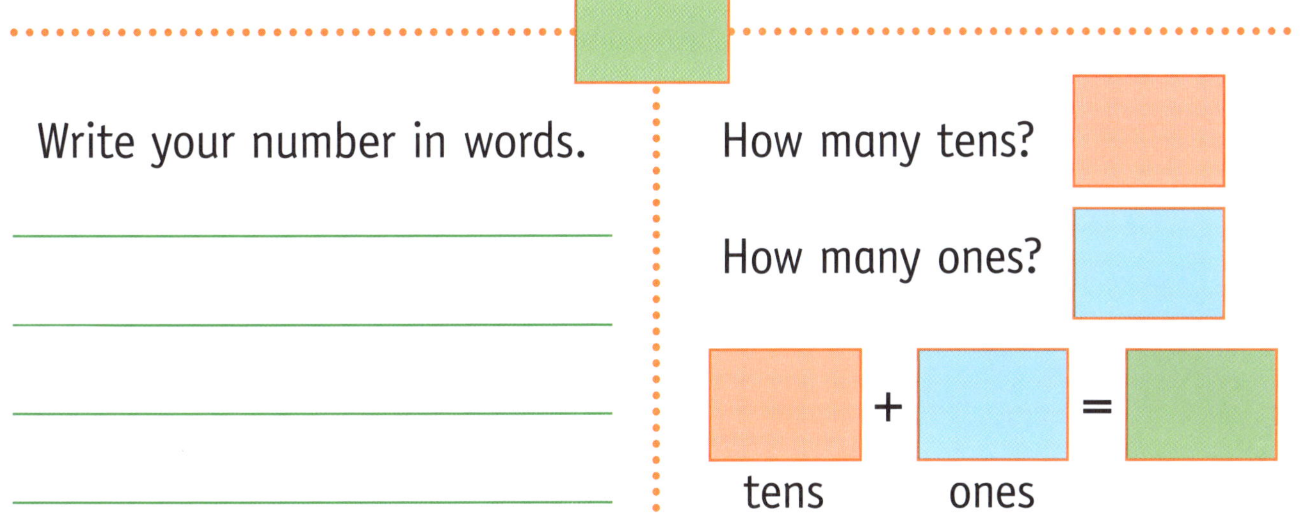

Draw your number using ten sticks and one blocks.

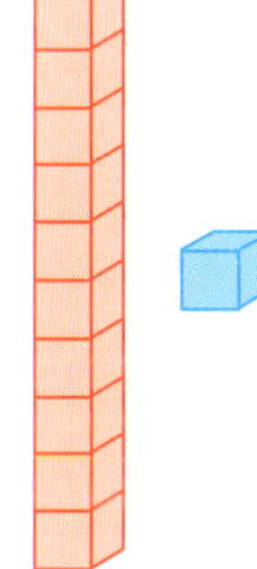

Fill in the number chart around your number.
Which numbers come before and after, above and below?

I can solve a problem by:

☐ identifying the tens and ones in a number. ☐ using many strategies.

Drawing shapes and measuring area

Area

Draw.

a square

a triangle

a rectangle

Colour each shape. Which shape is:

smallest?

largest?

Draw.

a small square

a large square

How many counters cover each square? Guess first then check.

small square		large square	
guess	check	guess	check

Area

Circle the smallest shape. ✗ Cross the largest shape.

How many cubes cover each shape?

green square		blue triangle		orange oval	
purple circle		yellow rectangle		red triangle	

How many small squares cover each shape?

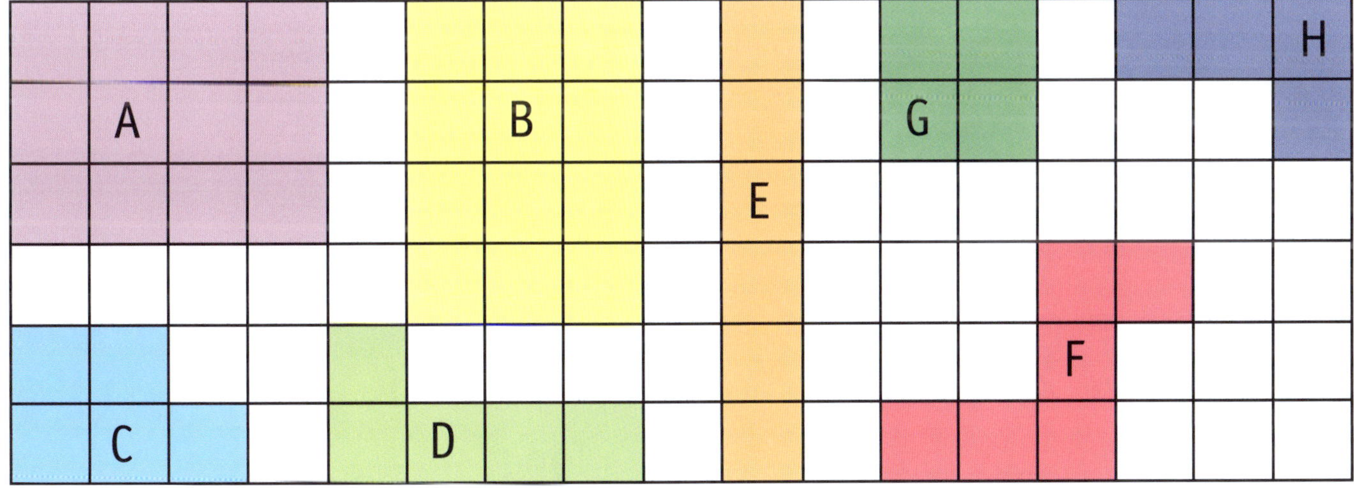

A		B		C		D		E		F		G		H	

Challenge! Which shapes above have the same area?

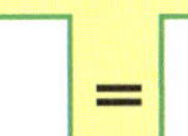

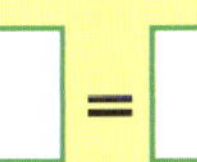

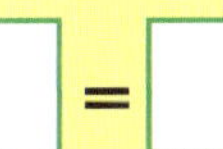

☐ = ☐ , ☐ = ☐ , ☐ = ☐ , ☐ = ☐

Length measurement

Length 

What is wrong with these paperclip measurements?

What is the correct measurement for each?

This is 2 paperclips long.

This is ______ paperclips long.

This is 4 paperclips long.

This is ______ paperclips long.

This is 3 paperclips long.

This is ______ paperclips long.

Why are there 2 different lengths for the same item?

This is 3 paperclips long and 7 blocks long.

Length units

If there is some length leftover, count it as **part** of a unit.

2 and **a half** paperclips long

Choose a unit: blocks  paperclips  counters

Why that unit? ______________________

Estimate, then measure.

	Estimate	**Measure**
	________	________
	________	________
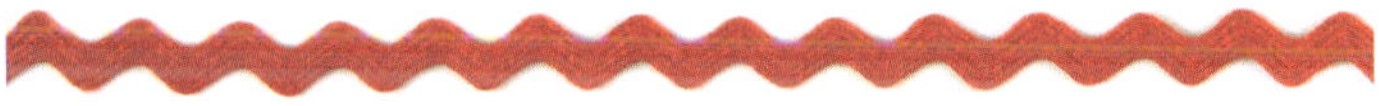	________	________
	________	________
	________	________

Challenge!

Draw a pattern that ends neatly at $5\frac{1}{2}$ paperclips in length.

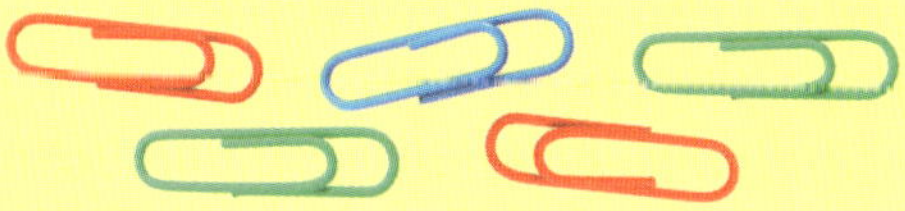

Mastery Checklist

I can:
- ☐ compare the areas of two or more shapes.
- ☐ measure area using squares.
- ☐ identify wrong use of length units.
- ☐ select units and measure length.

Problem solving

Five Town

All houses in Five Town cover 5 squares.
Each house is a different shape.
How many different houses can you draw?

House 1

I can solve a problem by:

☐ exploring areas on a grid. ☐ drawing a diagram.

AC9M1M01 Measurement **MA1-2DS-02** Two-dimensional spatial structure A • Area: Measure areas using uniform informal units
MA1-WM-01 Working mathematically • Apply mathematical techniques to solve problems

Hexagons

Hexagons have 6 straight sides.

Colour the hexagons.

Draw four different hexagons.

Challenge! Parallel lines are like train tracks. They are straight lines that never meet. Find the parallel lines on this page. Draw over them in red.

Flip, slide, turn

flip

flip it over

slide

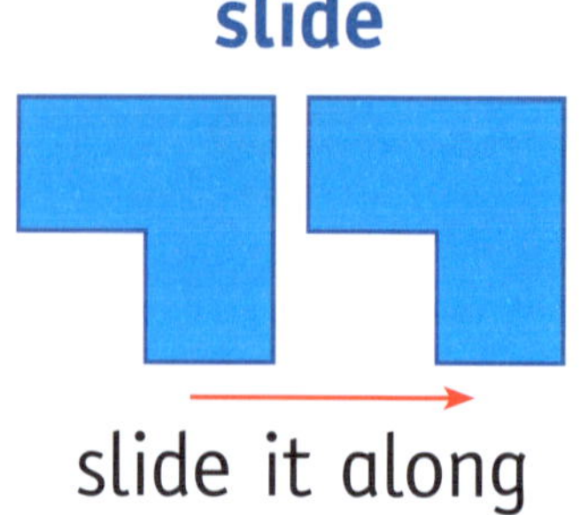

slide it along

turn

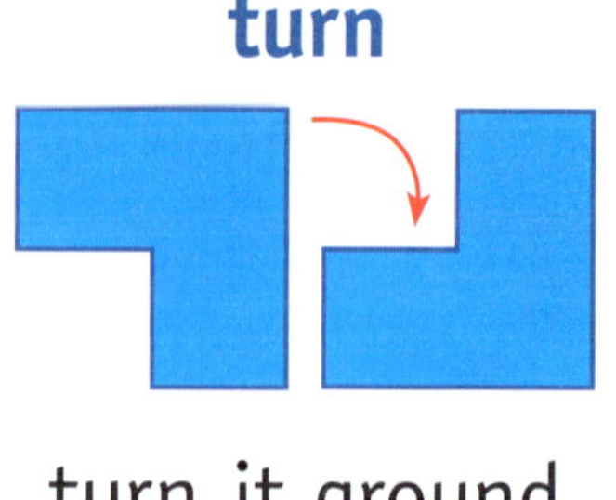

turn it around

1 How has the shape been moved? Write flip, slide or turn.

a

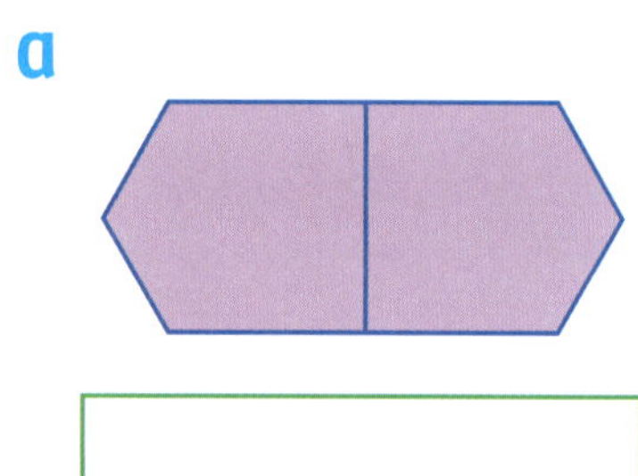

b

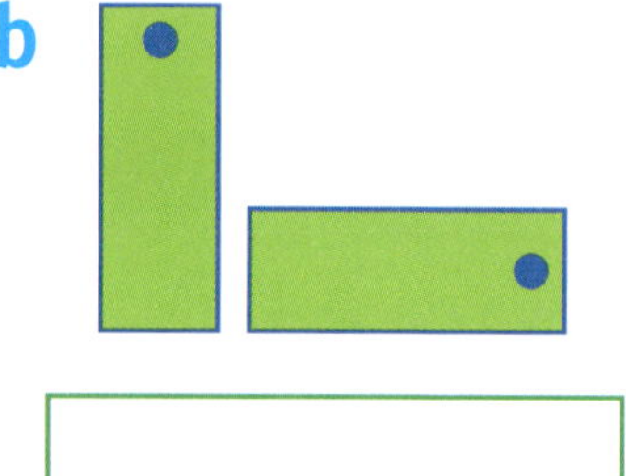

c

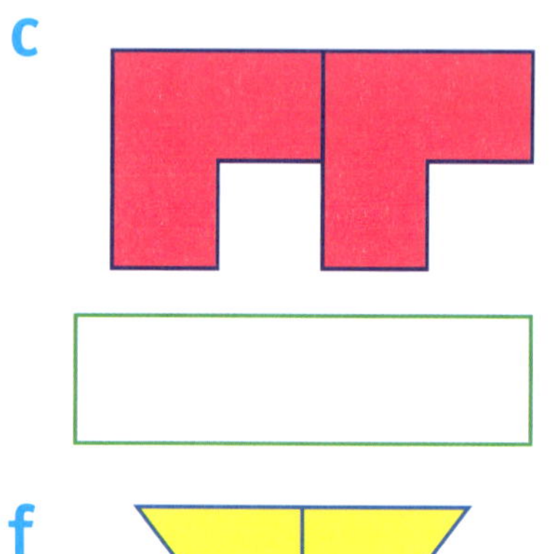

d

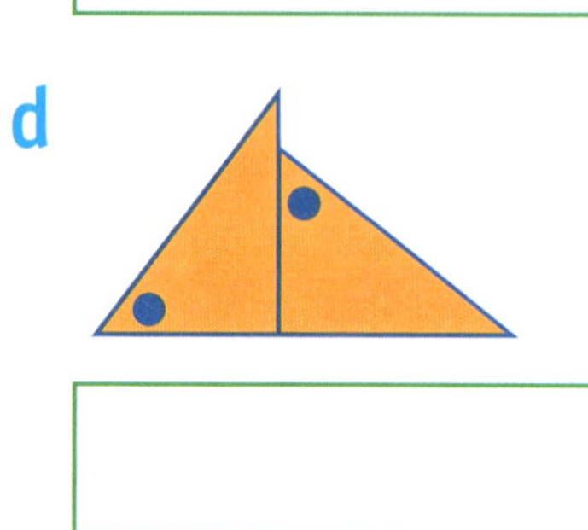

e

f

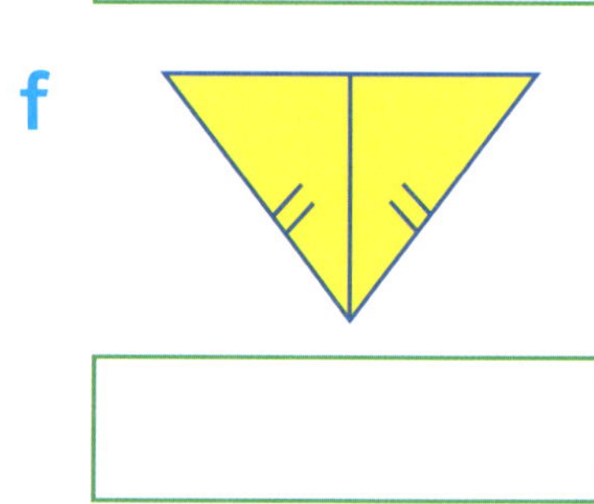

2 Continue each pattern.

a

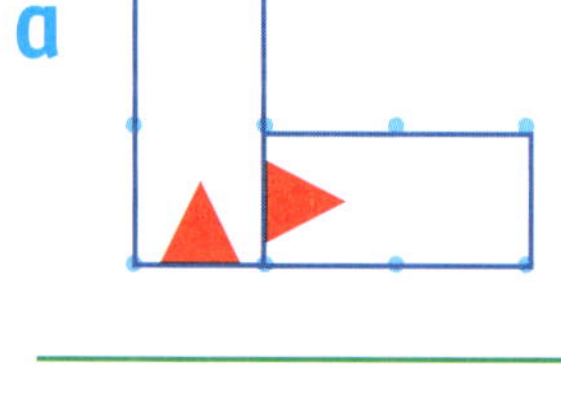

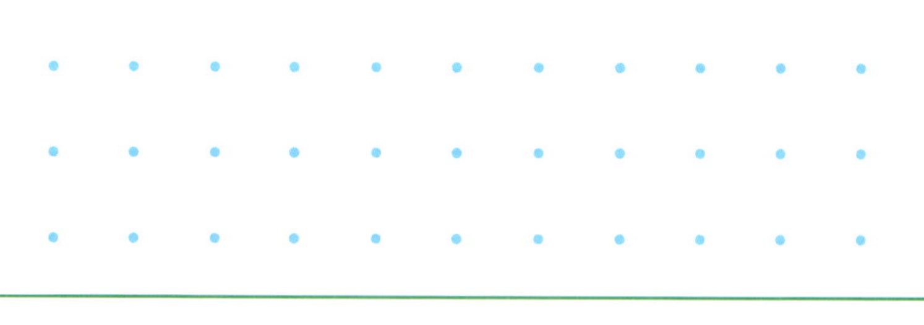

b

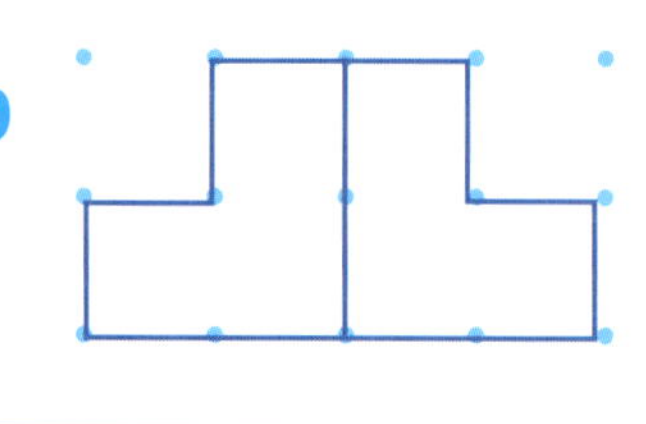

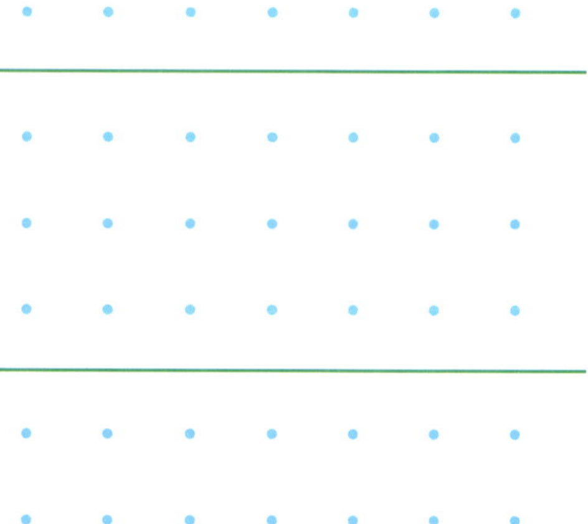

c

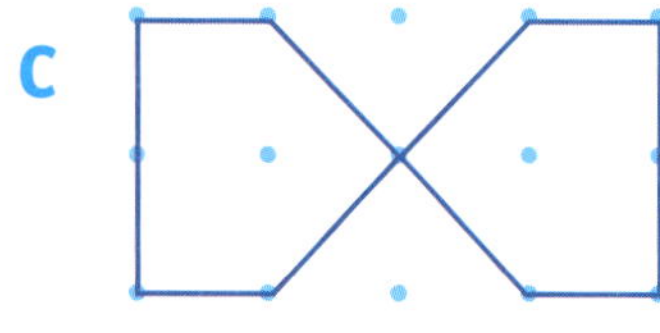

Symmetry

Use a mirror to help you.

Draw the other side of the picture.

Colour to make it symmetrical.

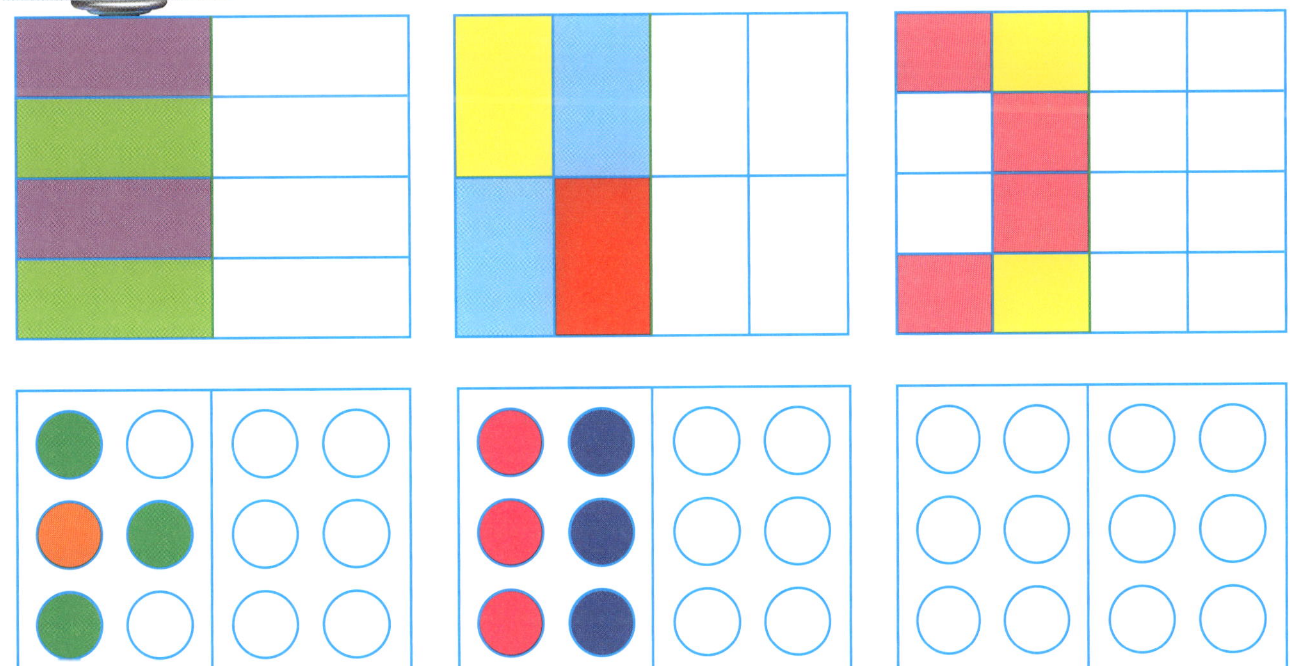

Count by 3s

1 How many?

a

2 sets of 3 wheels = ☐

b

3 groups of 3 balloons = ☐

c

4 sets of 3 legs = ☐

d

5 groups of 3 dots = ☐

2 a Draw 6 three-leaf clovers.

☐ leaves

b Draw 10 triangles.

☐ sides

3 Count in threes.

Equal rows

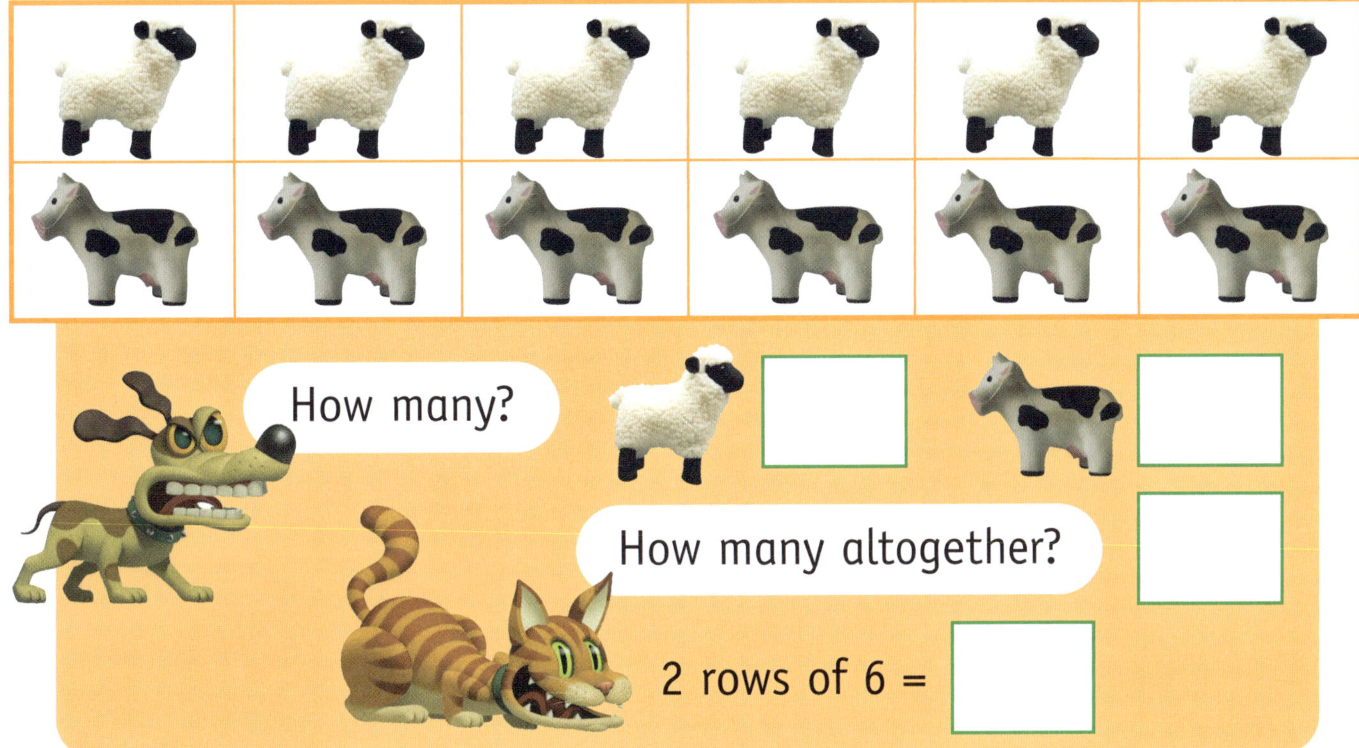

2 rows of 6 =

Draw 3 rows.

2 circle
2 triangle
2 square

How many shapes?

3 rows of 2 =

Draw 3 rows.

6 

3

How many faces?

3 rows of 3 =

Counting in fives

Count by fives

How many fingers?

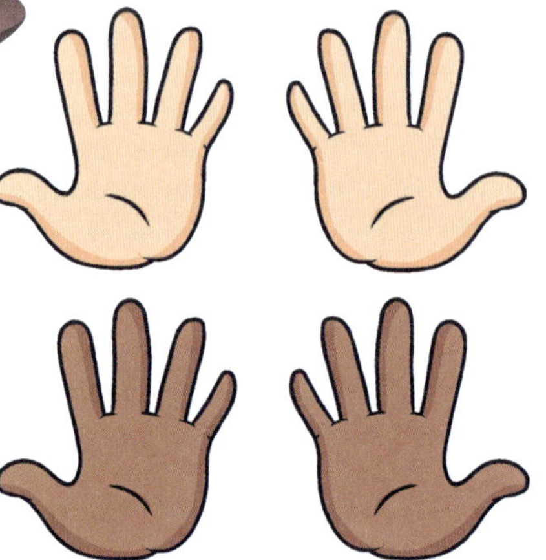

4 groups of 5 = ☐

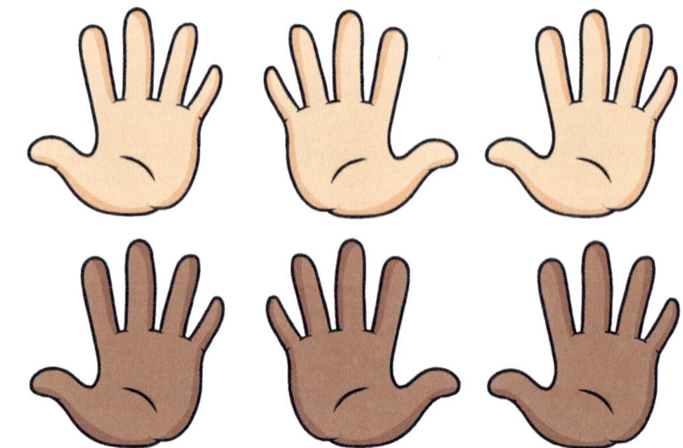

6 groups of 5 = ☐

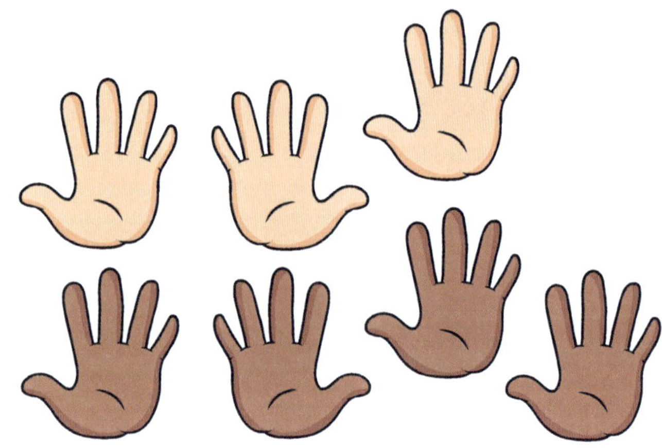

7 groups of 5 = ☐

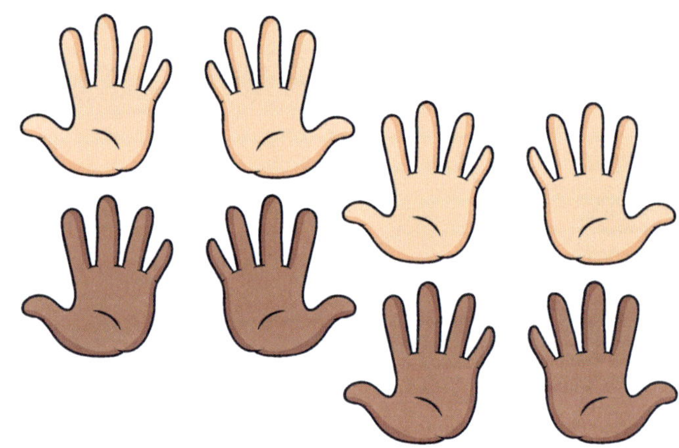

8 groups of 5 = ☐

Count in fives.

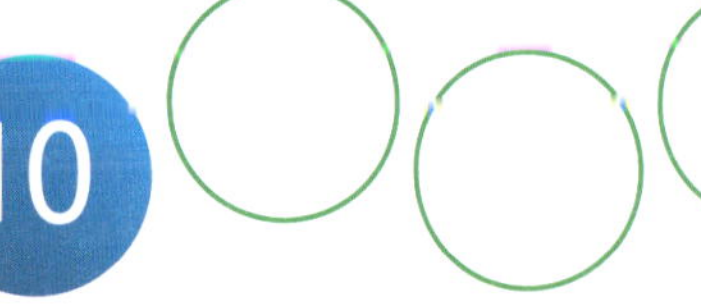

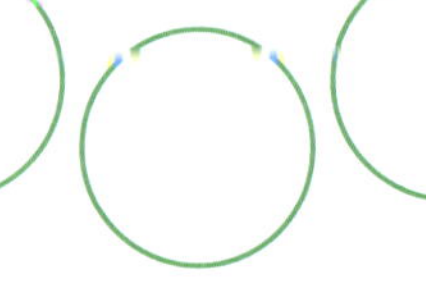

5 +5 → ☐ +5 → ☐ +5 → ☐ +5 → ☐ +5 → ☐

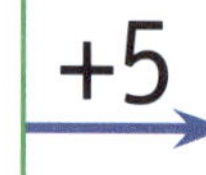

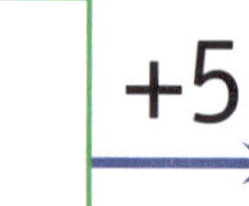

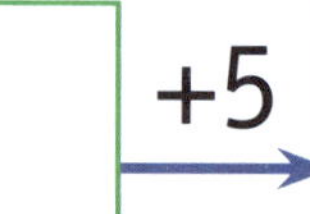

Multiplication as repeated addition

Count in twos.

2 + 2 = ☐

☐ twos are ☐

2 + 2 + 2 = ☐

☐ twos are ☐

2 + 2 + 2 + 2 = ☐

☐ twos are ☐

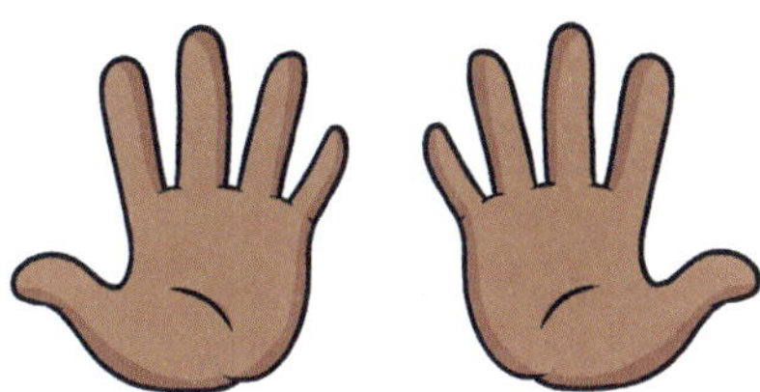

5 + 5 = ☐

☐ fives are ☐

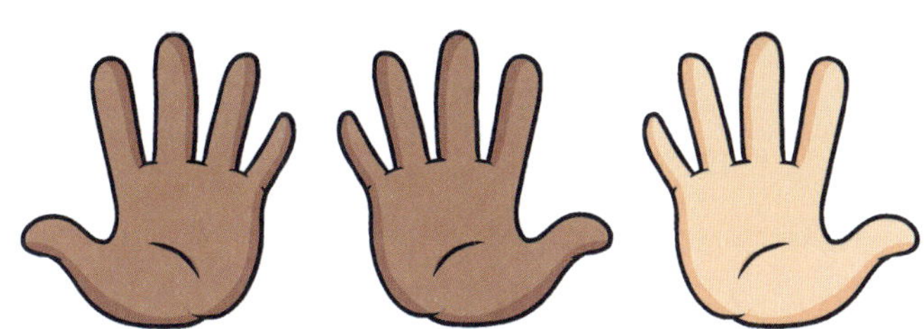

5 + 5 + 5 = ☐

☐ fives are ☐

Mastery Checklist

I can:
- ☐ make patterns using flip, slide and turn.
- ☐ finish designs with symmetry.
- ☐ count in 2s, 3s and 5s.
- ☐ add equal groups.

Your pet stick insect

Investigation 3

Draw your pet stick insect.

How long is your stick insect? Measure using blocks ________________

Draw a house for your stick insect.

AC9M1M02 Measurement **MA1-GM-02** Geometric measure A • Length: Measure the lengths of objects using uniform informal units
MA1-FG-01 Forming groups A • Model and use equal groups of objects to represent multiplication **MA1-WM-01** Working mathematically • Apply mathematical techniques to solve problems

Your pet stick insect

Investigation 3

Stick insects eat gum leaves. They also like twigs to walk on.

Your stick insect will eat 5 leaves every day.

Draw them in the table.

Monday	Tuesday	Wednesday	Thursday	Friday	Saturday	Sunday

Draw a branch that will feed your stick insect for a week.

To do this, I needed to:

- ☐ draw diagrams.
- ☐ measure length.
- ☐ fill in a table.
- ☐ count by 5s.

Revision

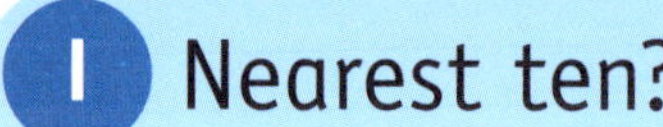

1 Nearest ten?

18 ☐ 23 ☐ 35 ☐

2 Write the missing numbers.

30 40 50 ☐ 70 80 ☐ ☐

3 Colour the hexagons.

4 Complete.

5 How many?

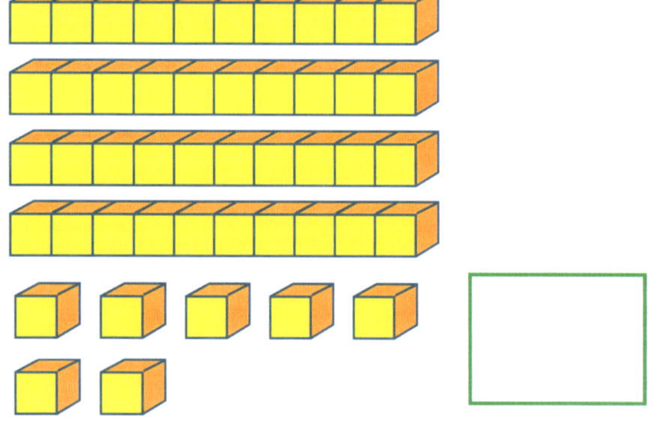

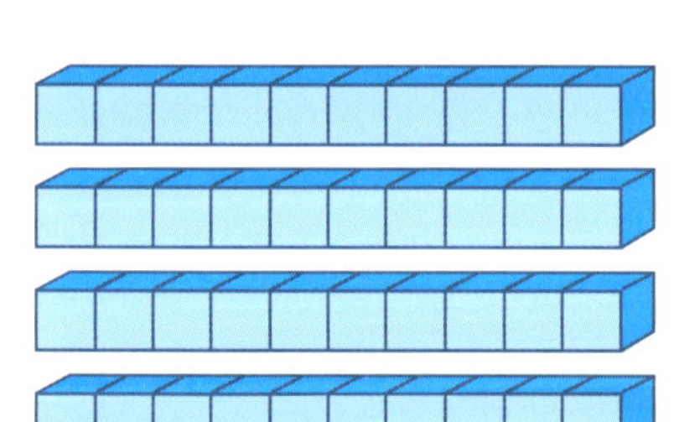

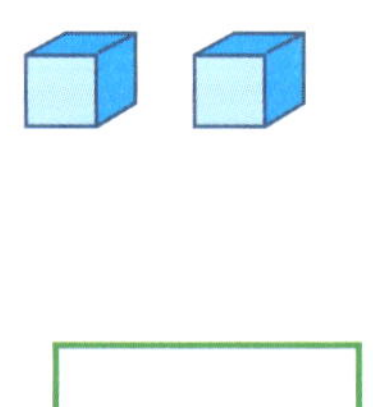

6 Order from smallest to largest.

smallest largest

Revision

7 How many wheels?

8 How long?

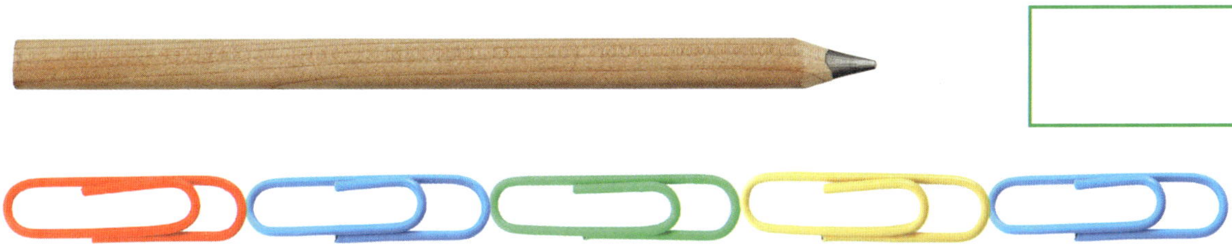

9 How many?

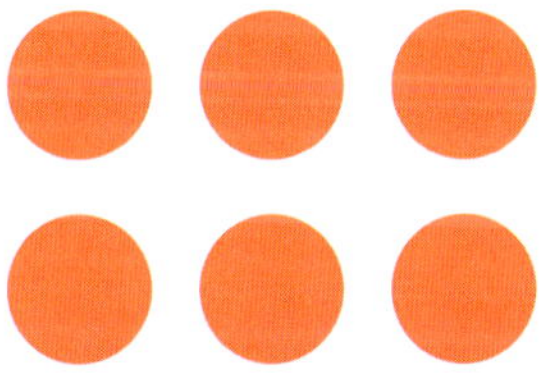

10 Which shape is:

biggest? smallest?

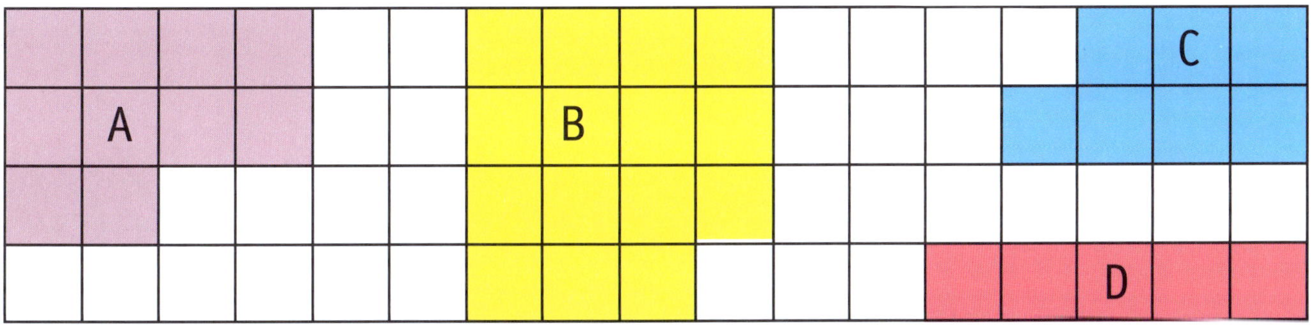

A B C D

Writing addition sentences

Write two additions for each picture.

2 + 4 = □

4 + 2 = □

□ + □ = □

□ + □ = □

□ + □ = □

□ + □ = □

Draw and write your own.

□ + □ = □

□ + □ = □

Challenge! Colour the butterflies that add to 6.

AC9M1N04 Number **MA1-CSQ-01** Combining and separating quantities A • Recognise and recall number bonds up to ten • Represent equality

Number facts

The first addition will help you answer the other two.

5 + 5 =

5 + 4 =

5 + 6 =

8 + 2 =

8 + 3 =

8 + 4 =

7 + 3 =

7 + 4 =

7 + 5 =

6 + 4 =

6 + 3 =

6 + 5 =

9 + 1 =

9 + 2 =

9 + 3 =

10 + 0 =

10 + 1 =

10 + 2 =

Challenge! 7 dogs, 3 mice, 8 birds, 2 cats

How many animals? 

Adding ten

Colour to add.

1	2	3	4	5	6	7	8	9	10	11	12	13	14	15	16	17	18	19	20

$10 + 3 =$ ☐ $3 + 10 =$ ☐

1	2	3	4	5	6	7	8	9	10	11	12	13	14	15	16	17	18	19	20

$10 + 5 =$ ☐ $5 + 10 =$ ☐

1	2	3	4	5	6	7	8	9	10	11	12	13	14	15	16	17	18	19	20

$10 + 8 =$ ☐ $8 + 10 =$ ☐

1	2	3	4	5	6	7	8	9	10
11	12	13	14	15	16	17	18	19	20

$6 + 10 =$ ☐

1	2	3	4	5	6	7	8	9	10
11	12	13	14	15	16	17	18	19	20

$4 + 10 =$ ☐

1	2	3	4	5	6	7	8	9	10
11	12	13	14	15	16	17	18	19	20

$9 + 10 =$ ☐

1	2	3	4	5	6	7	8	9	10
11	12	13	14	15	16	17	18	19	20

$10 + 10 =$ ☐

$7 + 10 =$ ☐ $2 + 10 =$ ☐

AC9M1N04 Number **MA1-CSQ-01** Combining and separating quantities A • Use advanced count-by-one strategies to solve addition and subtraction problems • Use flexible strategies to solve addition and subtraction problems

Adding tens using money

10	20	30	40	50	60	70	80	90	100

20c + 10c = ___ c   50c + 20c = ___ c

Write your own additions.

___ c + ___ c = ___ c   ___ c + ___ c = ___ c

___ + ___ = ___   ___ + ___ = ___

How much?

___   ___

Challenge! How much to buy 3 things from above?

___ + ___ + ___ = ___

Adding tens and ones

Add the tens, then the ones.

15 + 23	36 + 42	29 + 51
10 + 20 + 5 + 3	30 + 40 + 6 + 2	
30 + 8		

Add the tens, then the ones.

21 + 45 = 20 + 40 + 1 + 5 = 60 + 6 = ☐

52 + 18 = ____________________ = ☐

14 + 74 = ____________________ = ☐

33 + 67 = ____________________ = ☐

Challenge!

19 + 91

12 + 34 + 56

11 + 22 + 33 + 44

Mastery Checklist

I can:
- ☐ add numbers to 20.
- ☐ add tens.
- ☐ add two-digit numbers by splitting tens and ones.

Problem solving

Addition pairs

The numbers from 1 to 9 make pairs that add to 10.

1 + 9 | 2 + 8 | 3 + 7 | 4 + 6 | 5 + 5

Find pairs of two-digit numbers that add to 100.

11 + 89 = 10 + 80 + 1 + 9 = 90 + 10 = **100**

Is there a pattern to these pairs of numbers? ______________________

____

I can solve a problem by:

☐ adding tens and ones in two-digit numbers. ☐ writing number sentences.

Half hours

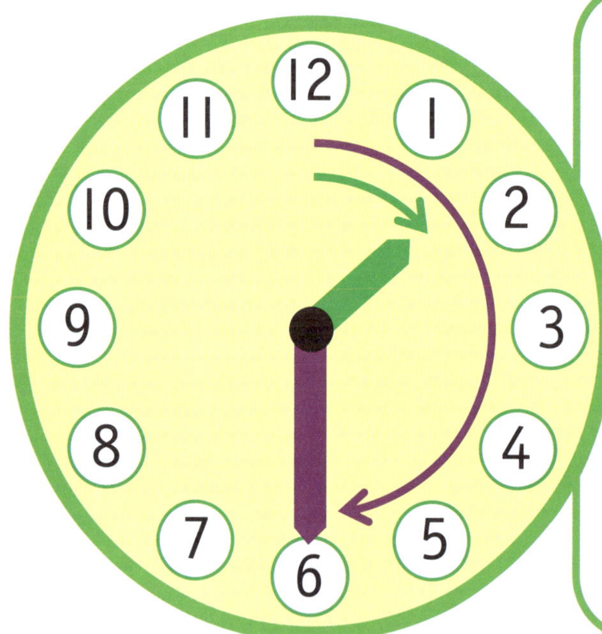

Half-past

Minute hand points to 6, a **half turn** around the clock. **Hour hand** is **halfway** between the last hour and the next.

Half-past 1

Minute hand points to 6. **Hour hand** is **halfway** between 1 and 2.

Draw on the minute and hour hands.

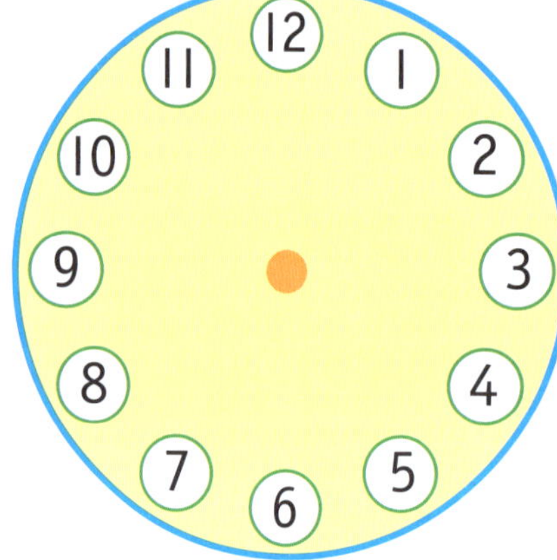

Half-past 4

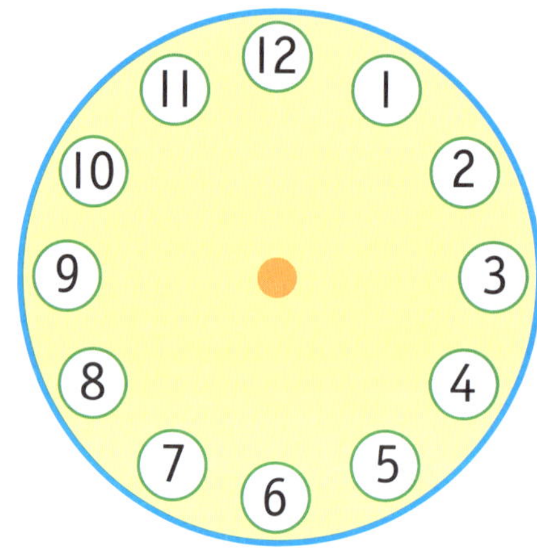

Half-past 9

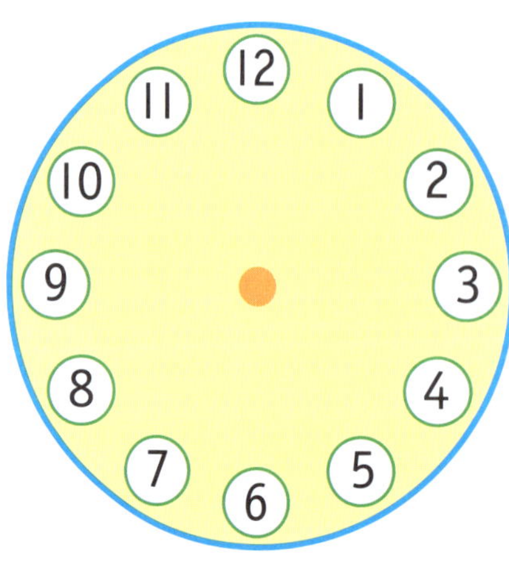

Half-past 11

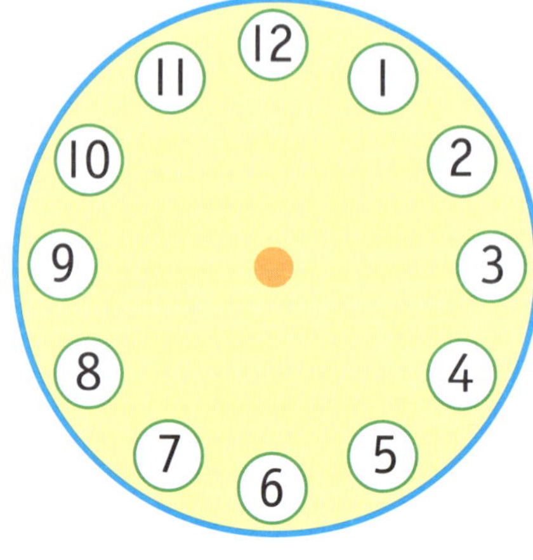

Half-past 6

Half-past

half-past ☐

half-past ☐

half-past ☐

half-past ☐

half-past ☐

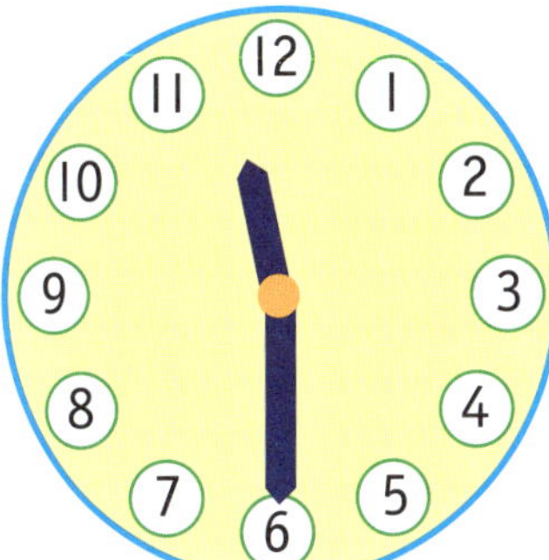

half-past ☐

Match.

half-past 10

half-past 7

half-past 1

half-past 6

O'clock and half-past

What time is it?

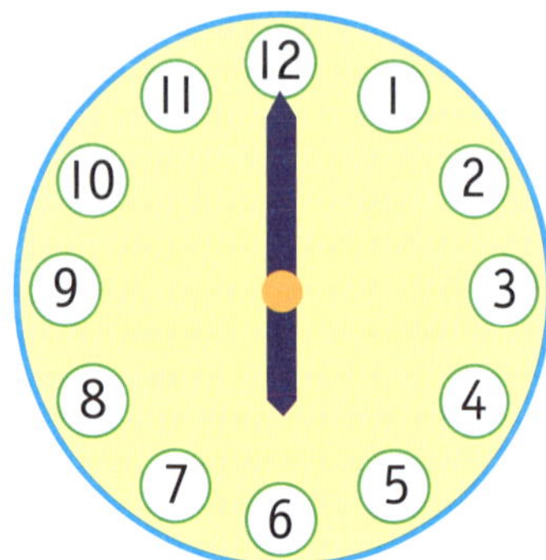

o'clock

half-past

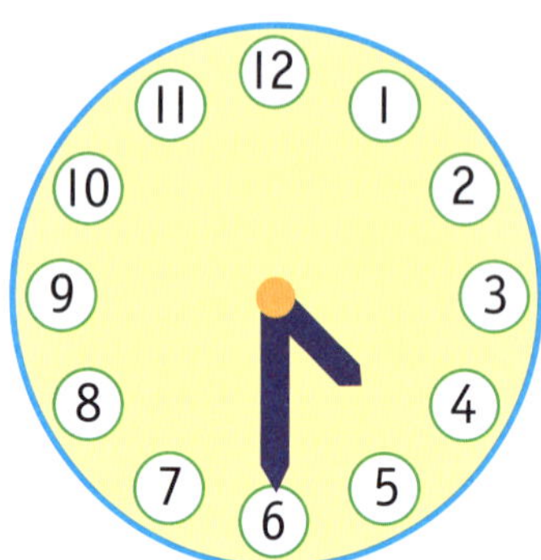

Challenge!

What is your favourite time?

Digital half hours

Half an hour

An hour is 60 minutes long.
Half an hour is **30 minutes**.
Half-past 1 is 1:30.
Half-past 5 is 5:30.
Half-past 12 is 12:30.

Fill in the missing times.

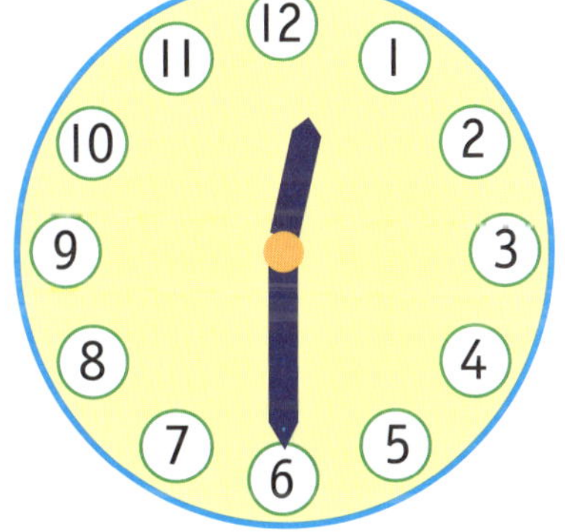

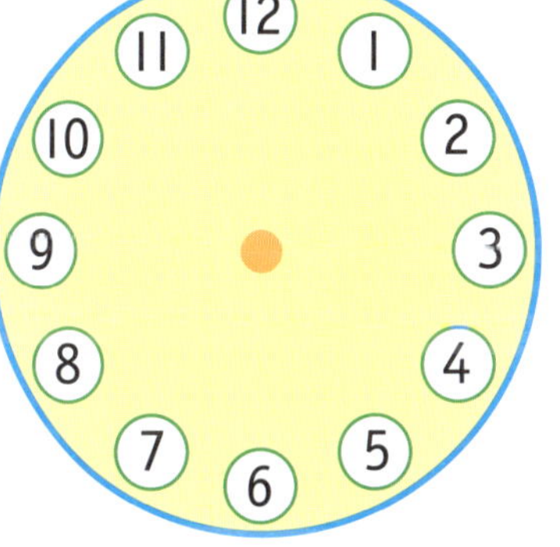

☐ :30

☐ :30

Mastery Checklist

I can:

- ☐ read clocks to the hour and half-hour.
- ☐ use 'o'clock' and 'half-past'.
- ☐ read digital time to the half-hour.

Equal parts

Fractions are equal parts.

Circle the shape that has equal parts. How many equal parts?

 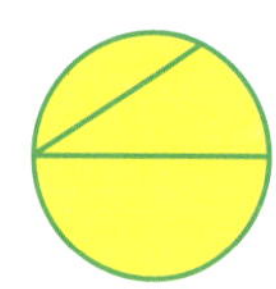

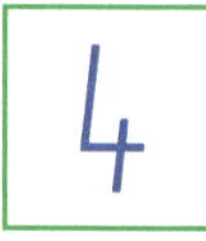 equal parts

 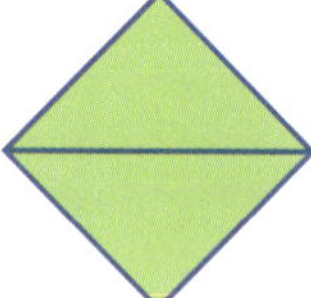

☐ equal parts

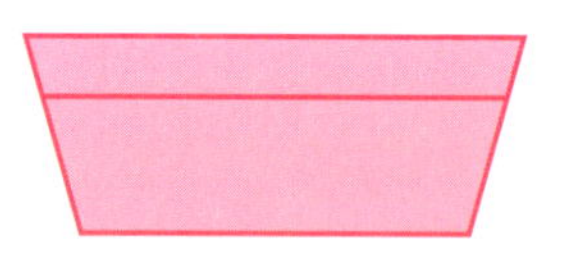 

☐ equal parts

☐ equal parts

☐ equal parts

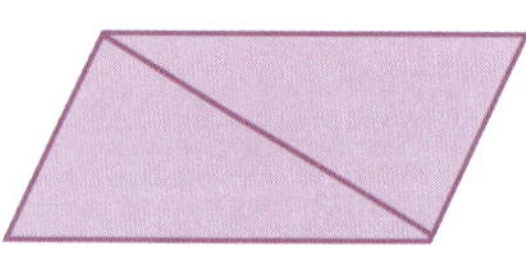

☐ equal parts

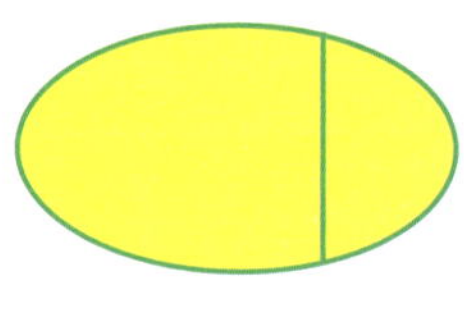 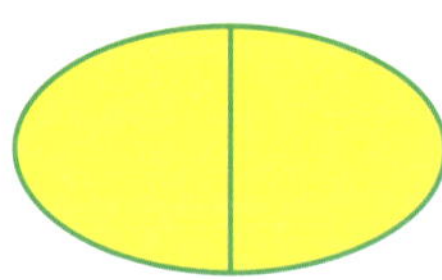

☐ equal parts

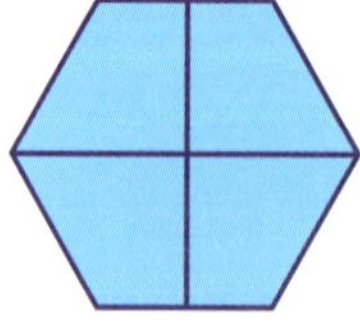 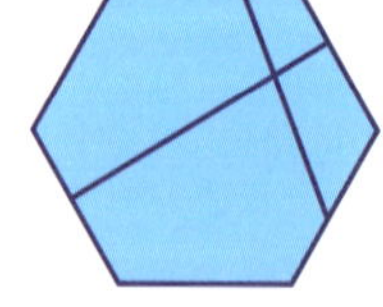

☐ equal parts

Can one half of a shape be larger than the other half? ____________

Why? ____

Quarters

Quarters are 4 equal parts.

1 whole = ☐ halves = ☐ quarters

Tick shapes that are cut into quarters.

Challenge!

Fold paper squares into quarters.
How many different ways can you find? 

Quarters

Colour one quarter of each shape.

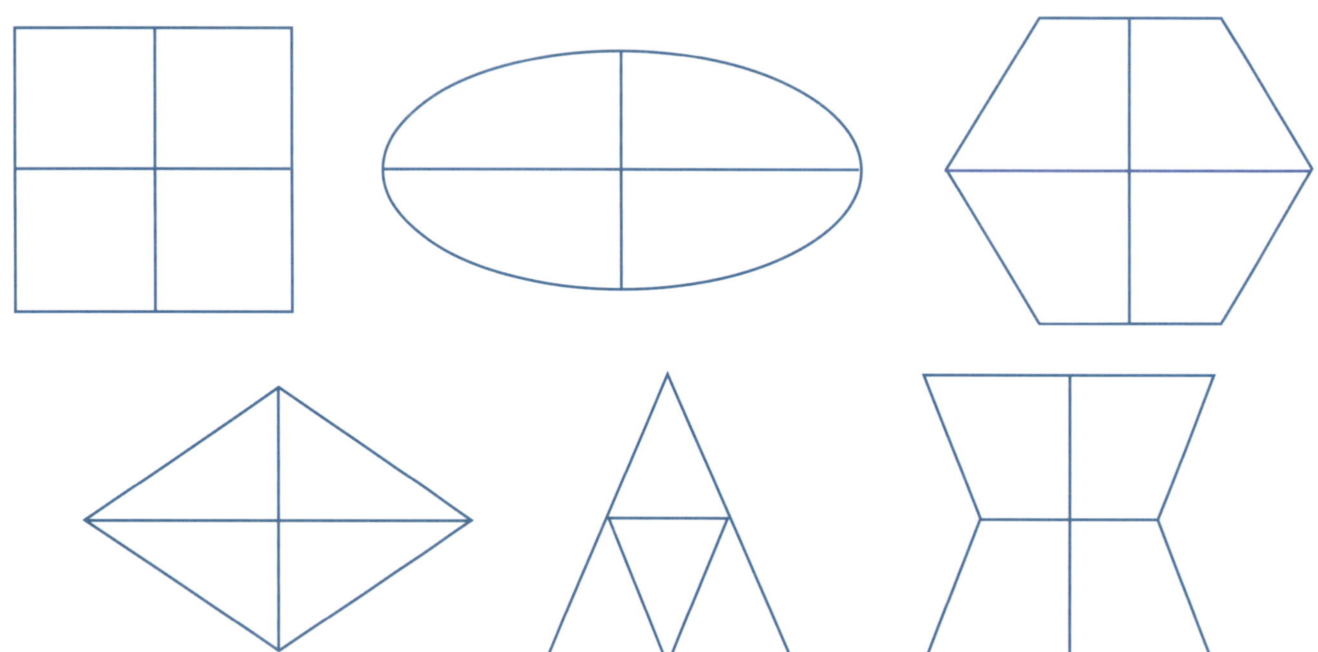

Cut each shape into quarters. Colour one quarter.

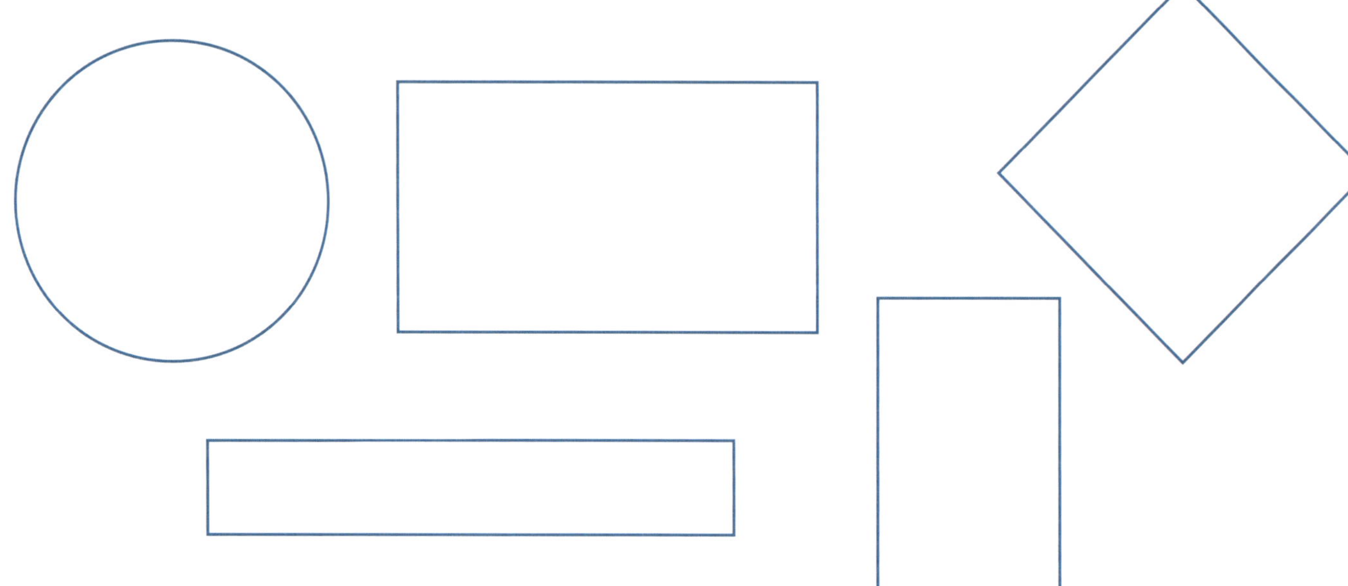

Challenge! Continue the pattern.

Halves and quarters

Tick the shapes that show halves.

Circle the shapes that show quarters.

Colour one half of each shape.

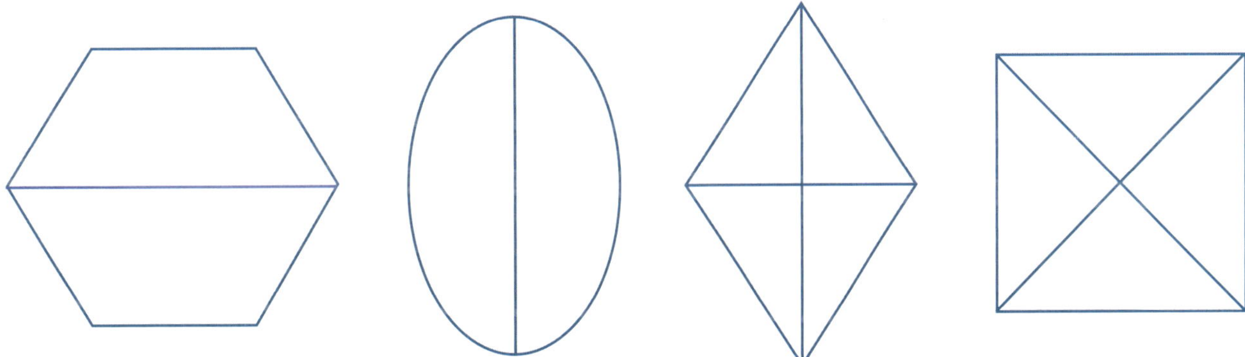

Challenge! Continue each pattern.

Fractions of lengths

How long is each ribbon?

Link the matching halves. How long is each ribbon in total?

a ______ b ______ c ______

Cut this ribbon in half. Cut each half in half.

What fraction is this ribbon cut into? ______

Cut these ribbons into quarters.

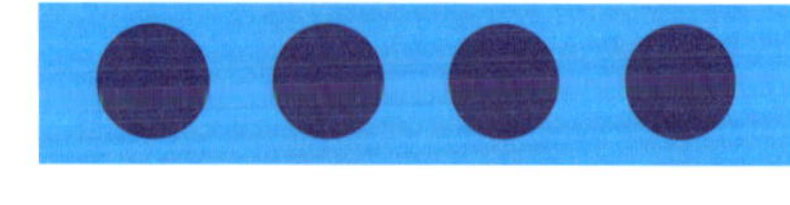

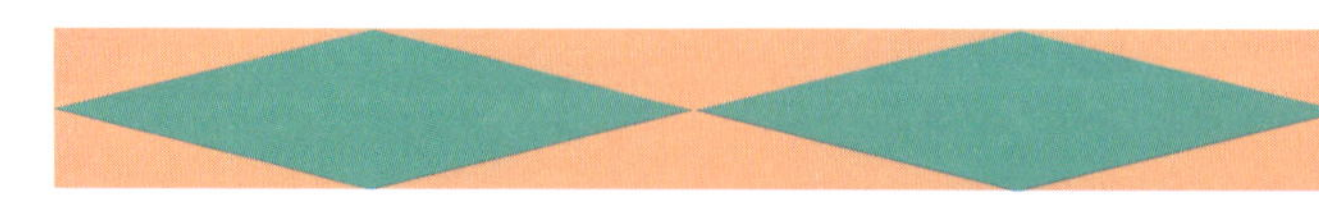

AC9M1M01 Measurement **MA1-GM-03** Geometric measure • Length: Subdivide lengths to find halves and quarters

Problem solving

Half of a group

Grab a handful of marbles, blocks or counters.
Draw them.
How many altogether? ☐
Circle half the group.

Half of ☐ is ☐.

Grab a smaller handful.
Draw them.
How many altogether? ☐
Circle half the group.

Half of ☐ is ☐.

Grab a larger handful.
Draw them.
How many altogether? ☐
Circle half the group.

Half of ☐ is ☐.

If you had an odd number, what did you do with the extra one?

____

____

I can solve a problem by:

☐ dividing a group in half. ☐ drawing a diagram.

Sorting data

How many balloons of each colour?

red	blue	pink	yellow

Write the balloon numbers in this table.

less than 10	more than 10

Challenge!

Sort the balloon numbers into odd and even.

odd	even

Mastery Checklist

I can:

- [ ] identify equal parts, halves and quarters.
- [ ] make halves and quarters of a length.
- [ ] show half of a collection.
- [ ] sort data into categories.

Problem solving

Graphing

Choose 3 colours. Write them in the table. Ask at least 10 people to answer this question. *Which colour do you like best?* Tally the answers.

Colours	Number of people

Draw a graph of your results. Add numbers and labels.

Number of people

Colours

I can solve a problem by:

☐ collecting data. ☐ making a graph.

Revision • Term 3

1 Colour one quarter.

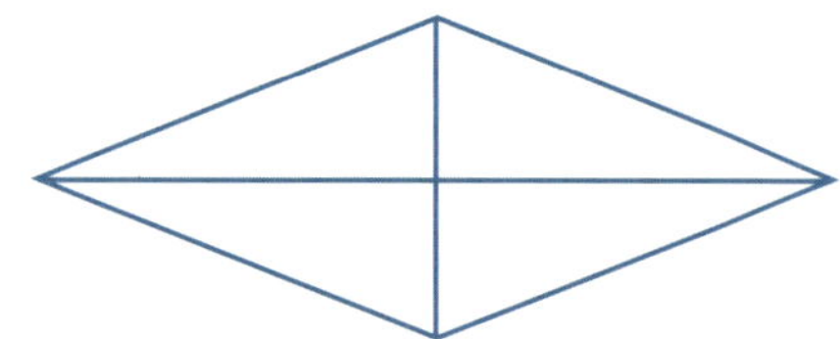

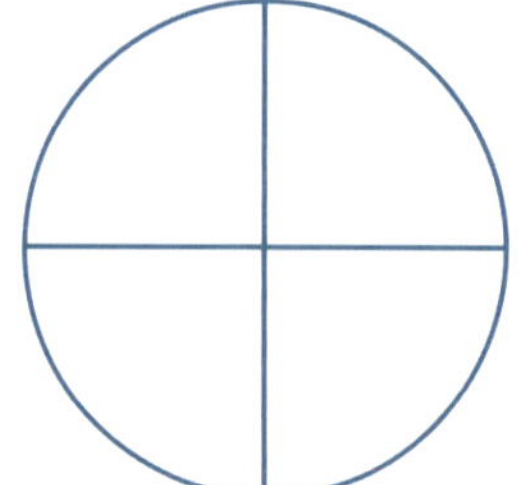

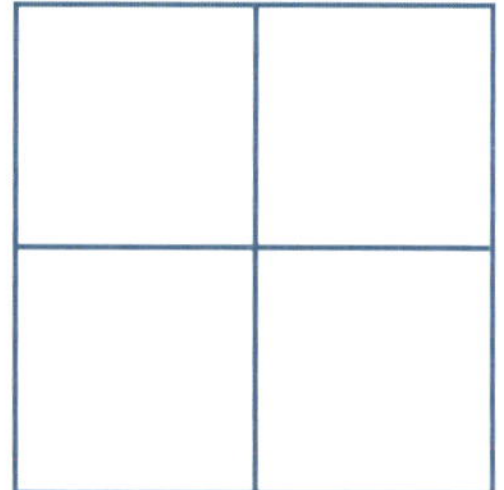

2 What time is it?

half-past ☐

half-past ☐

☐ o'clock

half-past ☐

3 **a** Half of 10 is 

b Double 5 is 

c 2 groups of 4 = ☐

d Half of 12 = ☐

4 How many?

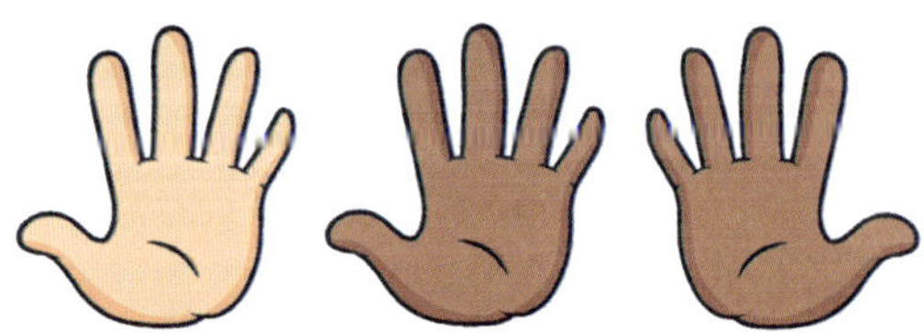

5 + 5 + 5 = ☐

3 + 3 + 3 + 3 = ☐

Revision • Term 3

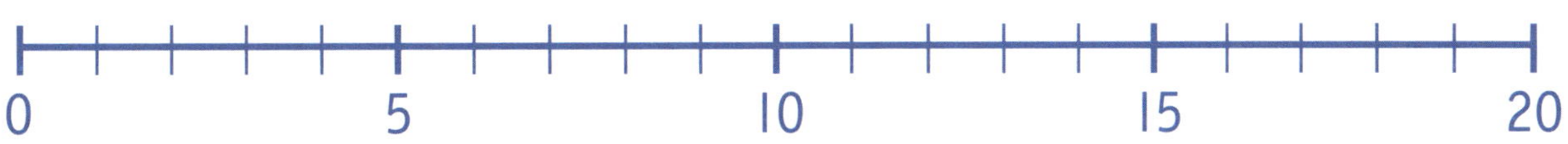

a 5 + 4 = ☐ b 8 + 2 = ☐ c 10 + 3 = ☐

d 5 + 10 = ☐ e 20 + 5 = ☐ f 30 + 1 = ☐

6 Where would you find 100 of these? Circle the correct answer.

in a bag in a shop under your bed

in the house in a plane in a park

in a car in a lake in a classroom

7 Add the tens, then the ones.

a 12 + 16 = ☐ b 25 + 44 = ☐

c 33 + 51 = ☐ d 64 + 36 = ☐

Place value

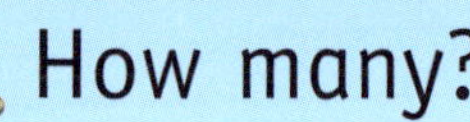

How many?

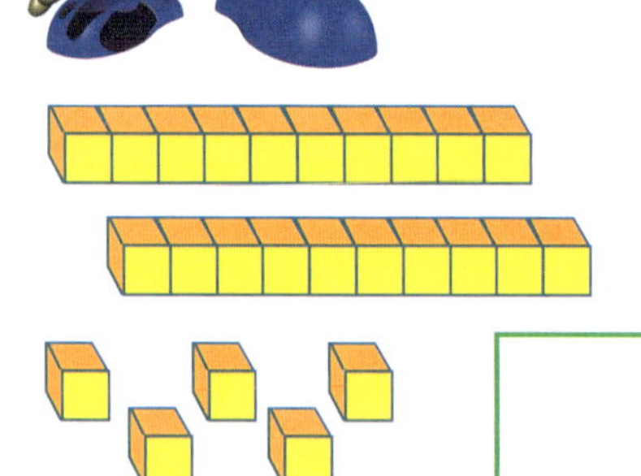
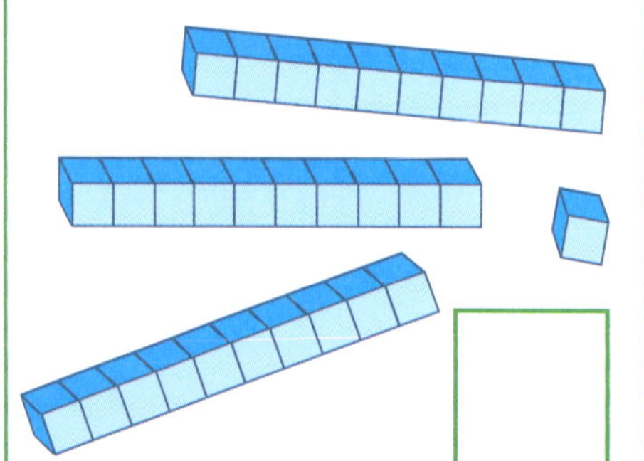
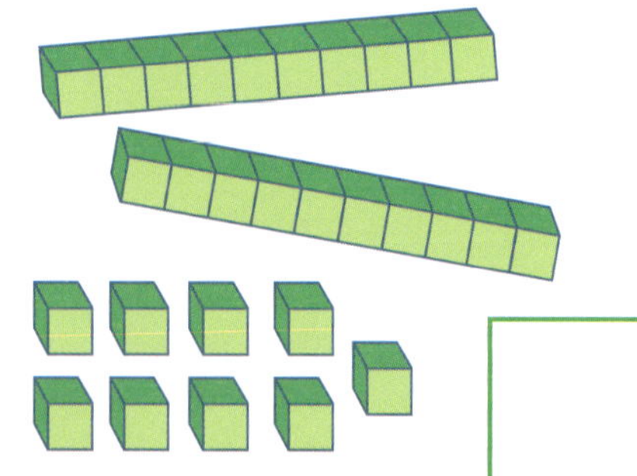
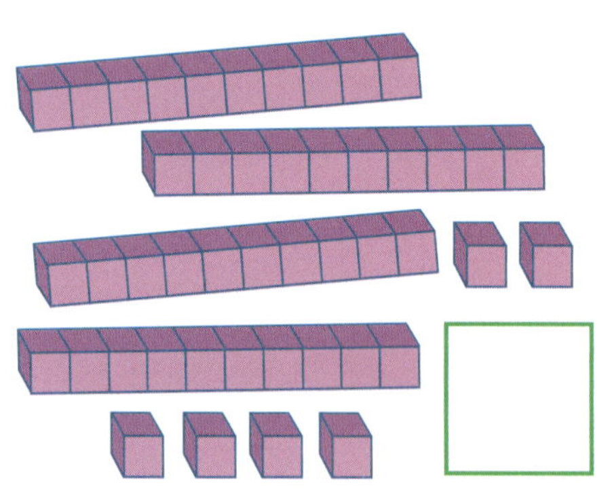
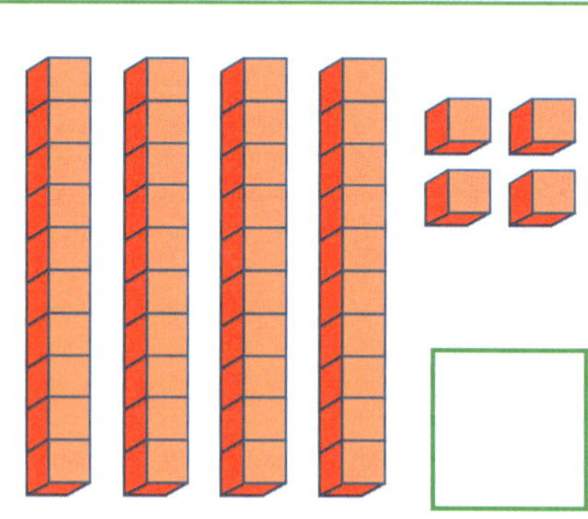
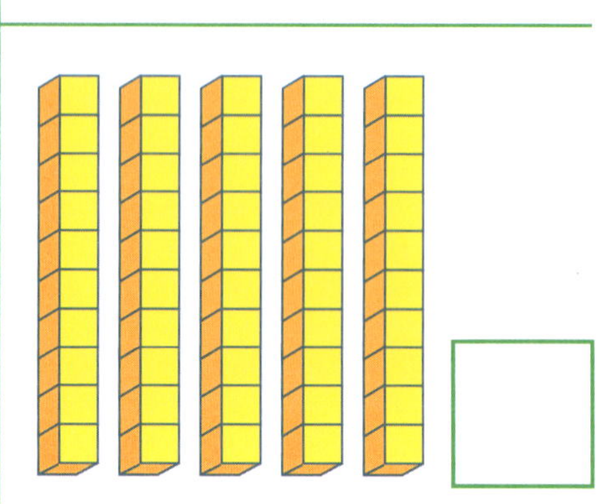

Write in order.

smallest

largest

Complete.

25 = 20 + 5

29 = ☐ + ☐

44 = ☐ + ☐

49 = ☐ + ☐

31 = 30 + ☐

47 = 40 + ☐

50 = ☐ + ☐

30 = ☐ + ☐

Place value

forty-five

45 = 40 + 5

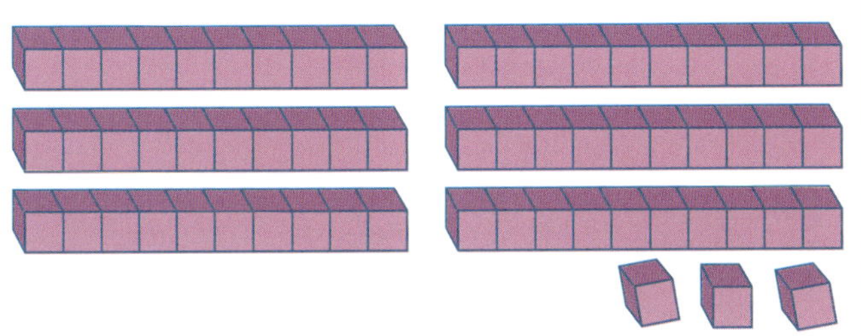

63 = ☐ + ☐

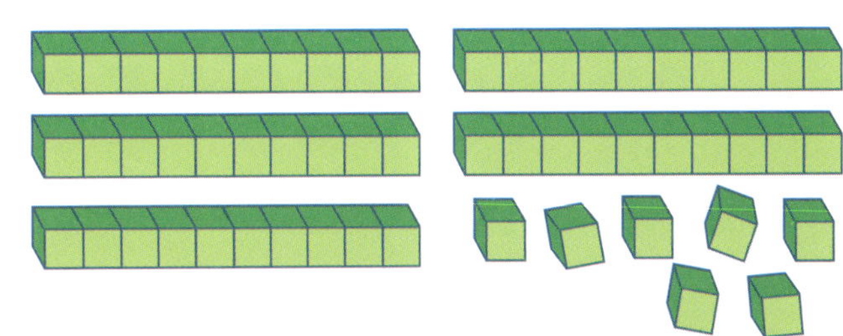

57 = ☐ + ☐

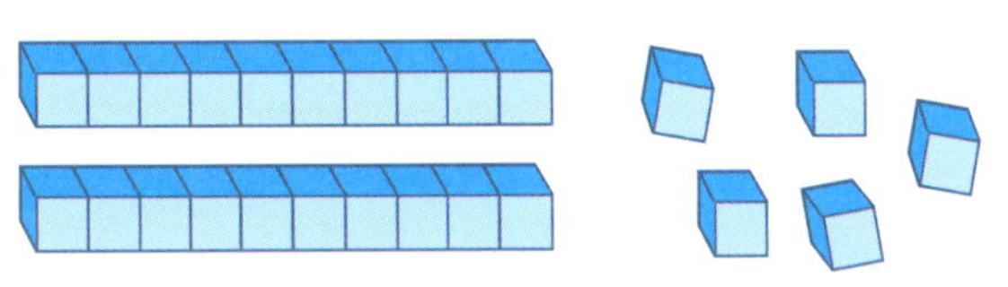

☐ = ☐ + ☐

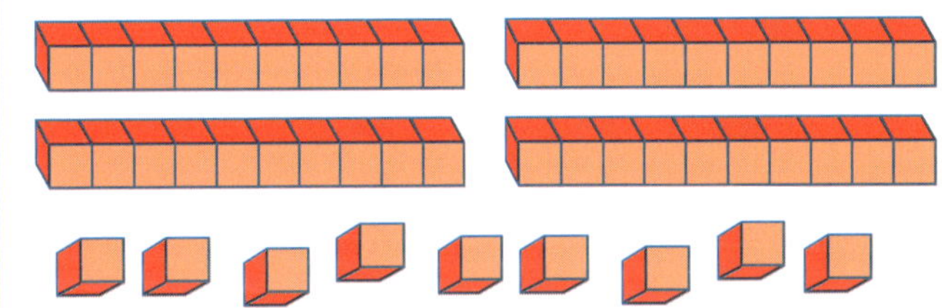

☐ = ☐ + ☐

91 = ☐ + ☐

69 = ☐ + ☐

28 = ☐ + ☐

53 = ☐ + ☐

37 = ☐ + ☐

84 = ☐ + ☐

75 = ☐ + ☐

99 = ☐ + ☐

Counting in tens

Count in tens.

0	10	20				60
40	50	60				
100	90	80				
60	50		30			

20 → add 10 → ◯ → add 10 → ◯ → add 10 → ◯

60 → + 10 → ☐ → + 10 → ☐ → + 10 → ☐

30 → take away 10 → ◯ → take away 10 → ◯ → take away 10 → ◯

70 → – 10 → ☐ → – 10 → ☐ → – 10 → ☐

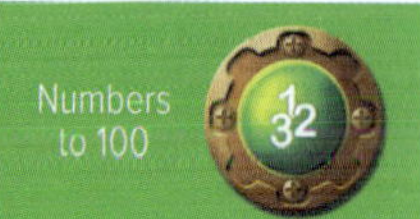

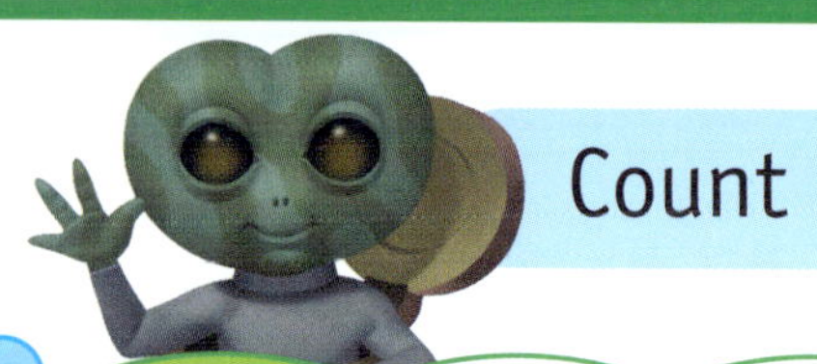

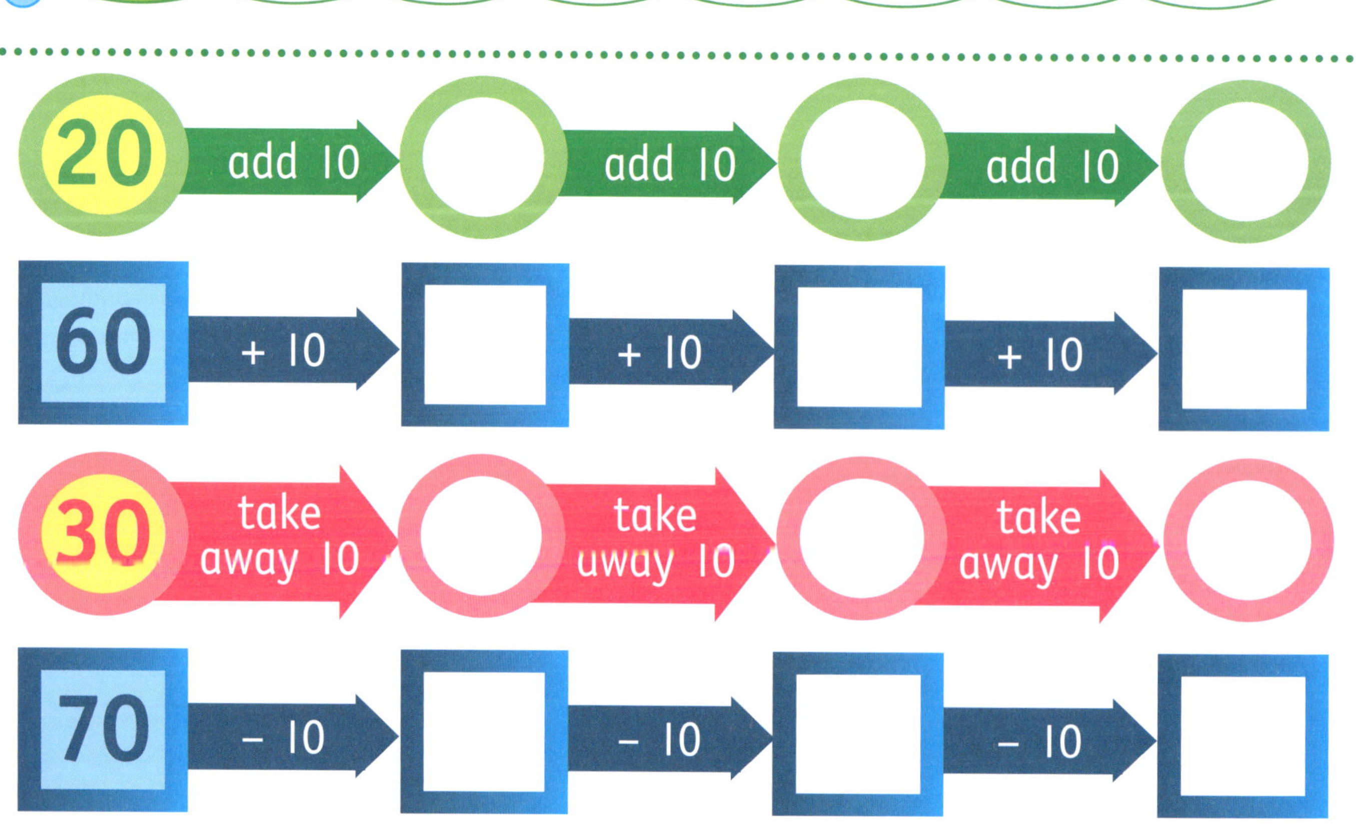

Number lines

Write the missing numbers.

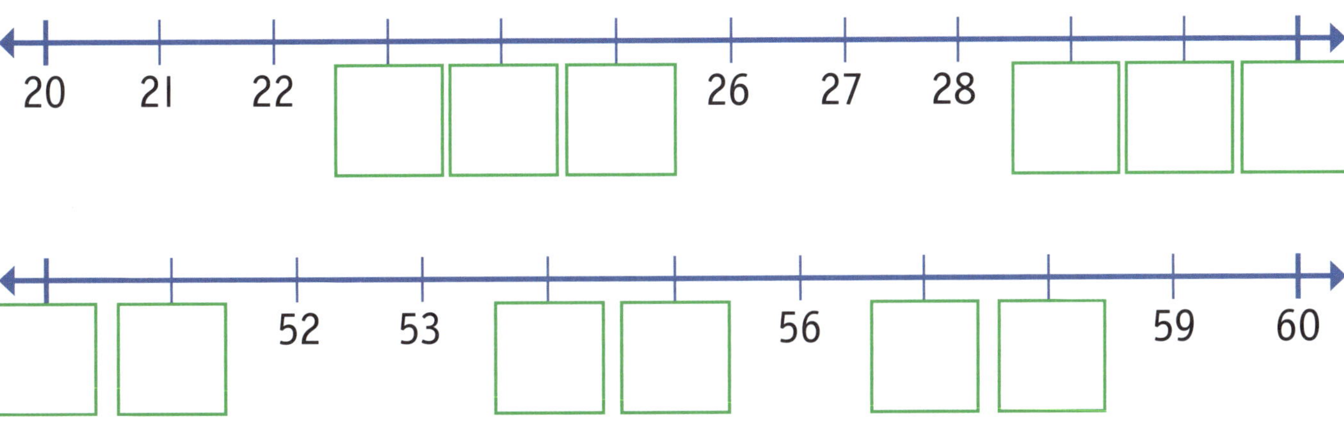

Fill in the tens.

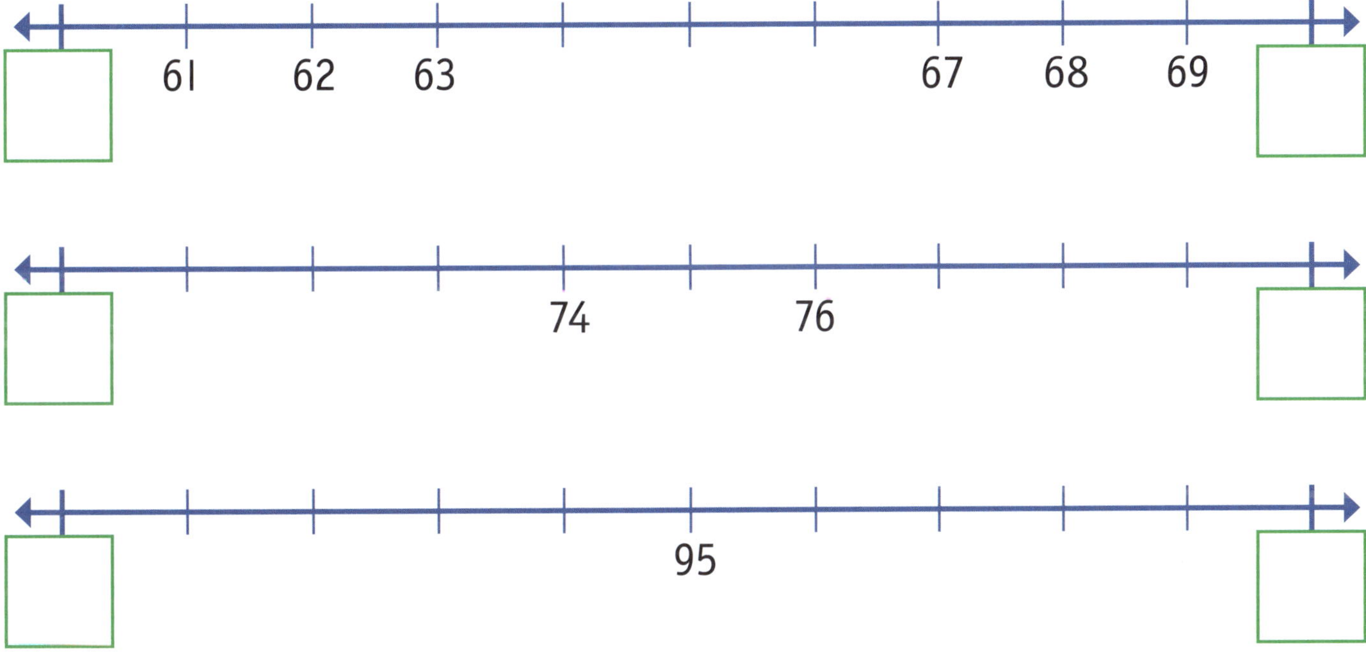

Count by tens.

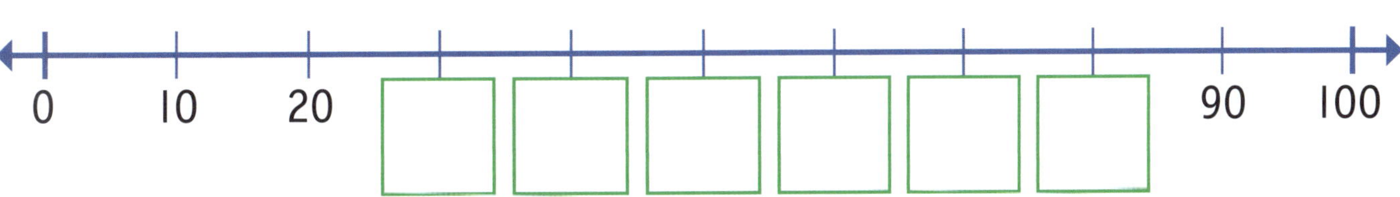

Draw and write each time.

I hour before		I hour after
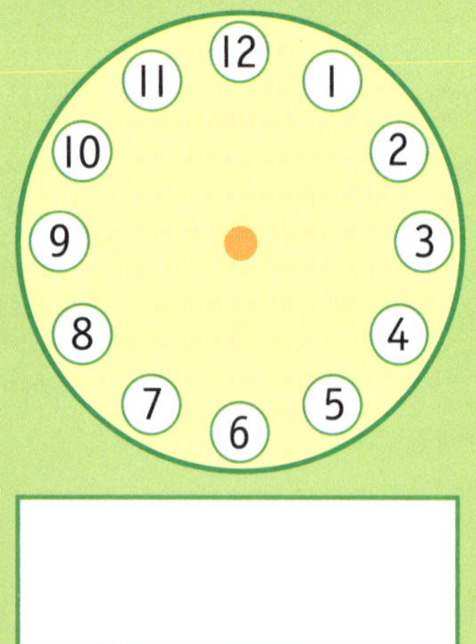		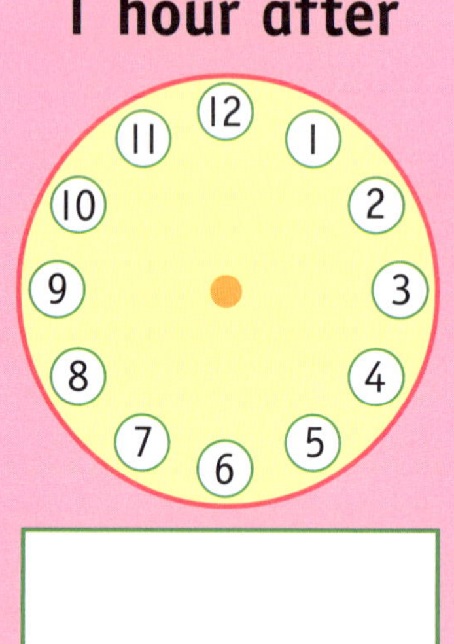
	6 o'clock	
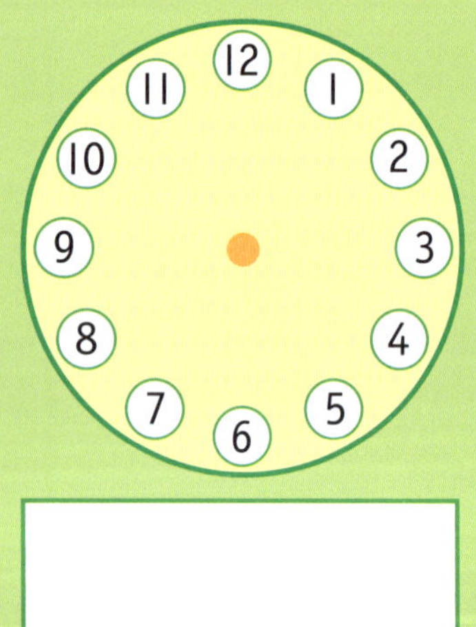		

Quarter past and quarter to

At a quarter past, the big hand has moved a quarter of the way around to the number 3.

The small hand is just past the hour.

A quarter past six

At a quarter to, the big hand sits on 9. It has a quarter of the way still to go.

The small hand is near the next hour.

A quarter to six

What time is it?

quarter past 7

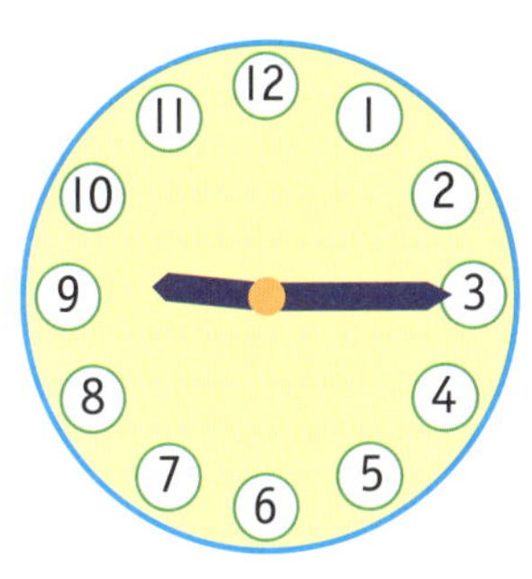

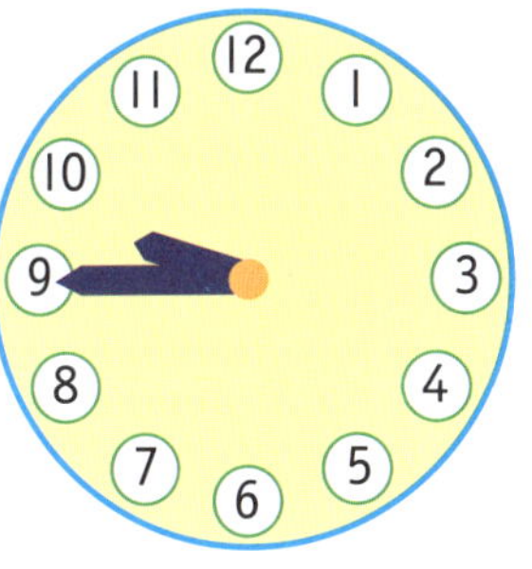

Calendar

Sunday	Monday	Tuesday	Wednesday	Thursday	Friday	Saturday
	1	2	3	4	5	6
7	8	9	10	11	12	13
14	15	16	17	18	19	20
21	22	23	24	25	26	27
28	29	30	31			

What day of the week is the

1st?

5th?

10th?

22nd?

25th?

31st?

How many? Saturdays? Wednesdays?

Challenge!

What number patterns can you see?

Mastery Checklist

I can:

- ☐ identify tens and ones.
- ☐ count by tens.
- ☐ read and write times.
- ☐ use a calendar.

My Favourite Date

What is your favourite day of the year? ____________________

What month is your favourite day in? ____________________

Fill in the calendar for the month of your favourite day.

Add your favourite day to the calendar.

Month:						
Sunday	**Monday**	**Tuesday**	**Wednesday**	**Thursday**	**Friday**	**Saturday**

What day of the week is your favourite day?

____

What is the number of your favourite day? __________

Fill in the date for your favourite day:

____________________	____________________	____________________
Day of the week	Number	Month

I can solve a problem by:

☐ identifying a date. ☐ using a calendar.

Subtraction

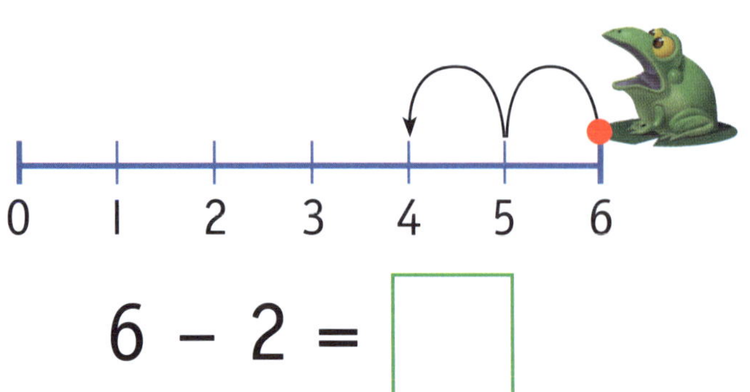

6 – 2 = ☐

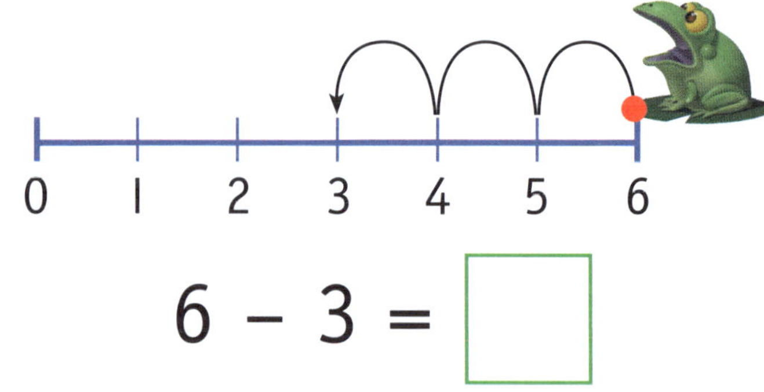

6 – 3 = ☐

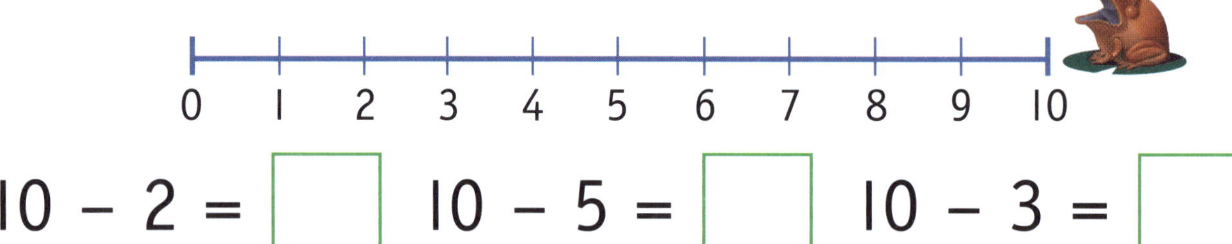

10 – 2 = ☐ 10 – 5 = ☐ 10 – 3 = ☐

How many dogs? ☐

9 – 3 = ☐ 9 – 5 = ☐ 9 – 6 = ☐

How many berries? ☐

8 – 4 = ☐ 8 – 2 = ☐ 8 – 7 = ☐

Subtraction

1 There were 10. How many left?

a

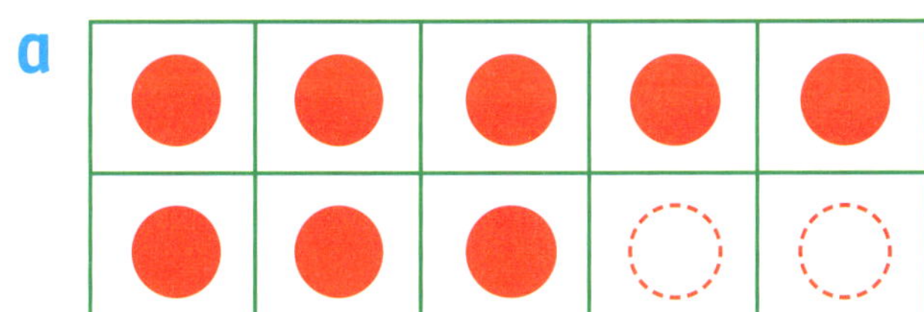

10 − 2 = ☐

b

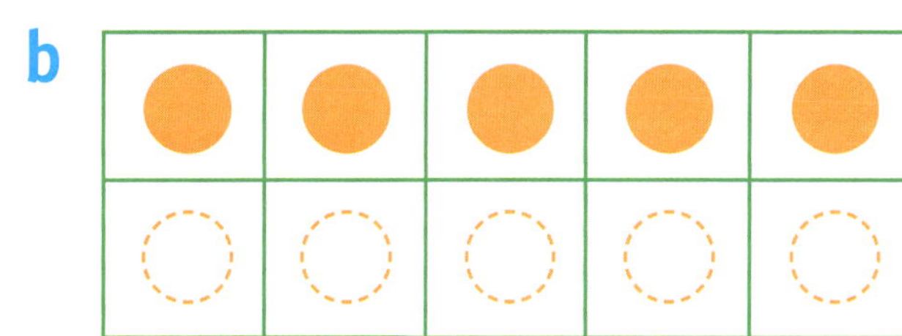

10 − 5 = ☐

c

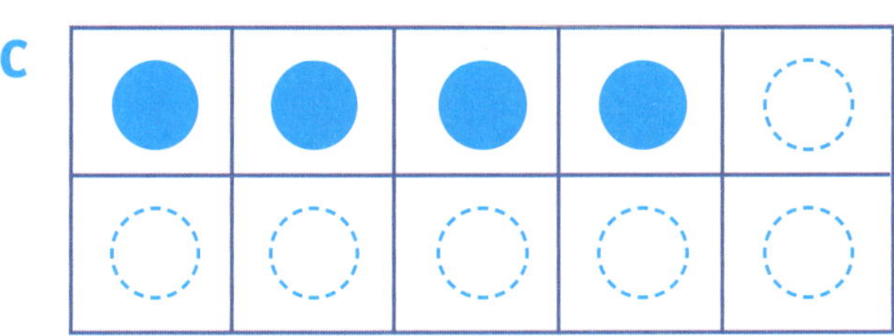

10 − 6 = ☐

d

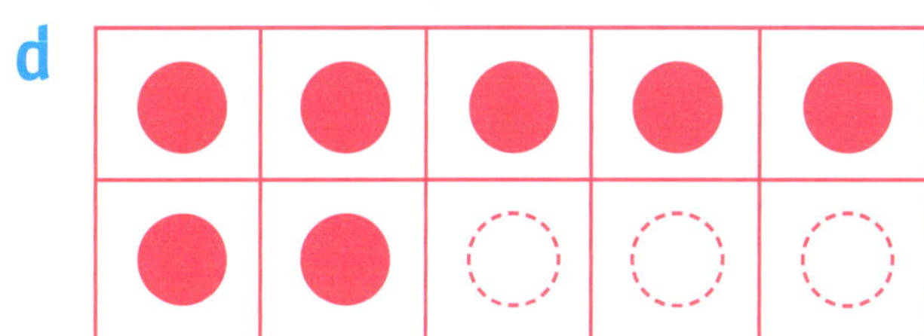

10 − 3 = ☐

e

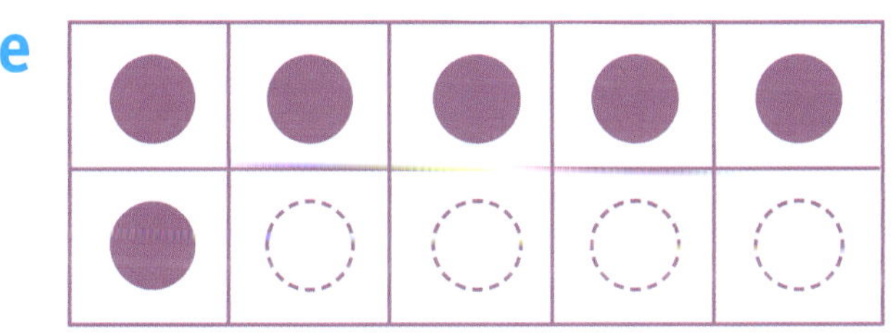

10 − 4 = ☐

f

10 − 7 = ☐

2 Draw and write your own number sentence.

a

10 − ☐ = ☐

b

☐ − ☐ = ☐

Change from ten dollars

Buy.

$2

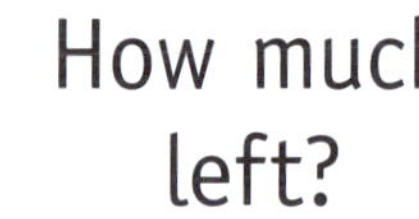

How much left?

$

$5

How much left?

$

=

You have	You spend	change

AC9M1N05 Number MA1-CSQ-01 Combining and separating quantities A • Use advanced count-by-one strategies to solve addition and subtraction problems • Recognise and recall number bonds up to ten

Subtraction

1 2 3 4 5 6 7 8 9 10 11 12 13 14 15

1 a $9 - 2 =$ ☐ b $10 - 4 =$ ☐

c $15 - 1 =$ ☐ d $15 - 3 =$ ☐

e $12 - 2 =$ ☐ f $11 - 3 =$ ☐

2 How much change?

You have  You spend  change 

You have  You spend  change

You have  You spend  change 

You have  You spend  change

You have  You spend  change 

You have  You spend  change

Addition and subtraction

Addition and subtraction are related.

3 + 2 = 5

5 – 3 = 2

1 Write the subtraction.

a

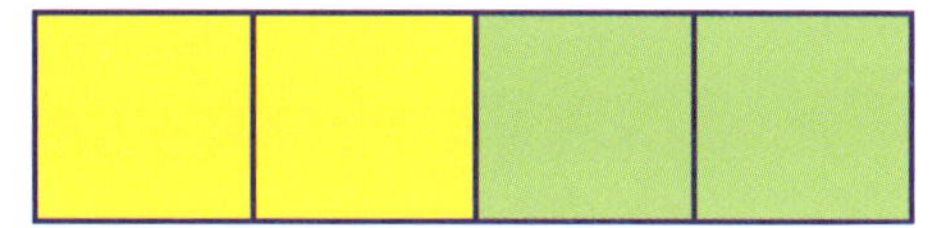

2 + 2 = ☐

☐ – ☐ = ☐

b

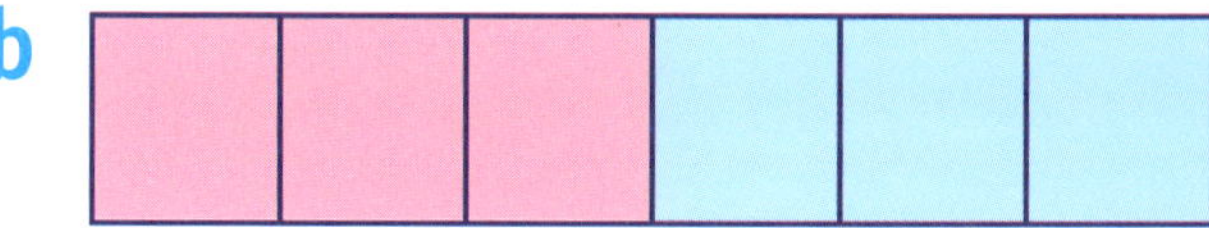

3 + 3 = ☐

☐ – ☐ = ☐

c

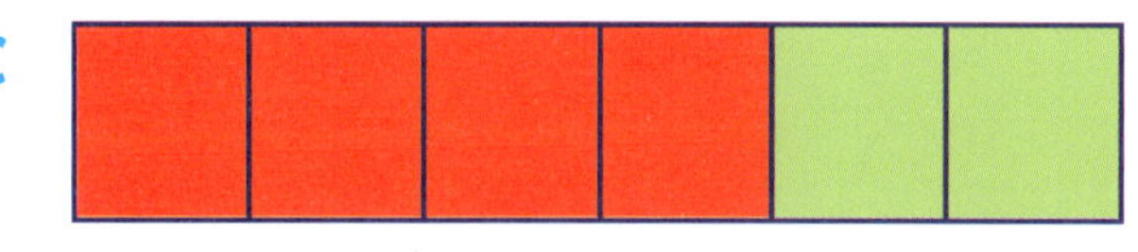

4 + 2 = ☐

☐ – ☐ = ☐

d

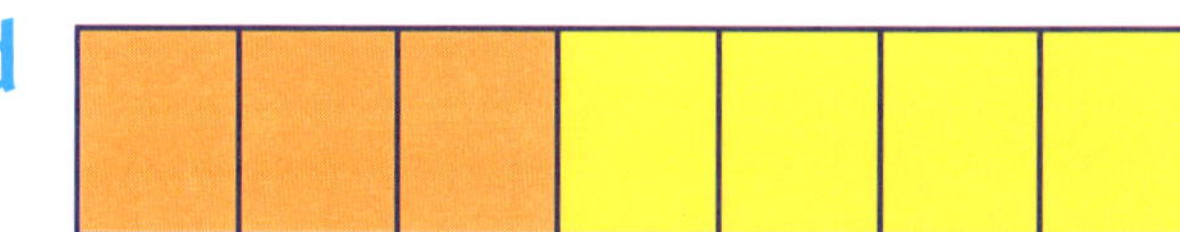

3 + 4 = ☐

☐ – ☐ = ☐

2 Colour and write your own.

a

☐ + ☐ = ☐

☐ – ☐ = ☐

b

☐ + ☐ = ☐

☐ – ☐ = ☐

Number sense – part and whole

Break each group into two smaller numbers.

1 Write a number sentence. Use + or –.

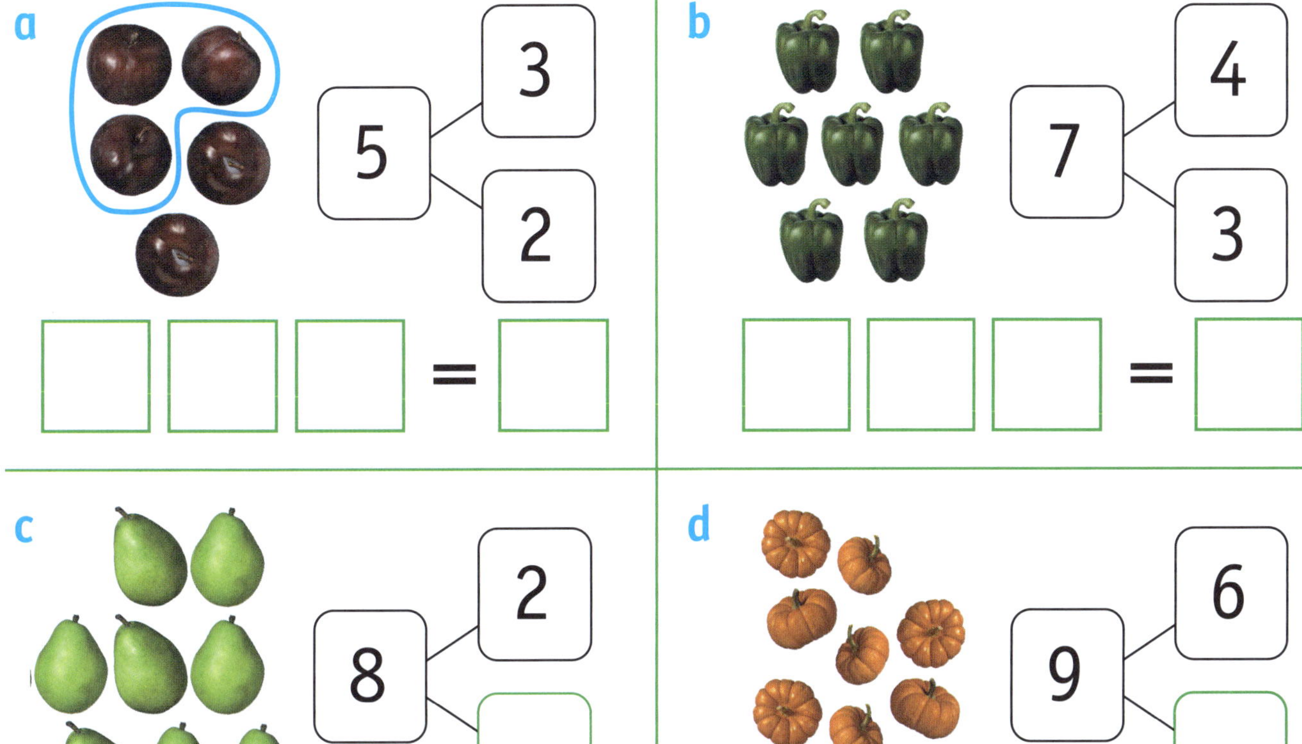

2 Write two number sentences.

Mastery Checklist

I can:
- ☐ count back to take away.
- ☐ identify pairs of numbers that make 10.
- ☐ add money and find the change.
- ☐ solve subtraction problems.

Problem solving

Subtraction

Draw and write your answers.

1 10 marbles.
4 roll away.
How many left?

10 -

2 10 cakes.
7 get eaten.
How many left?

3 9 pencils.
2 get broken.
How many left?

4 14 presents.
I open 7.
How many are left to open?

5 I have $20.
I spend $7.
I get $3 from Dad.
How much do I have now?

6 15 cars.
9 drive away.
How many cars left?

I can solve a problem by:

- [ ] counting back to take away.
- [ ] drawing a picture and writing an equation.

AC9M1N05 Number **MA1-CSQ-01** Combining and separating quantities A • Use advanced count-by-one strategies to solve addition and subtraction problems • Recognise and recall number bonds up to ten **MA1-WM-01** Working mathematically • Apply mathematical techniques to solve problems

Volume

Volume and capacity

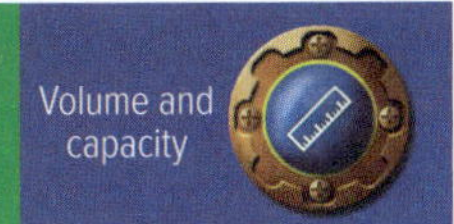

Order from 1–3. 1 takes up most space. 3 takes up least space.

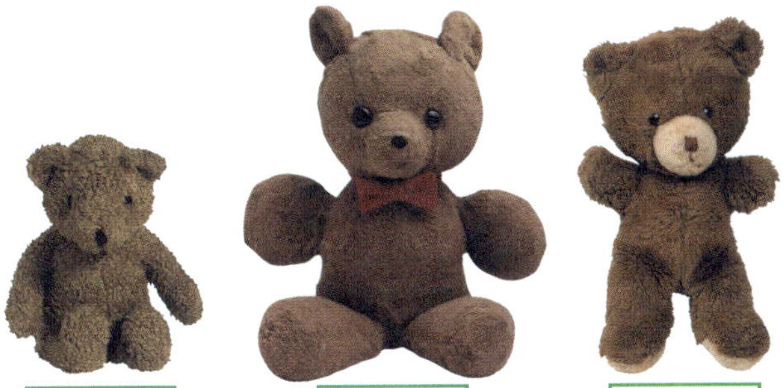

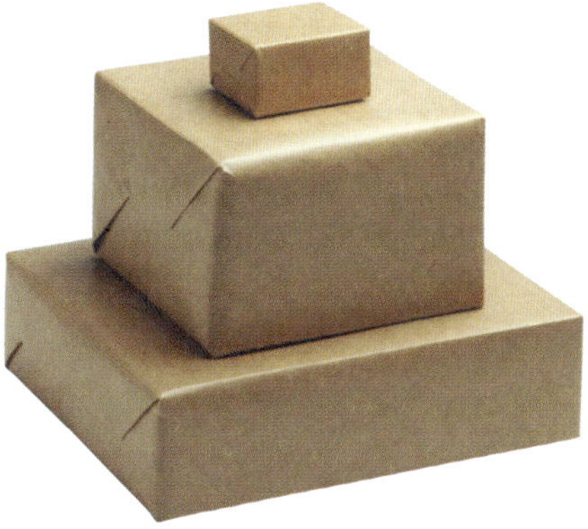

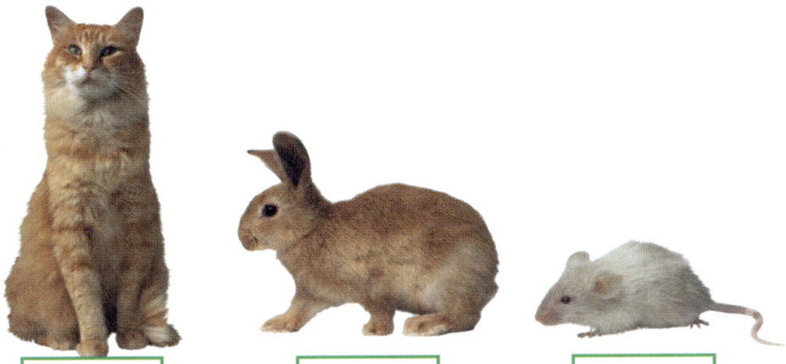

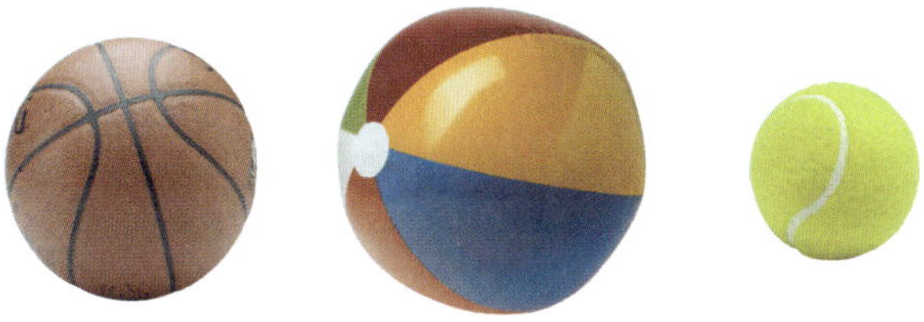

Build each model. How many blocks?

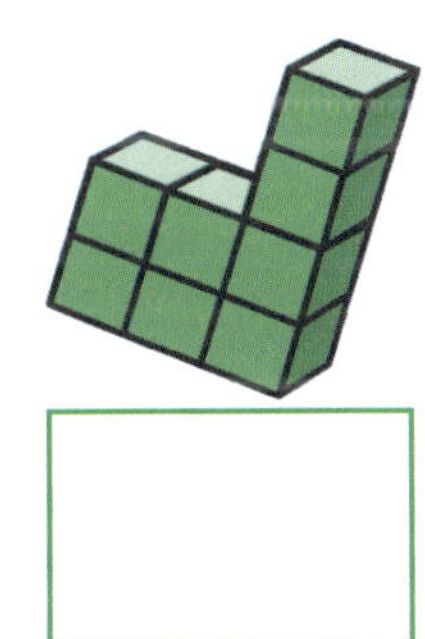

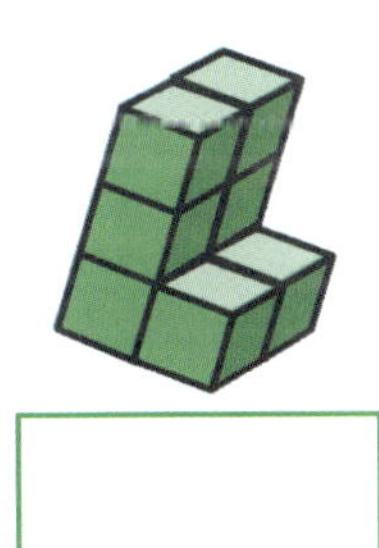

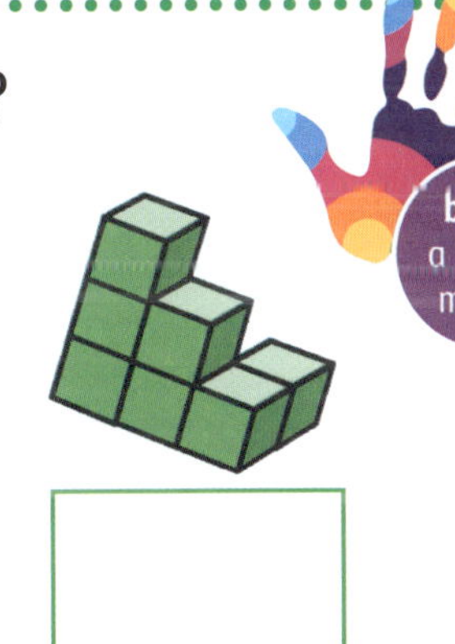

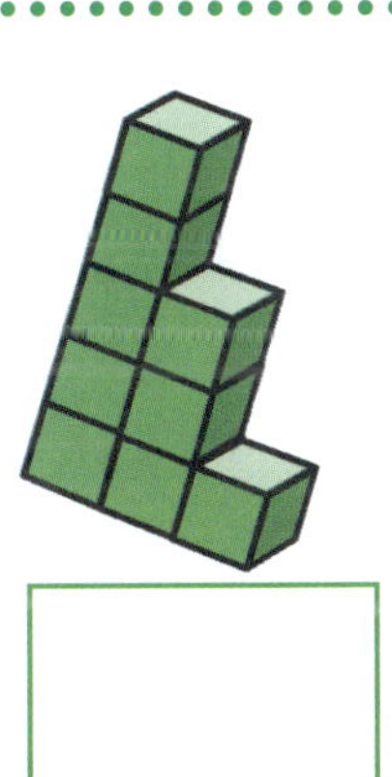

Tick ✓ models with the same number of blocks.

Challenge!

Draw the new water level.

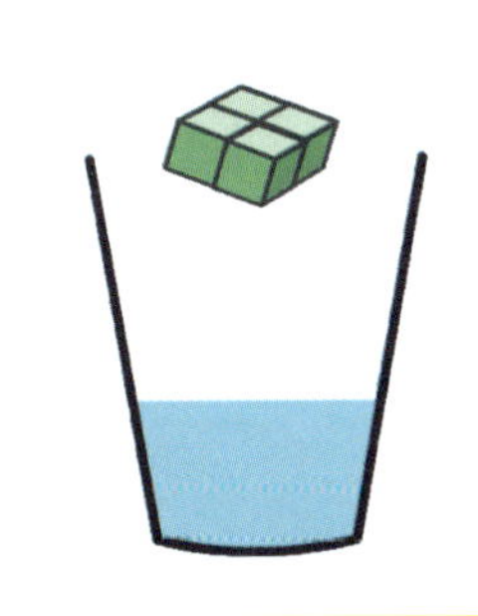

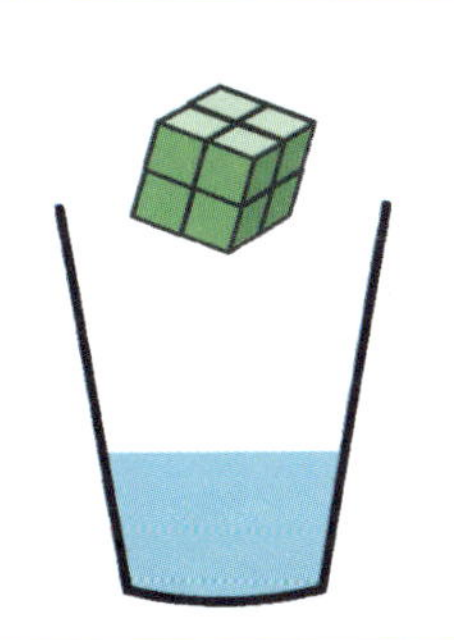

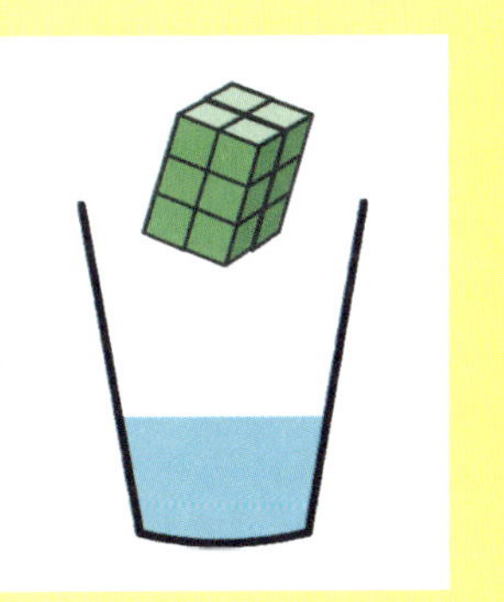

Capacity using blocks

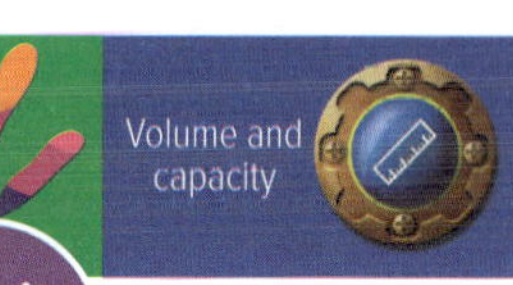

capacity in blocks

How many [block] fit inside? Guess first, then count.

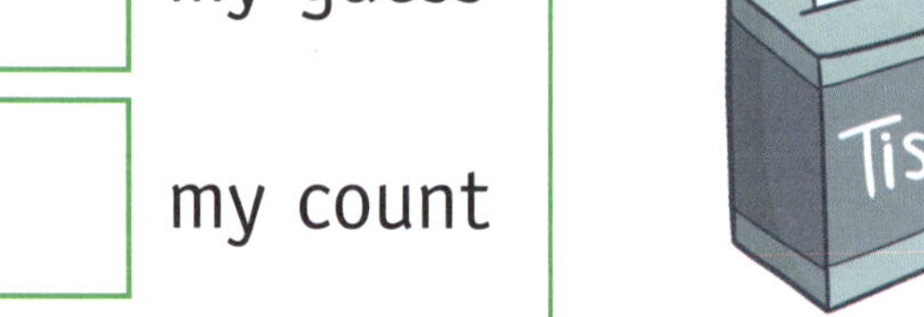

my guess

my count

my guess

my count

my guess

my count

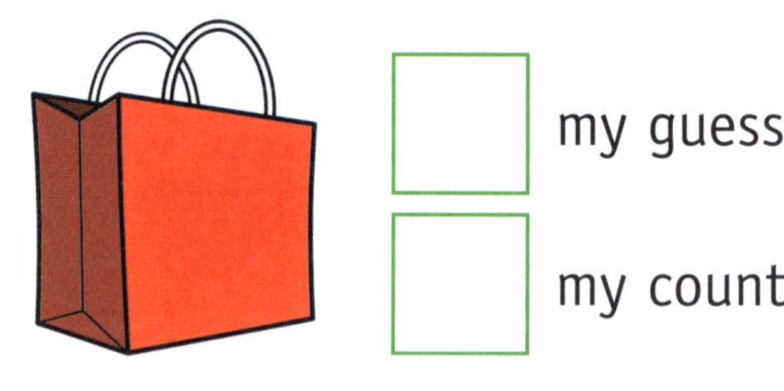

my guess

my count

Order things from 1–4. 1 = holds the least, 4 = holds the most.

Draw two containers that hold about the same.

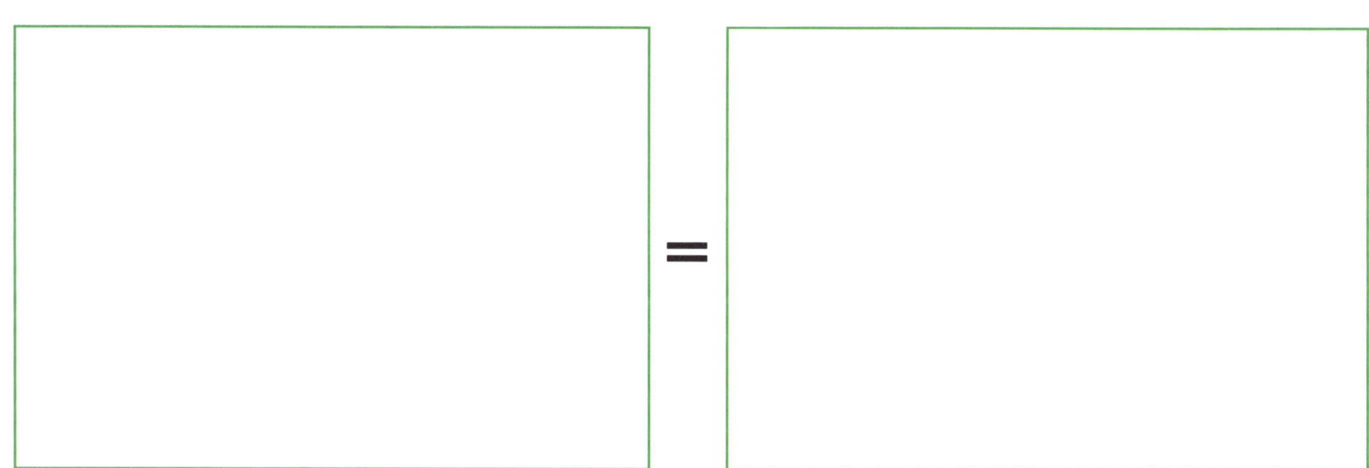

Challenge! How many blocks in a handful? Pick up blocks with one hand. Count. Try again.

AC9M1M01 Measurement **MA1-3DS-02** Three-dimensional spatial structure A • Volume: Measure the internal volume (capacity) of containers by packing

Packing cubes

Which item is best for measuring the capacity of a box?

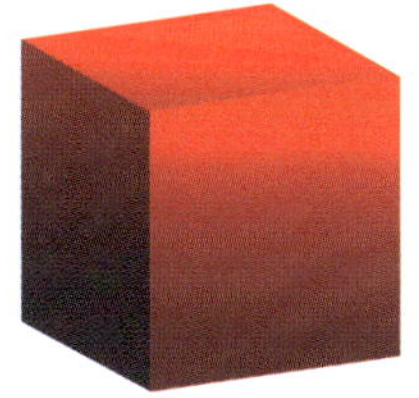

Why? ______________________________

____

Circle the box with correct packing.

A

B
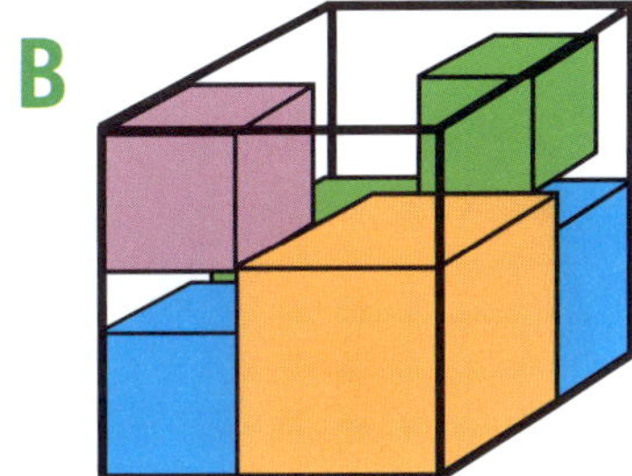
C

Why are the other two not correct?

____

____

____

What is the capacity of the box? __________ cubes

What was tricky about counting the cubes in this box?

____

____

____

Estimating capacity

1 Estimate how many  each one will hold.
Circle your estimate.

2 Make your own estimates. Then measure to check.

Measuring capacity

Why are there 2 different capacities for this jug?

____

____

Number these from smallest (1) to largest (5) capacity.

What is tricky about ordering these capacities?

____

____

Mastery Checklist

I can:
- ☐ measure volume using cubes.
- ☐ measure capacity correctly using cubes.
- ☐ estimate and measure capacity in cups.

Block it out

Investigation 4

volume in blocks

Use 8 blocks to make a rectangular prism.

How many blocks wide? ________ How many blocks long? ________

Draw your rectangular prism:

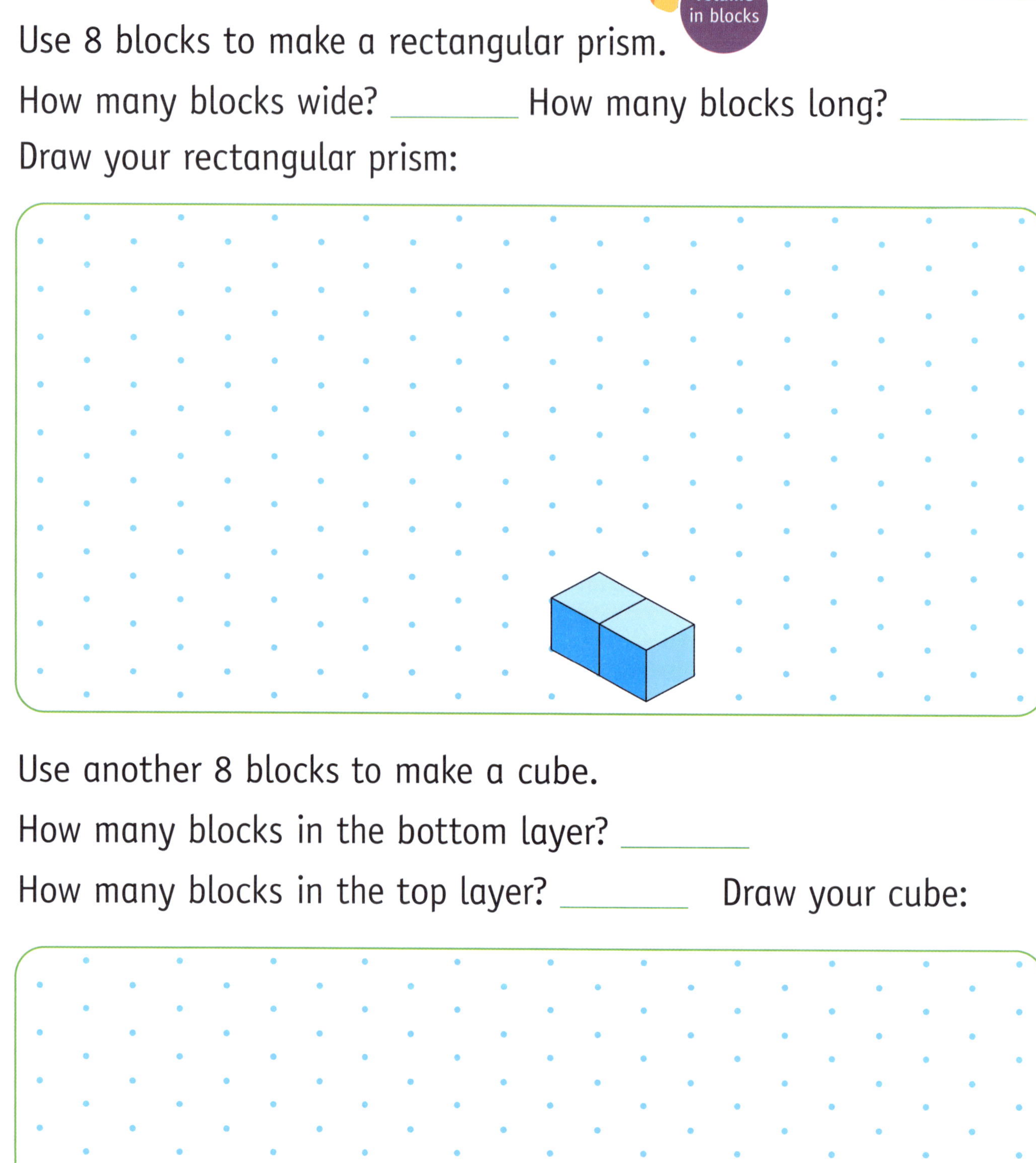

Use another 8 blocks to make a cube.

How many blocks in the bottom layer? ________

How many blocks in the top layer? ________ Draw your cube:

AC9M1M01 Measurement **MA1-3DS-02** Three-dimensional spatial structure A • Volume: Construct volumes using cubes
MA1-WM-01 Working mathematically • Apply mathematical techniques to solve problems

Block it out

Investigation 4

Use a new number of cubes to make 2 different rectangular prisms.

How many cubes in each prism? ______

Draw your 2 rectangular prisms:

building prisms

To do this, I needed to:

- [ ] take three different rectangular prisms and a cube.
- [ ] construct volumes using cubes.
- [ ] measure volume in cubes.
- [ ] draw rectangular prisms made from cubes.

I enjoyed this task!

☆☆☆☆☆

Revision

1 Order from smallest to largest.

16 82 60 37

☐ ☐ ☐ ☐

smallest largest

2 Complete.

30 add 10 → ☐ add 10 → ☐ add 10 → ☐

3 Fill in the tens.

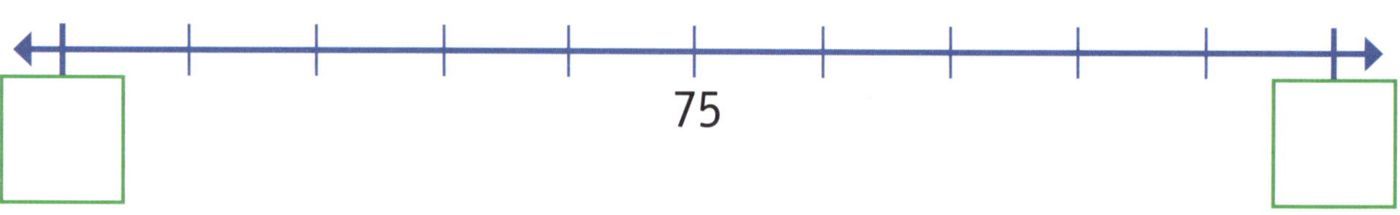

4 How many?

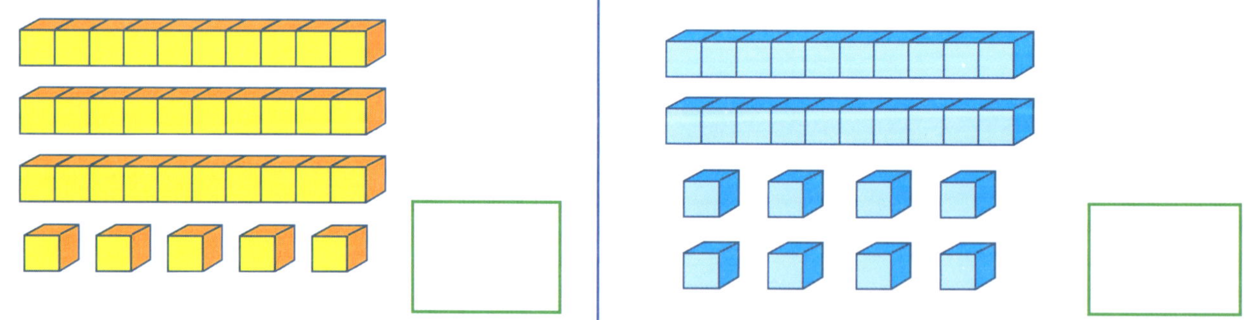

5 What is the volume?

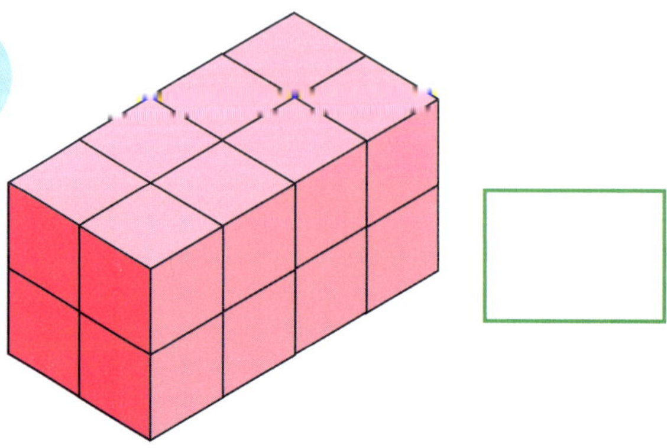

Revision

6 Circle pairs that add to 10.

4	8	2	4	1	5	7	1	5
10	0	5	9	5	6	3	5	9
8	5	6	8	3	10	4	6	8
9	1	4	2	7	0	3	7	2

7 How much? ....

$

Change?

8 What is the time? ....

1 hour before

:

1 hour after

:

9 Complete. ....

5 + ☐ = 10   10 − 5 = ☐

8 + ☐ = 10   10 − 8 = ☐

Sharing into equal groups

Circle two equal groups. How many in each group?

Share equally.

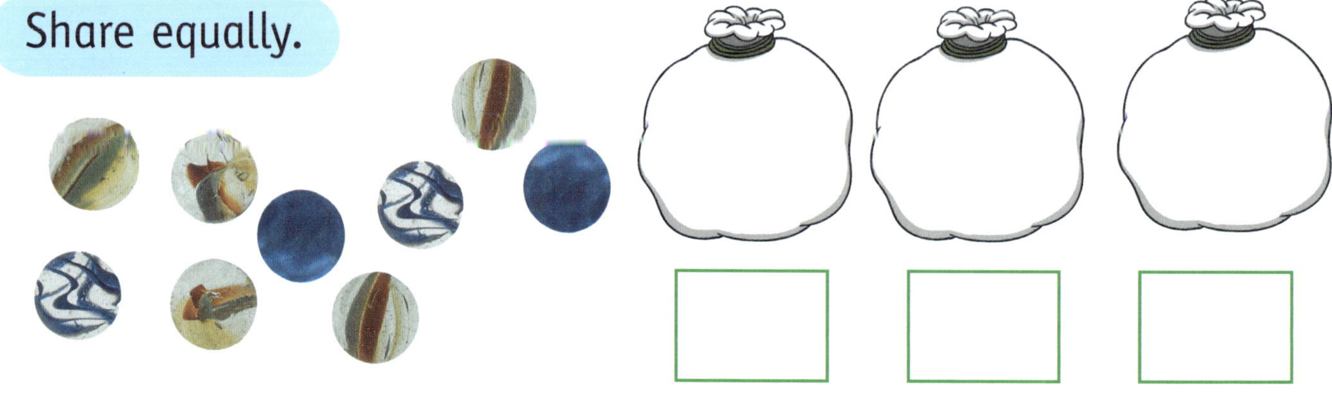

Making groups

How many?

How many groups of 2?

How many groups of 5?

How many groups of 3?

How many groups of 10?

Equal groups

How many groups of 2?

☐ groups of 2 = ☐

☐ groups of 2 = ☐

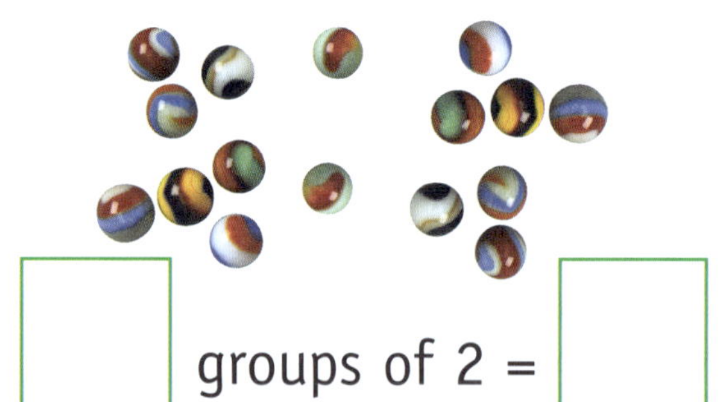

☐ groups of 2 = ☐

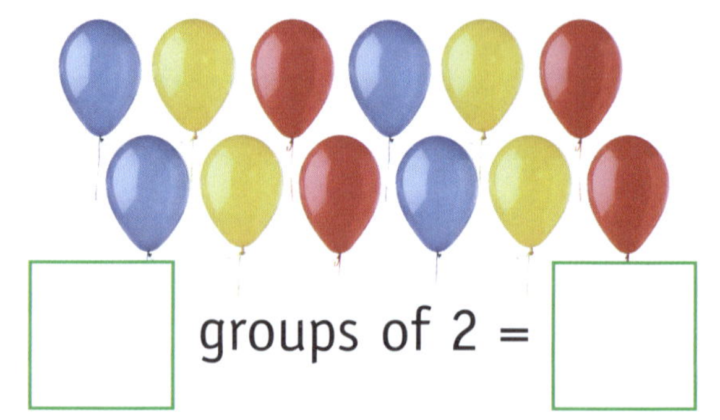

☐ groups of 2 = ☐

How many groups of 3?

☐ groups of 3 = ☐

☐ groups of 3 = ☐

☐ groups of 3 = ☐

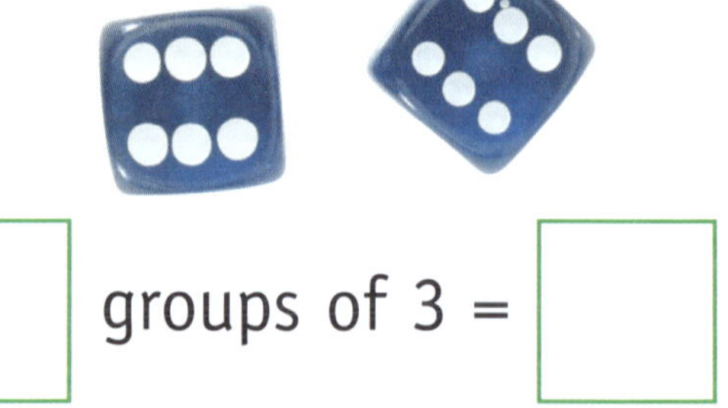

☐ groups of 3 = ☐

Challenge!

How many ways can you share 12 equally?

☐

Sharing

Share equally.

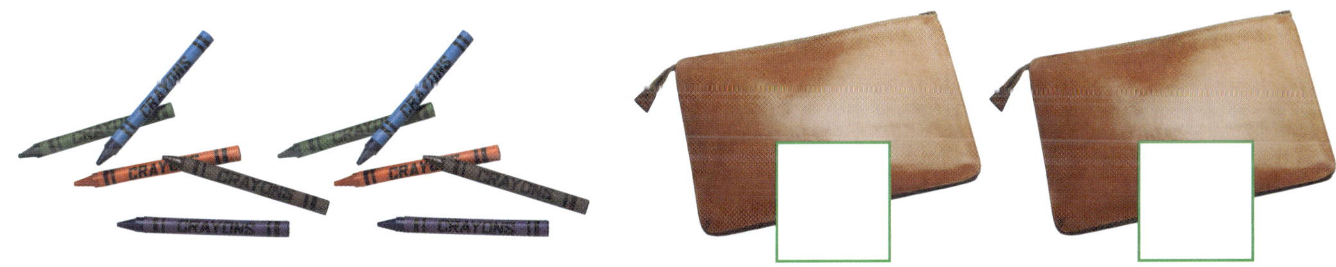

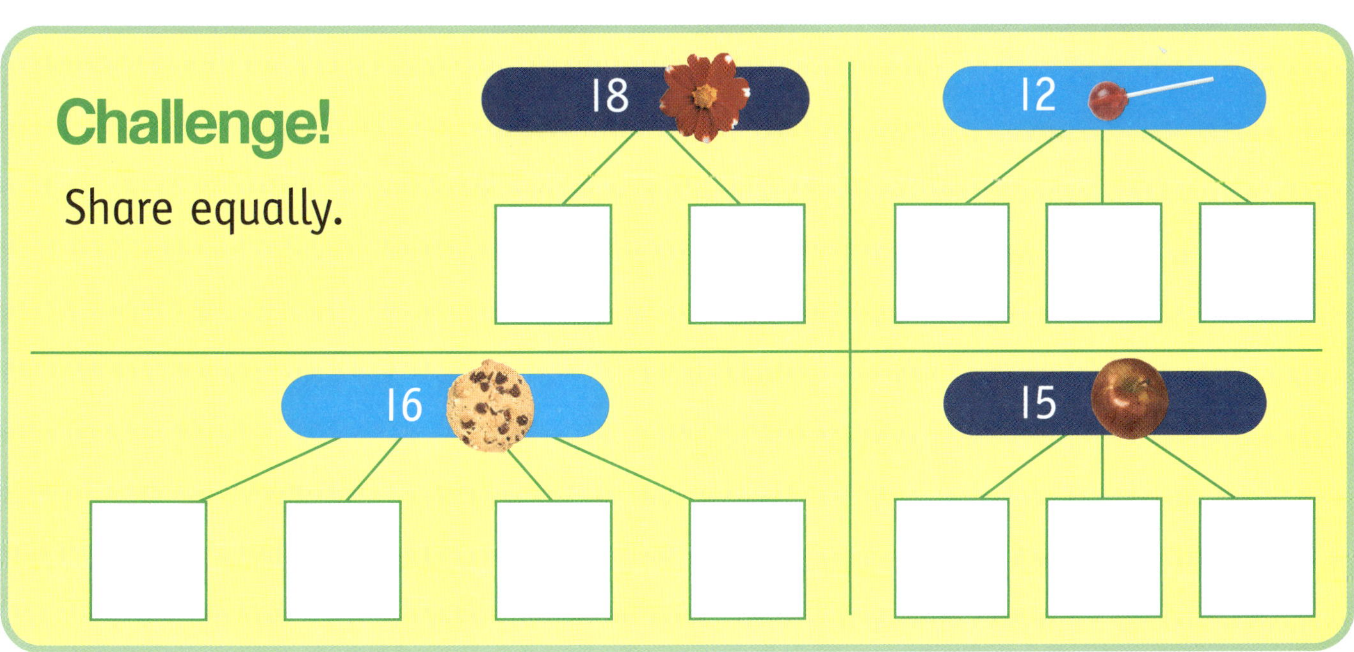

Problem solving

Class groups

The children in class 1B formed groups of 4.

There was 1 extra child. How many children could be in 1B?

Draw and write your answer. There can be more than one answer.

I can solve a problem by:

☐ making groups and adding 1 more. ☐ drawing a diagram.

AC9M1N06 Number **MA1-FG-01** Forming groups A • Model and use equal groups of objects to represent multiplication • Recognise and represent division
MA1-WM-01 Working mathematically • Apply mathematical techniques to solve problems • Communicate their thinking and reasoning coherently and clearly

Measuring

Which tool would you use to measure each? Write its name.

tape measure

jug

clock

ruler

teaspoon

calendar

scales

How tall I am.

____

Remembering my birthday.

____

The milk to make a cake.

____

How wide my book is.

____

The sugar needed to make a cake.

____

Sugar for Grandpa's tea.

____

Time to cook the cake.

____

Comparing mass

Write or draw 4 items into the item boxes.
Predict which item will be heavier in each pair.
Use an equal-arm balance to check.

Items to compare		**Predict:** Which is heavier?	**Measure:** Were you right?
Item 1	Item 2		
Item 1	Item 3		
Item 1	Item 4		
Item 2	Item 3		
Item 2	Item 4		
Item 3	Item 4		

Challenge!

Order the items from heaviest to lightest.

Mastery Checklist

I can:
- ☐ share items into a number of equal groups.
- ☐ share items into groups of a certain size.
- ☐ choose the right tool for measuring.
- ☐ use an equal-arm balance to compare masses.

Problem solving

Group mass

How many dumplings weigh the same as a bun?

2 rolls weigh the same as 1 bun.

4 rolls weigh the same as 2 tarts.

3 dumplings weigh the same as 1 tart.

☐ dumplings weigh the same as 1 bun.

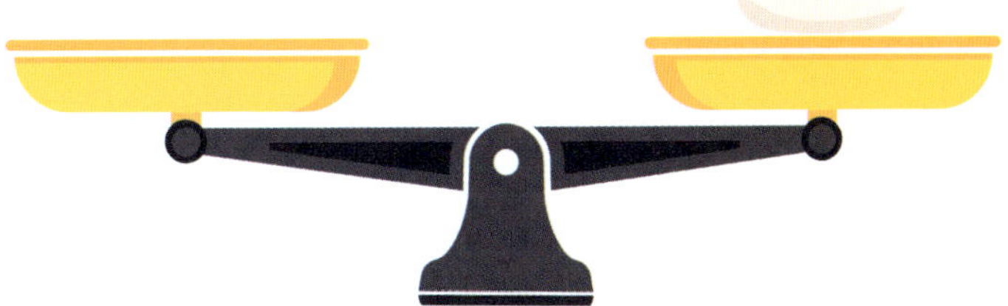

I can solve a problem by:

☐ comparing the mass of groups of objects. ☐ using logical thinking.

2D or 3D?

1 Colour the **2D shapes** in **green**. Colour the **3D objects** in **blue**.

A B 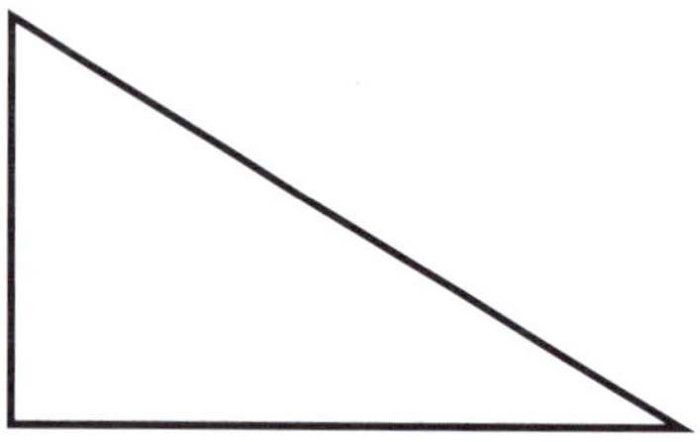 C

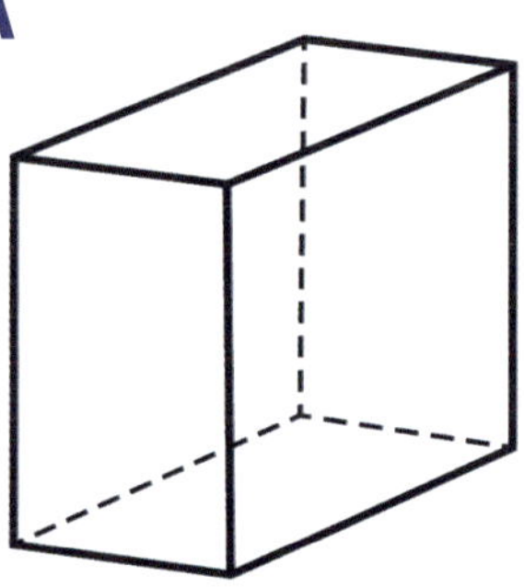

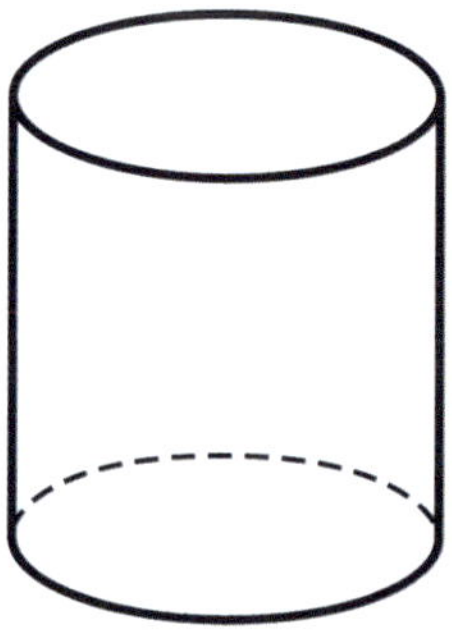

D E 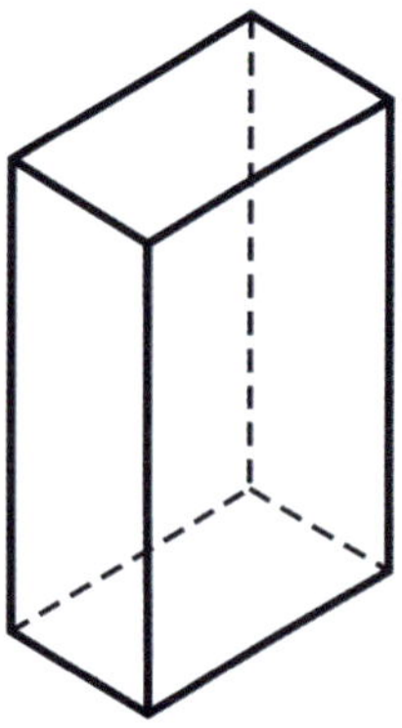 F 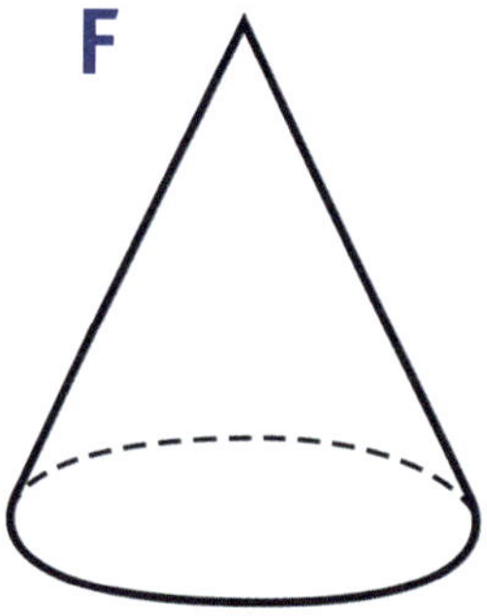 G

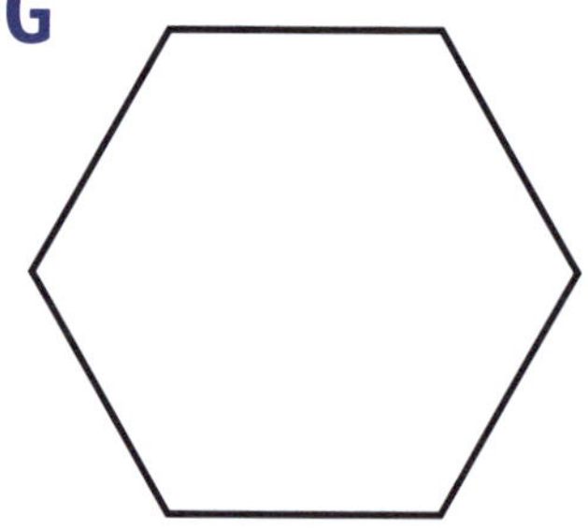

H I 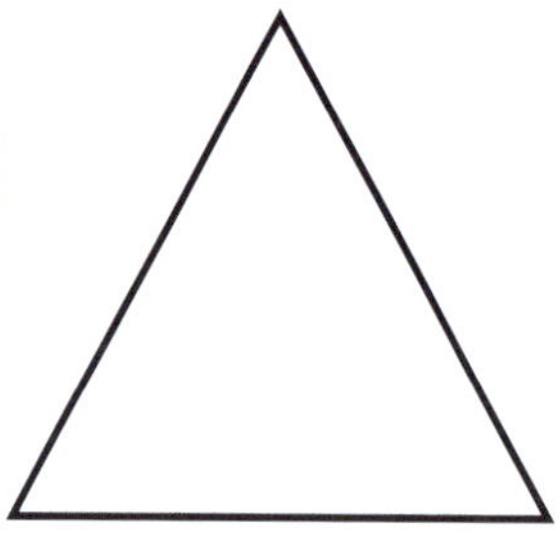 J

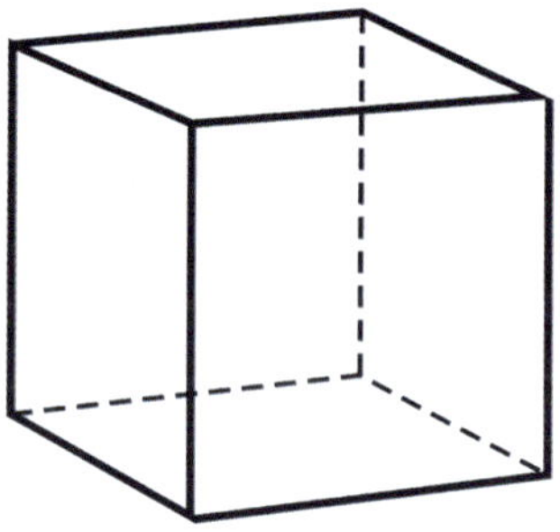

2 Can you name each shape and object?

A ______________________ B ______________________

C ______________________ D ______________________

E ______________________ F ______________________

G ______________________ H ______________________

I ______________________ J ______________________

Faces of 3D objects

Find and draw around each shape.

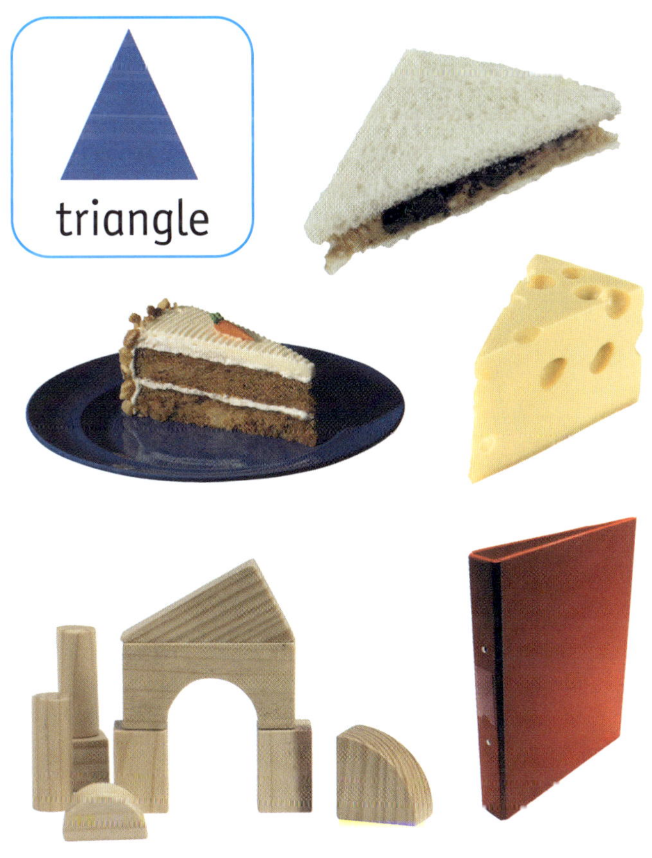

3D objects and faces

Faces are flat surfaces.

1 Colour the shape drawn.

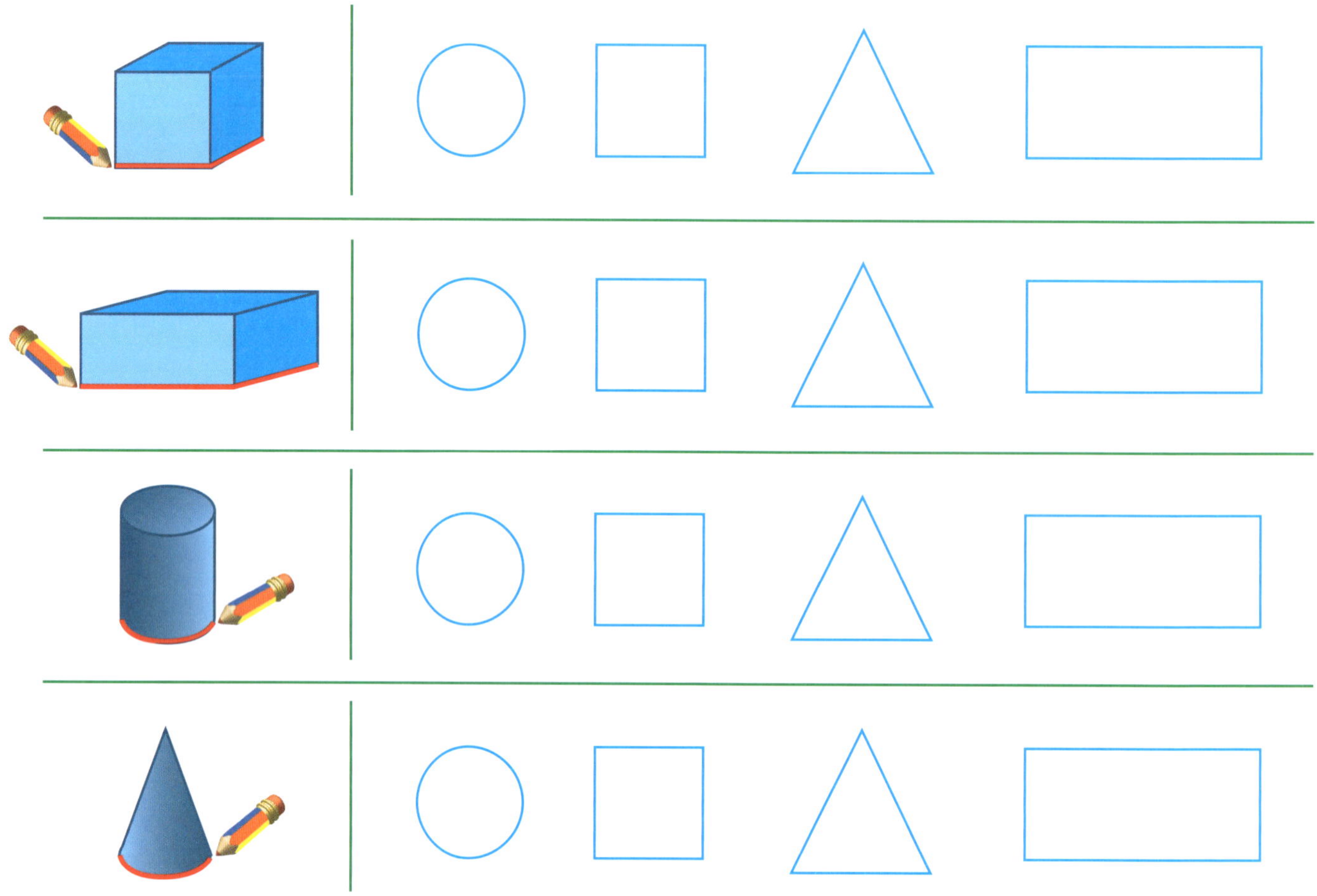

2 Circle objects that have a flat surface that matches.

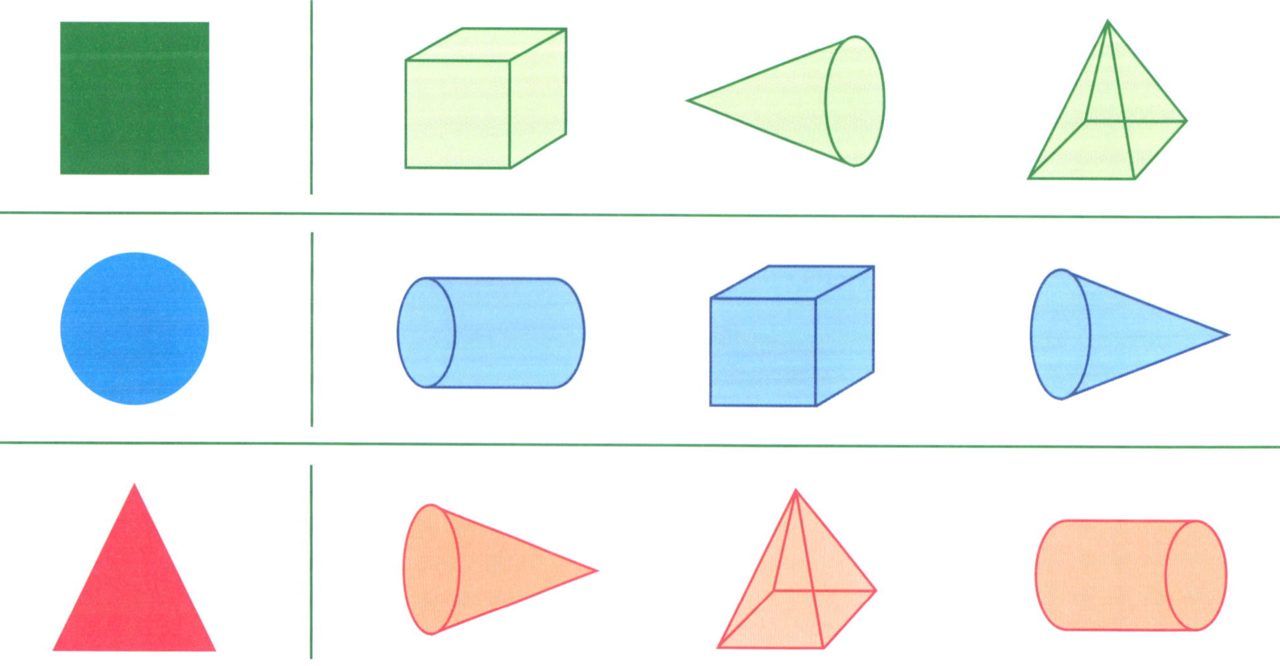

3D objects – faces and corners

How many faces?

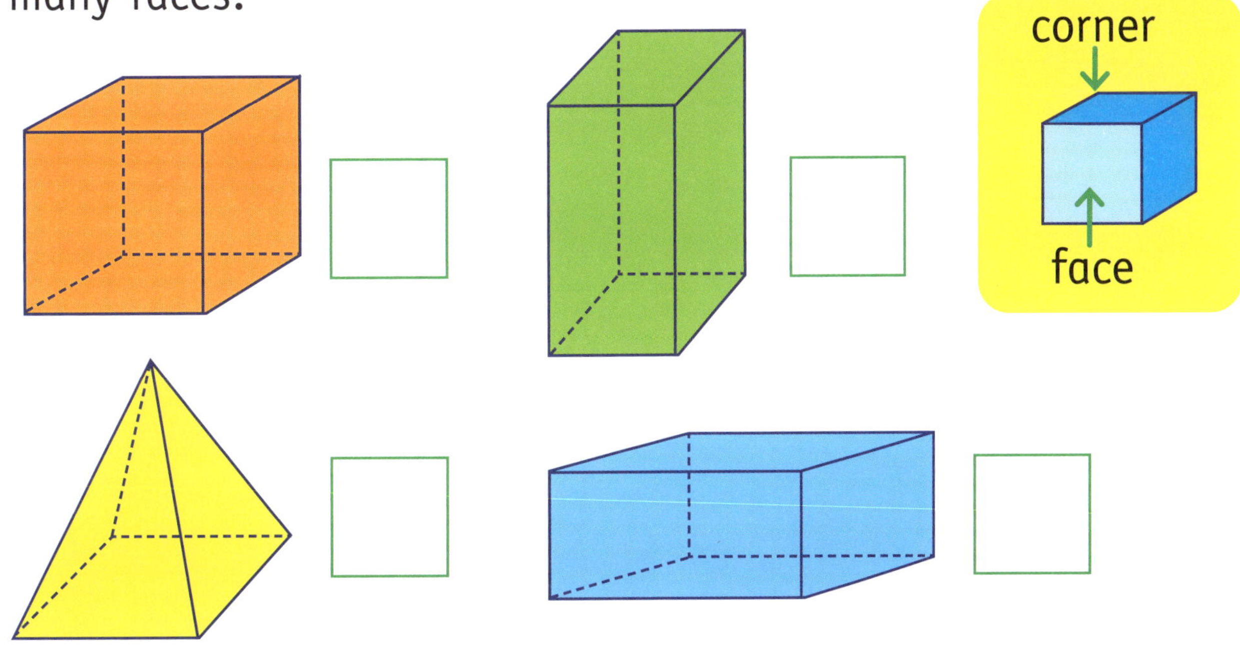

How many corners?

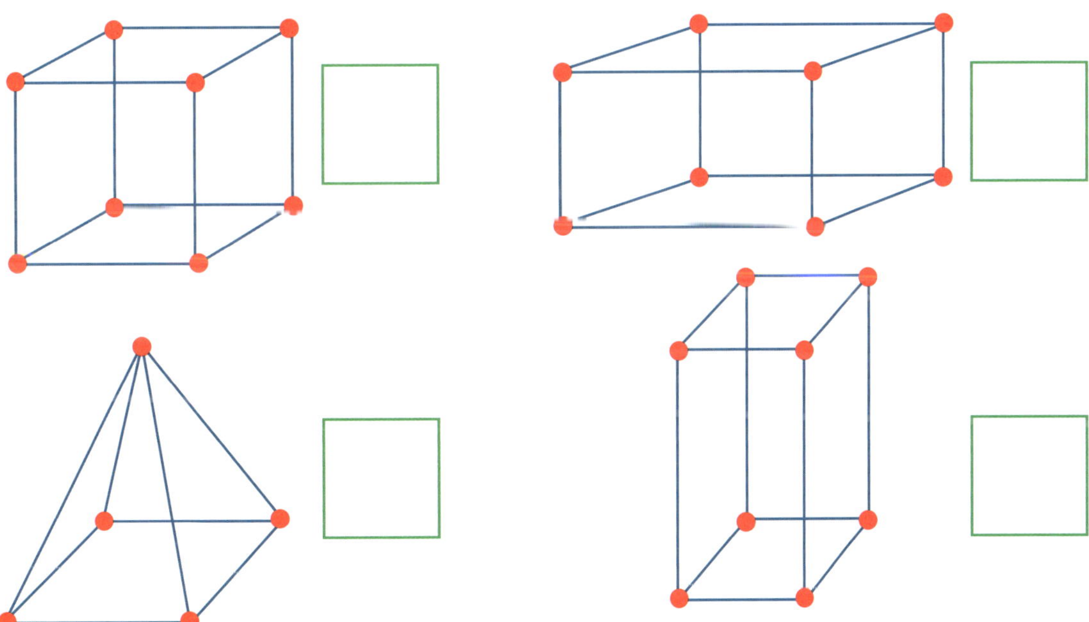

Challenge!

Make your own shapes. Label them.

Mastery Checklist

I can:

- ☐ identify 3D objects and 2D shapes.
- ☐ identify the 2D shapes of faces on 3D objects.
- ☐ count faces and corners on 3D objects.
- ☐ describe 3D objects.

Problem solving

Name the 3D object

Draw each 3D object and name it.

2 circle faces.
1 curved surface.
No corners.

6 square faces.
8 corners.

Describe two 3D objects.
Ask a friend to draw and name your shapes.

I can solve a problem by:

☐ describing 3D objects. ☐ drawing a diagram.

AC9M1SP01 Space **MA1-3DS-01** Three-dimensional spatial structure A • 3D objects: Sort and describe three-dimensional objects
MA1-WM-01 Working mathematically • Apply mathematical techniques to solve problems • Communicate their thinking and reasoning coherently and clearly

Reading tables and graphs

1 This table shows the number of books read by Blue Group.

Name	Books read	Number
Jake	📖📖	2
Lana	📖📖📖📖	4
Alex	📖📖📖📖📖📖	6
Madison	📖📖📖	3

How many books did Madison read? ____________

Who read the most books? ____________

Who read 4 books? ____________

How many books did Alex and Jake read altogether? ____________

2 Colour 1 ☐ for each book read.

Number of books	Jake	Lana	Alex	Madison
6				
5				
4				
3				
2				
1				

The language of chance

Describe each sentence. Use one of these.

unlikely | likely | very likely

Chance describes how some events are more or less likely.

Tomorrow

you walk to school

you ride to school on a horse

you come to school in a car

This week at school

your class has a party

you write your name

you talk to the principal

This weekend

you play sport

you go shopping

you fly to the moon

Revision • Term 4

1 Share equally.

How many carrots? ☐

How many each? ☐

2 Circle the heavier one.

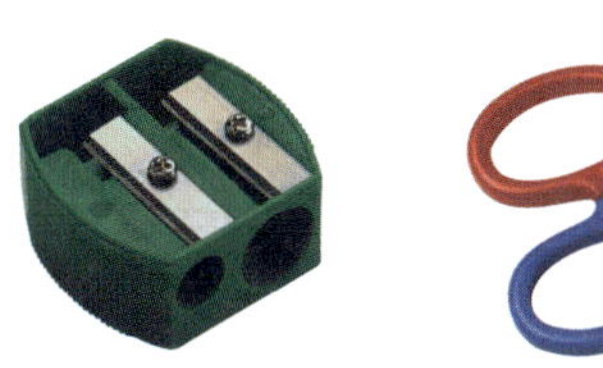
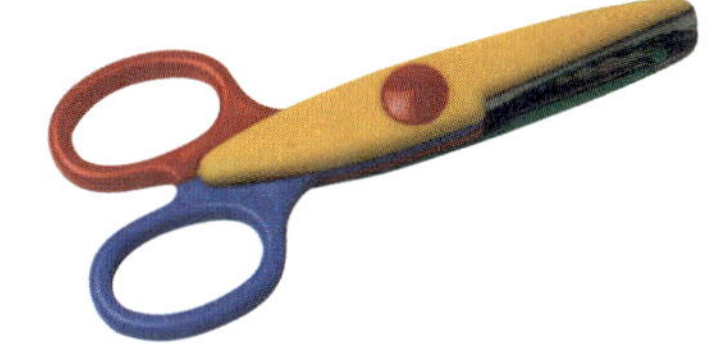

3

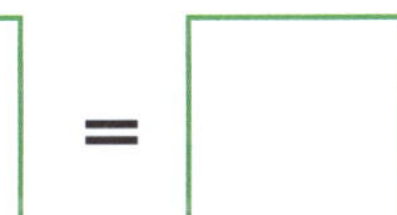

☐ – ☐ = ☐

☐ – ☐ = ☐

4 Circle the object.

8 corners.
2 square faces.
4 rectangle faces.

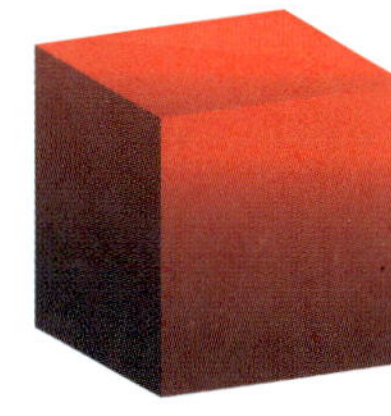
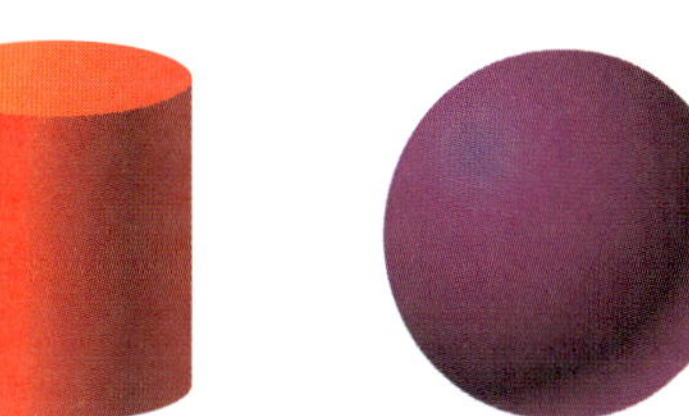

5

spend 

change $ 

spend 

change $ 

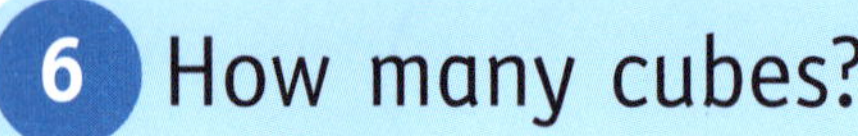

6 How many cubes?

Circle the one that takes up the most space.

7 Write likely or unlikely.

8 How many groups of 2?

☐ groups of 2 = ☐